The National Board for Prices and Incomes

JOAN MITCHELL

The National Board for Prices and Incomes

FOREWORD BY
THE RT HON. AUBREY JONES PC

Secker & Warburg · London

First published in England 1972 by
Martin Secker & Warburg Limited
14 Carlisle Street, London W1V 6NN

SBN: 436 28252 6

Printed in Great Britain by
Willmer Brothers Limited, Birkenhead

Contents

PART IV

Conclusions

Appendixes

Foreword

by The Rt Hon. Aubrey Jones PC

Dr Joan Mitchell and I were founder-members of the National Board for Prices and Incomes. She came from the Labour Party, I from the Conservative. The composition of the Board at its foundation in the spring of 1965 was, in terms of party affiliation, roughly 50–50. And it was still much the same when the abolition of the Board was announced after the General Election of June 1970. Throughout those five-and-a-half years no minority report was issued by any member of the Board, nor did any fundamental rift appear between members of different party allegiance. This is a fact of no mean interest. And to me the significance of the Board was more political than economic.

It was an observation of politics that induced me to accept the Chairmanship of the Board. I had seen at least two Conservative Governments deliberately encourage inflation in an attempt to facilitate the re-election of the party on which they were based. Not only was this nationally damaging, but it also appeared to me in personal terms to be a futile exercise. I was to live to see the Labour Government of 1966–70 do much the same. And it has yet to be shown that its Conservative successor is not still prone to the identical weakness.

Amidst this flux the National Board for Prices and Incomes represented the beginnings of an attempt to introduce at any rate one element of stability. It was concerned with the distribution of income as between wages and salaries on the one hand and profits on the other. The struggle over this distribution is a cause, possibly in our time it has become the most important cause, of inflation. A push upwards by trades unions on pay causes firms to push prices upwards against consumers; similarly a push upwards on prices provokes a push upwards in pay, with further effects on prices. There would be little point at any one time in trying to identify which was the chicken and which the egg; indeed I doubt whether one could.

Be that as it may, the Board tried to deal with this problem by investi-

vii

gating, at the instance of the Government, particular cases of prices and incomes in the light of rules agreed upon initially between the Government, firms and trades unions. I do not myself believe that the rules were necessarily fair to all parties, nor would I consider it desirable that they should be fixed for all time. The fact, however, that there was a set of rules agreed to by firms and trades unions had a considerable symbolic importance. And the obligation placed upon the Board to examine cases in the light of the rules played a significant part in maintaining its cohesion.

Like any other new institution the Board found itself inserted into a society littered with all other kinds of institutions, owing their inspiration to different stages of history and, because of their age, regarding themselves as above the rules. The most notable of these were the various bodies of conciliation and arbitration accustomed to splitting the difference between an employer's and a union's view of a proper pay settlement, regardless of the implications of the split for the consumer.

Between 1965 and 1968 some progress was made, inevitably slowly, in assimilating these other institutions to the Board. Then, at the end of 1968, the crack came. In the middle of that year the late Lord Donovan had issued his report on trades unions and employers' associations. He had diagnosed the industrial relations problem of the United Kingdom as one of short, sporadic but frequent unofficial strikes. In the light of the public preoccupation with unofficial strikes both the political parties, at roughly the same moment of time, placed the strike problem at the top of their list of priorities.

The Labour Government introduced its White Paper *In Place of Strife*. It let go of its prices and incomes policy; despite this it failed to carry through *In Place of Strife*, and this failure, combined with the imminence of the election, made it impossible to resume a dialogue with the trades unions on a distribution of the national income between pay and profits. The Conservative Government, in its turn, repeated precisely the same pattern of events. It abolished the Prices and Incomes Board; it introduced the Industrial Relations Act modelled on American legislation pre-dating by some decades an awareness of the prices and incomes problem; and by so doing it heightened its difficulty in talking to the trades unions about pay and prices.

Clearly strikes are important. What legislation about strikes does, however, is to change somewhat, lengthen perhaps, the channels through which negotiations take place. It does not necessarily ensure that the final outcome of the negotiations is any fairer to the consumer, or that there is any greater agreement on the distribution of pay between different groups of workers or between pay and profits. Nor can we console ourselves with the thought that in the longer term we may have a more orderly system of industrial relations at the risk of a more disorderly one in the short term. For the short term problem is one of inflation; and inflation feeds upon itself—it escalates.

We pride ourselves that our political system is a stable one. In fact, by proving unable to cope with the problem of inflation it makes for instability—economic (what else is stop-go?), social and ultimately political. The National Board for Prices and Incomes was one small attempt to deal, in agreement, with a major national problem that the political system has put off and, by putting off, aggravated. For this reason I believe something like the Board, however disguised, will return. Those who wish to prepare for the future would do well therefore to read Dr Mitchell's book.

17 May 1972

The research work, of which this book forms a part, was supported by a grant from the Social Science Research Council.

Introduction

This book gives an account of how the prices and incomes policy worked out through the activities of the National Board for Prices and Incomes. It records mainly what the Board thought of its functions and what its conclusions were. The Board thought long and hard and applied itself to a great number of cases. In six years, from 1965 to 1971, it produced 170 reports, from the pay problems of 28 limbfitters in one company to productivity agreements and food-distribution costs in general. Two other tasks are not attempted here: to criticise the Board's mode of thought or operation, or to analyse the consequences of the Board's recommendations, except where second (or even third or fourth) references enabled the Board to follow up its own recommendations.

The Board had its share of personalities, and the strengths and weaknesses of working relationships often affected the way conclusions were reached, and occasionally the nature of the conclusions. Nevertheless, the Board always made itself collectively responsible for its conclusions, and the collectiveness became more effective as time went on. The most important personality in the early work was the Chairman, Aubrey Jones, whose guiding hand could clearly be seen in the reports. But after about fifty reports, the contributions of individuals were absorbed more thoroughly into the collective work and wisdom of the whole. The reports no longer showed much evidence of particular authorship or leadership for the last half of its life. By the time it had been decided to supersede the Board in 1969, it had become a mature and experienced institution, able to carry on its distinctive work, through changes of staff or Board members. When it was eventually disbanded in 1971 (some months after the decision to dispense with it), an organisation with expertise, competence and *élan* of rare quality in the Government machine was lost.

Hereafter, the Board is referred to as the Prices and Incomes Board, PIB for short, as it was known to the press and the staff. We begin the PIB's history with a brief account of the prices and incomes policy. Then follows an account of the PIB itself. Parts II and III summarise the results of its deliberations, on prices and incomes respectively. There were four criteria in the policy White Papers for distinguishing cases in which exceptional price increases might be justified. It might appear therefore that the PIB's reports ought to be grouped according to these four types of case. But in practice there was a clearer distinction in the nature of the investigations or in the reports, between private- and public-sector cases, and between types of activity in the private sector. Part II therefore distinguishes labour-intensive manufacturing industry, distribution and services, and other (mostly capital-intensive) manufacturing in the private sector; and all public-sector cases are dealt with together.

Though the issues discussed in the income reports correspond more closely to the rules distinguished by the criteria for exceptional treatment than in the prices reports, many concerned more than one of the criteria. Moreover, the PIB's primary interest in productivity meant that most cases were related in some way to this theme, even when they were clearly also about low pay, or another exceptional case. In many salary cases, pay could not be related to performance in the same way as in most wages cases. Hence all salary cases are dealt with as one group. The early incomes cases were distinct, since they were establishing the ground rules by which the PIB would function. Part III therefore begins with an account of the reports in which first principles were discussed, particularly about the norm for pay. It is followed by those which principally established the PIB's concern with pay and productivity. Thereafter follow chapters on productivity agreements, low pay, comparability and the market, and pay structures.

Part IV draws some general conclusions, as much about the policy as about the PIB. The PIB reports referred to are listed at the end of each chapter.

Part 1

The Prices and Incomes Policy

1

Prehistory

Prices and incomes policy as an accepted part of the Government's responsibility for economic management has a history going back at least to 1948. During the first post-war Labour Government, Sir Stafford Cripps (Minister of Economic Affairs and Chancellor of the Exchequer, 1947–48) tried voluntary restraint on personal incomes. But its effects were soon attenuated, and the policy was finally killed by the devaluation of 1949. Mr Selwyn Lloyd, Chancellor of the Exchequer in a Conservative Government, tried a pay pause in 1961, which soon collapsed because it only had effect on relatively weakly organised public-service employees. The first to attempt to formulate an incomes policy for cases, independently of the Government, was the National Incomes Commission, also set up by a Conservative Government in 1962. But this was doomed to ineffectiveness when the TUC and the larger unions refused to take part in it or to give evidence to it.

Successive Governments had accumulated experience of abortive incomes policies. But as expectations of continually rising income were firmly established, inflation was more likely and a remedy became more urgent. Governments were bound to be concerned about prices and incomes in the private as well as the public sector, since bursts of inflation have been accompanied by balance of payments crises. An incomes policy could be regarded as an instrument for correcting or avoiding balance of payments crises, as well as for removing a hindrance to faster growth. Growth without inflation, and hence without balance of payments crises, was still the aim of economic management throughout the 1960s. The idea of economic planning was received in unlikely places with a new respect: the National Economic Development Council was instituted, a policy arising directly out of the balance of payments crisis of July 1961. The NEDC consisted of industrialists, trade-union leaders, chairmen of nationalised industries and academic economists, sitting with Government Ministers under the chairmanship of the Chancellor of the Exchequer. Businessmen as well as trade-union leaders were inclined to favour planning as a means to growth, and pressed increasingly to be consulted by the Government over economic policy matters. NEDC was both the means of consulting industry and trades unions, and of drawing up a plan for economic growth.

Having begun planning, NEDC turned to discussing problems that would need to be solved to make the plan possible. One of the most important of these was avoiding cost-induced inflation, to prevent a worsening balance of trade or too high a proportion of the gross national product going to consumption, rather than to investment or public expenditure. Increases in incomes ought to be kept down to the likely rise in output per head. Prices, it was thought, would not go up so readily if incomes did not rise so fast. Equally, increases in incomes would not be so aggressively pursued, nor achieved so often, if real income was not eroded so fast by rising prices.

Restraining the increase in income to the rate of increase in productivity would only restrain prices effectively if markets were competitive. Otherwise, stable or falling labour costs per unit of output might merely mean higher profit margins. The trade unions would not agree to any agreements likely to have this effect, since they feared a reduction of real incomes. They were also unwilling to see a larger share of the national income go to profits. Hence their aim was to strike a bargain: a policy for incomes, a euphemism for restraint on collectively bargained incomes, provided there was a corresponding policy for profits.

Between 1962 and 1964, the problem was discussed in an increasingly desultory and inconclusive way. There must be a general election sometime in 1964, and evidence was accumulating that the new Government would be formed by the Labour Party. The theme of the Labour Party's propaganda from 1962 to 1964 was Britain's needs for "modernisation". This meant economic planning to direct resources to more desirable objectives nationally, and more Government intervention in particular places, with particular objects, depending on the problems needing solution. NEDC was a suitable instrument for planning purposes, as it would allow the close association of trades unions and business with the new policy.

It had become clear both through the discussions at NEDC, and through various proposals by the Labour Party, that direct or reciprocal restraint on incomes and profits was not practicable. The "other half" of the incomes policy would have to be prices policy, rather than profits policy. This would have its own logic anyway, since an important part of the objective of the dual policy was to safeguard the real incomes of trade-union members. This would be achieved, at least partly, by price stability.

One of the first members of the new Labour Government was George Brown, as First Secretary of State and Minister of Economic Affairs. His main job was to prepare a National Plan, and to design and operate a prices and incomes policy. Two key things were already agreed: the policy was to consist of general restraint on prices and incomes, the degree of restraint on incomes being determined by the rate of increase in productivity. Secondly, the details of the policy would be agreed between the Government, trades unions and employers jointly. The discussions of October to December 1964 went on between George Brown and his advisers in the Department of Economic Affairs, and the leaders of the trades unions and business. But many of the people involved were also members of NEDC, and their experience of previous NEDC discussions and knowledge of one another helped to get the new discussions with DEA more quickly to a conclusion, embodied in the Statement of Intent. The policy itself would take weeks more of hard bargaining; but real progress had been made. Hence the Statement of Intent, in simple but more dramatic language (for a Government document) than a policy statement, committing no-one yet to anything specific.

After a preamble on the objectives of Government policy (faster growth, full employment, social justice) and the conditions for achieving them (stronger balance of payments, more exports, higher productivity), the Statement of Intent continued:

5   We, Government, management and unions, are resolved to take the following action in our respective spheres of responsibility.
6   The Government will prepare and implement a general plan for economic development, in consultation with both sides of industry through the National Economic Development Council. This will provide for higher investment; for improving our industrial skills; for modernisation of industry; for balanced regional development; for higher exports; and for the largest possible sustained expansion of production and real incomes.
7   Much greater emphasis will be given to increasing productivity. Government will encourage and develop policies designed to promote technical advance in industry, get rid of restrictive practices and prevent the abuse of monopoly power and so improve efficiency, cut out waste, and reduce excessive profits. More vigorous policies will be pursued designed to facilitate mobility of labour and generally to make more effective use of scarce manpower resources, and to give workers a greater sense of security in the face of economic change. The Government also intend to introduce essential social improvements such as a system of earnings-related benefits in addition to the improvements in national insurance benefits already announced.
8   The Government will set up machinery to keep a constant watch on the general movement of prices and of money incomes of all kinds and to carry out the other functions described in paragraph 10 below. They will also use their fiscal powers or other appropriate measures to correct any excessive growth in aggregate profits as compared with

the growth of total wages and salaries, after allowing for short-term fluctuations.

9 We, the representatives of the TUC, the Federation of British Industry, the British Employers' Confederation, the National Association of British Manufacturers, and the Association of British Chambers of Commerce accept that the major objectives of national policy must be:

to ensure that British industry is dynamic and that its prices are competitive;

to raise productivity and efficiency so that real national output can increase, and to keep increases in wages salaries and other forms of incomes in line with this increase;

to keep the general level of prices stable.

10 We therefore undertake, on behalf of our members, to encourage and lead a sustained attack on the obstacles to efficiency, whether on the part of management or workers and to strive for the achievement of a more rigorous standard of performance at all levels; and to co-operate with the Government in endeavouring in the face of practical problems, to give effective shape to the machinery that the Government intends to establish for the following purposes:

(i) to keep under review the general movement of prices and of money incomes of all kinds;

(ii) to examine particular cases in order to advise whether or not the behaviour of prices or wages, salaries or other money incomes is in the national interest as defined by the Government after consultation with management and unions.

The Statement ended with an expression of "mutual confidence" in the achievement of the aims (see Appendix A for the full Statement).

It was sometimes lost sight of later in the history of the policy that it was originally conceived clearly in the framework of a National Plan, and against a background of rising production and incomes. The emphasis was also clearly on productivity. It was assumed that the obstacles to efficiency lay within the control of managements or workers, leaving only very general policies like the control of monopoly to the Government.

The national interest in price and income determination was acknowledged, as well as a promise to support an institution for investigating cases. The national interest might override the particular interests of unions or firms. Industry, competitive though its markets might be, did not necessarily achieve price stability, nor maximum efficiency. Equally, the unions did not necessarily either induce efficiency by forcing up wages, nor coax it out of their members by negotiating better conditions. Sectional interest aggregated did not achieve the national interest.

The national interest in efficiency was emphasised. The national interest in equity was not so clearly recognised—somewhat surprisingly perhaps for one of the first major productions of the new Labour Government. Equity between one broad group and another, between wage and salary earners on the one hand and the receivers of profits on the other, was mentioned; but not the equally important matter of equity between one wage or salary earner and another.

Deciding the national interest was not to be the prerogative of Government, even though the prices and incomes policy was the central part of the Government's economic policy. NEDC was both to consider reports about "general prices and incomes behaviour" and their implications for the national interest. Most of the members of the NEDC who were not members of the Government, were those trade-union leaders or employers who would, on days when NEDC was not in session, be taking part in decision-making about prices and incomes—the very process that had failed so far to serve the national interest adequately. To make a change, a real bargain, serving the interests of all three parties and requiring concessions from all three, would have to be reached. Moreover, the bargain had to be sufficiently plain to induce managers and unions to change their behaviour radically. The White Paper on the *Machinery of Prices and Incomes Policy* (Cmnd 2577) appeared on 11 February 1965. The policy, its principles and standards had still to be drafted. Meanwhile a suitable Chairman for this unique and powerful body had to be chosen. It became known that the employers' representatives had refused to agree to anyone but a businessman for the chairmanship. Fortunately the trades unions were not so intransigent. Nevertheless, the particular businessman had to appear sympathetic enough to their interests to extract their consent. The choice was Aubrey Jones, Member of Parliament, an ex-Minister of the Conservative Government, managing director of Staveley Industries, reputedly left-wing (within the Conservative Party), an early participant in informal discussions on prices and incomes policy among influential politicians (another of whom had been George Brown).

A Royal Warrant setting up the National Board for Prices and Incomes as a Royal Commission was signed on 17 March and the name of the Chairman announced a few days later. The policy to apply and the other members of the Board were announced in the House of Commons on 8 April, and published in a White Paper, *Prices and Incomes Policy* (Cmnd 2639).

2

The Political Framework: Powers and Influence

The prices and incomes policy was treated with seriousness and urgency by all the parties to it. But whether anything different resulted from the advice of the PIB depended only on the force of publicity, or the moral and political predilections of trades unionists and managers. Government policy could be made to bear in the public sector. But a policy having effect on the public sector only would penalise public-sector employees, and lead to a similar decline and fall that Selwyn Lloyd's pay-pause had suffered. There were no powers whatever to implement the policy.

George Brown considered that he was sponsoring a campaign in public education. Providing the PIB produced sensible reports, the public would recognise them to be so, and would support the conclusions. The parties to wage or price decisions would be persuaded by sweet reason, backed up by public approval, to serve the national interest. Early success would be signified by increasing willingness to seek the PIB's advice, and to adapt decisions to the advice given. There was plenty of sympathetic public interest, but the goodwill was not universal. There were trades unionists, employers and politicians, who thought the whole thing nonsense, and some determined to oppose it. Even some supporters of the policy were nevertheless suspicious of political interference with collective bargaining or price determination. It was vital that as many trades unionists as possible should understand the purpose of the policy, and actively support its implementation. The leaders participating in formulating the policy was not enough. Pay negotiations occur at many levels, and settlements depend in the last resort on what the workers will tolerate. To involve the pay negotiators with the policy, two conferences were held in the spring of 1965, one of union executives, and one at the TUC. The Government's prices and incomes policy and the TUC reports on it were both supported by an overwhelming majority.

There was no doubt about the general goodwill of the great majority of trades unionists at that stage.

The policy seemed to have got off to a good start, and the PIB appeared to be an appropriately influential body. It was independent of parties and the Government, and had its own staff. Its status as a Royal Commission made it clear that it would not look to any department for guidance, still less for instruction. It would communicate directly with the public at large—for that is what reporting to the Sovereign in fact involved. It was to apply a policy described in very general terms to particular cases. The cases would be referred by the Government, but the conclusions would be public.

However, a number of obvious weaknesses in an entirely voluntary policy appeared almost as soon as the PIB started work. These could only be remedied by acquiring powers by legislation. Only income settlements already made, and price increases already effective were being referred. It was difficult or impossible to withdraw wage or salary increases once the extra payments had started, however outrageous they might be in the light of the policy rules. Many prices could not quickly be brought down once they had been put up, inconsistent though they might be with the policy, if only because calculating new price lists or schedules of charges, notifying customers, and reprinting was time-consuming and expensive. The PIB's task was to show how costs could more effectively be absorbed; and its advice was more useful before price or wage changes had been made than afterwards.

The PIB's status as a Royal Commission was not entirely satisfactory either. Its powers to require evidence were constitutionally vague, in practice probably non-existent. Making all reports to Her Majesty was administratively awkward and time-wasting. It was a cumbersome device when many of the cases required urgent decisions.

The Government was anxious to have definite developments in the policy to show publicly by the time the political parties held their annual conferences in the autumn of 1965. It had been returned in the previous year with a very small majority, which it wanted to increase as soon as possible. Getting on in a purposive way with new ideas was one way to build up support. Also, in the background there were unwelcome signs of a renewed weakness of sterling. This and evidence of the continuing increase in the flow of incomes goaded Ministers and officials alike into hastening measures to make the incomes policy more effective.

George Brown announced on 2 September that some powers would be taken. Advance notification of proposed price and pay increases would be required by statute. Any proposed increase could be referred to the PIB; and while it investigated the case, the increase would have to be deferred. The announcement was made at the TUC annual conference, in a speech in which George Brown promised not to activate the powers unless it proved necessary, nor without prior consultation with the

TUC and CBI. The TUC duly gave its support to the strengthened policy. The delegates then went on to approve a very important development: that all pay claims from member unions would be referred to the TUC first before they were negotiated.

A new White Paper, *Prices and Incomes Policy, an Early-Warning System* (Cmnd 2808) appeared in November 1965. The new system was to be introduced immediately by agreement, as the powers could not be created for a few months. Though they had agreed to the general principles, it had not been possible for the Government to get the positive approval of either the TUC or the CBI to the details. The White Paper merely recorded that discussions had been held with them.

Early warning was supposed to apply to every decision or settlement on pay or prices. But as soon as legislation was proposed, administrative problems emerged. It was impossible to record every price change, let alone examine it. There are several million changes in a year, many of them seasonal and many of them of quite trivial importance. There are not so many pay settlements, though how many there are depends on how a settlement is defined. Local or company agreements over piece rates or bonuses may involve few workers, and happen frequently. It is not always apparent whether such settlements involve changes relevant to the policy rules or not. A system had to be devised to give warning of a reasonable number of cases, small enough not to be burdensome to managements or departments, but large enough to include cases significantly influencing national trends.

On prices, the general aim was to include goods and services "of particular economic significance", or consumer goods which were important elements in the cost of living. It would not apply to prices influenced by short-term changes in demand and supply, or depending mainly on import costs. Food needed special treatment, because of its importance to the cost of living. It would be subject to "constant watch" by the Ministry of Agriculture, Fisheries, and Food. In addition, there were goods where such great difficulties arose in establishing whether prices had increased or not, that they had to be left out. Where the product frequently changed in content, where many small firms were involved, or where custom-made equipment or goods were sold at prices individually negotiated, prices could not be effectively monitored. The limitations were formidable, especially in manufacturing.

Any enterprise producing goods specified in the White Paper (including nationalised industries and Government Departments), was to give four-weeks notice of an intention to raise prices, supported by a justification in terms of the policy. Departments receiving such notice would have four weeks to decide whether the case was to be referred to the PIB. If it was, the proposed increase was not to be made until the PIB reported. The whole standstill period would not exceed three months. This effectively gave the PIB two months for its investigations, a formidable limit on some of its early-warning cases.

There were five Government Departments principally concerned—the Ministry of Agriculture, Fisheries and Food; the Board of Trade; the Ministry of Technology; the Ministry of Public Building and Works, and the Ministry of Power. They now needed divisions or sections that would have responsibility for prices and incomes generally. This in itself was a major step forward for the policy. As there were specific tasks to perform, the precise rules of prices and incomes policy had to be studied since these had been embodied in the law. Few, if any, of these departments were well equipped to do the job. Investigating whether a company had a case for a price increase within the rules involved accounting and economic expertise as well as knowledge of the particular circumstances of the firm or industry. This was not readily available in all Government Departments, especially not in administrative divisions. However, to get price policy considered at all in relation to Government-to-industry dealings was a step forward.

Where goods were reasonably uniform, unbranded, but produced by many different firms of varying size, only firms above a certain size were required to give early warning. Fortunately (from the administrative point of view), not many of the products mentioned on the early-warning lists were produced in many varieties by many firms. Where there was either strong price leadership or only a few firms, prices moved together in the same direction very quickly, and often by very similar amounts. (The early-warning lists are reproduced in Appendix B.)

But unlike price cases, many pay claims would already have been reviewed before they came to the Government. The TUC set up its own "vetting" committee to examine them, to refer them back with comments, or to approve them. Exactly what was to happen where claims were not approved was not made clear. There could only be discussions between claimants and members of the General Council of the TUC. Member unions were to wait five weeks between notification and pressing claims to allow all this to be done. Only unions or staff associations not affiliated to the TUC would notify the Ministry of Labour directly of claims, and report to them on the progress of negotiations.

Pay cases did not present the same administrative complications as prices. There was only one department concerned, the Ministry of Labour. This department too was forced to take a rather more serious view of incomes policy than it had previously done, and to handle more work. Employers were to report both claims and settlements, the CBI collecting information from its members on national claims affecting more than 1,000 workers, and firms not belonging to the CBI reporting direct to the Ministry of Labour. The treatment of pay claims after they had reached the administration was rather different from that of prices.

The Government would consider whether the settlement was "likely to be consistent with the principles laid down in Cmnd 2639", or whether the case should be referred to the PIB. There was no mention of a standstill while the claims were considered by the Ministry of Labour. It was only when cases were referred that the parties would be expected to "suspend further action" until a report had been made. Reports would take two to three months.

There were now, in effect, three parallel organisations examining pay claims. Any case could, in principle, be referred to the PIB. But most claims were dealt with by the TUC, or by the Ministry of Labour. So long as the standards used were the same no great difficulty would arise. But if different interpretations of the standards were adopted, there would be danger of conflict and injustice for the victims. This happened to some extent after 1967, when there was a difference of view between the TUC and the Government on the standard to be adopted, based on a different view of economic problems and prospects.

The early-warning arrangements remained in force, with extensions to the lists, until early in 1970 (see Appendix C). They were then brought to an end as a statutory requirement, though voluntary early warning was supposed to continue to the end of the PIB's existence.

When early warning first started early in 1966, the Department of Economic Affairs was preparing the first Prices and Incomes Bill, introduced into the House of Commons in February 1966, just before the announcement that Parliament would be dissolved. Few General Elections can be said to be about any specific issue, but by introducing the Bill just before the election, the Government kept the prices and incomes policy in the forefront of discussion. Equally no Government in the UK can really claim to have a mandate for any particular measure. But the new Labour Government elected in March 1966 could claim public approval for pursuing its prices and incomes policy as much as any Government ever can.

A serious division between Government and part of the trade-union movement came to the surface soon afterwards. The Transport and General Workers' Union had consistently opposed such a policy. Nevertheless its leader, Frank Cousins, became a member of the new Government as Minister of Technology. But early in July 1966, when a Prices and Incomes Bill was once again under discussion, he resigned from the Government. The anti-incomes policy view among trades unionists had gained an important spokesman, then still in the House of Commons.

Frank Cousins declared his objections when the Bill was debated. He was attacking what was to him a "wrong philosophy"—the belief that there was a significant general relation between productivity and wages. His prescription was that "we should all look at the isolated cases". Wages should be related to performance in the most detailed way, case by case, aiming not at a "different division of the same kind of cake", but a "division of a larger cake". Employers and workers ought to work out productivity deals, so that output would rise together with wages. Stopping the "wage adjustment cycle", as he called it, would achieve nothing, because it would not induce increased production.

These were persuasive arguments, and in harmony with a trade-union leader's function of looking after his members' interests. They were also in harmony with the PIB's role and attitude. The PIB examined pay case by case, and insisted that pay be related to performance. The division of opinion was really over the interest of the consumers, and questions of national economic management. Productivity and pay moving closely in step might leave little scope for greater stability of prices, bearing in mind the activities where performance could not be improved quickly. The policy was to insert a new influence on behalf of consumers. But the second weakness of productivity deals alone was more important to the Government: increases in aggregate incomes might still far outstrip increases in output or the amount available for personal consumption, even though pay and performance were carefully related wherever they could be. The Government and trades unionists of this way of thought had begun to argue about different things, which could be consistent or inconsistent according to the circumstances, and the circumstances would make their views increasingly difficult to reconcile.

The Prices and Incomes Bill, reintroduced in July 1966, first made the PIB into a statutory board, set out its method of operation, and gave legislative effect to the current White Paper on prices and incomes policy as its terms of reference. Part II made the early-warning arrangements a statutory requirement, and established reserve powers to impose a standstill on any price or income referred to the PIB. This was all as before; but an early-warning arrangement for dividend distribution had been added. Profits and dividends had been rising strongly in 1965–66. Neither taxes nor prices policy appeared to have induced any restraint.

Meanwhile the Chancellor of the Exchequer and the Prime Minister were increasingly preoccupied with the state of the international reserves, which had begun once more to slip away. On 14 July the Prime Minister made a statement on the economic situation, the main point of which was to announce an urgent review of economic policy. The House then went on to the second reading of the Bill. The policy review showed that inflationary pressures were accumulating and sterling continued to weaken. The Government decided to maintain the current value of sterling at \$2.80. The only remedy left was to impose generally deflationary measures with great speed. The new policy was announced on 20 July; but it consisted not merely of the usual deflation of demand. There was to be a general standstill on all prices and incomes—a freeze —to accompany credit restriction and cuts in Government expenditure —another squeeze.

This was not the first time such a policy had been considered; there were advocates of a freeze for incomes in 1965. But it was ruled out of the question then, because neither the trades unions nor industrialists would accept it, and the policy was to be a voluntary one. When it was clear that there would have to be a freeze, there was a furious controversy for a time over whether it should be imposed for six or twelve months. In the end a compromise was reached. There would be six-months' freeze, followed by six-months' "severe restraint". The policy was now entirely imposed by the Government. Neither the general principle nor the details were negotiated or agreed with trades unions or industrialists. Neither could very actively oppose the policy because of the obviously serious economic situation. But though acquiescence was forthcoming for the freeze, this did not remove the disappointment of George Brown himself, and many other of the original supporters of the policy. The prices and incomes policy had become much more a part of national economic management than of general industrial reform.

The statement of 20 July was received with a profound sense of shock, as much due to the circumstances as to the standstill itself. Looking back on it, the reaction seems understandable, but perhaps mistaken in respect of the freeze. There is rather more justice in a standstill for everyone alike, than for weaker attempts at restraint whereby the law-abiding are restrained, and the self-seeking gain yet more advantage. It was also a much more definite policy for prices, known and understood much more widely than the heavily qualified "stability", with obscure rules about when prices might be increased.

However the standstill was the end of George Brown's hopes and intentions of operating a prices and incomes policy in an environment of steadily increasing real income. The policy and the powers for its enforcement were now part of an immediate effort to restore balance of payments equilibrium. A gradual, voluntary, expansionary policy was not possible. It seemed for twenty-four hours that the First Secretary would resign from the Government. He did not; he exchanged offices with Michael Stewart, then Foreign Secretary. But before the exchange actually took place, he had to steer a transformed Bill through the committee, report, and third-reading stages to its enactment, as the Prices and Incomes Act 1966.

The Bill as originally put before the House did not provide powers to enforce a freeze. A fourth part had to be added, with two major developments. The Government would acquire powers "to make orders (subject to negative resolution by either House of Parliament) directing that specified prices or charges, or specified rates of remuneration shall not be increased from the date of the order without Ministerial consent". The powers would be brought into operation by Order in Council, and would lapse automatically after twelve months. Secondly, the Government would take powers to enforce recommendations of the PIB, where the parties concerned did not agree to do so.

While the amended Bill was going through, it had to be decided exactly what would be frozen. In spite of the apparent simplicity of a standstill, there was still a deal of interpretation to be done, mostly in respect of incomes, the details of which were set out in the White Paper *Prices and Incomes Standstill* (Cmnd 3073), published before the end of July.

Increases in pay or reductions in hours were generally to be included. But payments which did not constitute an "increase in pay" in this context were quite considerable, including expenses, commissions, piece-work earnings (while piece *rates* remained the same), overtime and profit-sharing, "genuine promotion" and, most controversial of all, increments due on incremental scales. Another thorny problem was what to do about the existing agreements for increases in pay, beyond what was sanctioned by the policy rules. "Existing commitments" were to be honoured after a uniform delay of six months. More than 25 per cent of workers were covered by existing commitments of one kind and another, and this fact alone made it impossible to allow them to be honoured, regardless of the standstill. There would then have been no standstill. A uniform delay was also desirable, to maintain a modicum of fairness between workers covered by existing commitments and those closely behind them, though not past the crucial qualifying date. For the rest no new agreement could take effect before 1 January 1967, with very few exceptions. The same rules would apply to arbitration awards, and any other employment income, whether settled by collective bargaining or not. Fees for professional services were specifically included. All other money incomes, including dividend distributions, were also subject to the standstill, unless companies could make a case to the Government that exemption was "imperative". Such cases might be referred to the PIB, though none ever were.

On prices all that needed to be done was to specify which prices were included in the standstill, and to extend the early-warning system appropriately. All enterprises had to give early warning, excepting food which was subject to constant watch, and enterprises employing less than one hundred workers and not already in the early-warning schedule. Rent and rates were specifically included this time.

For all the vehemence of the debate in Parliament and the loud protests of trades unionists and industrialists, the standstill was accepted remarkably well; once the Act was passed, there were remarkably few efforts to defy it. The Government now had power to impose a Standstill Order in the case of any pay or price increase, regardless of whether the case was referred to the PIB or not. Only fifteen such Orders were made, seven of them in the standstill period up to 31 January 1967 and eight more in the period of severe restraint up to 12 August 1967 when the powers lapsed (see Appendix D1, page 281 for details). One of them related to prices, and 14 to incomes; but only some 36,000 workers were covered by all of them, out of a working population of 23 million. The powers to enforce the PIB's recommendations were never used. (It must also be noticed that any imaginary subservience of public authorities to Government policy is belied by the appearance of no less than three of them [the Metropolitan Police Receiver, Birmingham Corporation and the Royal Borough of Rothesay] among the defiant ones. There were, as we shall see, many more such pieces of evidence that public authorities are no better or worse, as a group, than private-sector groups, at any rate in respect of prices and income policy.)

The short list of the unrelenting opponents understates the extent of attempts to break the standstill. It does not reveal cases where claims were pursued or price increases contemplated in defiance of the stand-still, only to be postponed after pressure from Government Departments.

However it was after the policy was backed by statutory powers that conflict between the Government and some of the unions became more acute. While the policy remained voluntary, the difference remained a difference of opinion, and the dissenting unions merely continued to press pay claims on any grounds they chose. The TGWU, for instance, continued to press for higher wages through productivity increases, putting the greatest pressure on the least efficient employers. It aimed to establish an effective minimum wage by these tactics. Differences over national policy made relations between the TGWU and the Government, and between it and the PIB uneasy, though not as grim as might have been expected. The first of the cases referred to the PIB, road haulage, embroiled the TGWU willy-nilly with the policy (see page 53). But the PIB recommended nothing contrary to TGWU policy. Conflict appeared more sharply in 1966 over the busmen. A London busmen's pay agreement was referred to the PIB in the last days of the voluntary period. The new agreement provided an above-norm increase in pay, due to be copied by municipal and company busmen in the provinces, according to previous routines. The PIB managed to approve the London increase, but recommended that only the norm should be paid to other busmen, unless productivity agreements justifying more could be negotiated. Further trouble was put off by the standstill, as the provincial agreements were not made in time to escape the freeze.

The Association of Supervisory Staffs, Executives and Technicians (now the Association of Supervisory, Managerial and Technical Staffs) also opposed incomes policy. It was a small, but fast-growing union, representing a group of people who resented doing less well, or no better than manual workers. A policy involving squeezing or preserving existing differentials between the lower- and higher-paid jobs would not enable them to do any catching-up. It was not surprising therefore that this was among the most aggressive opponents of the policy and the PIB. But it only came into direct conflict with the PIB over the smallest case ever referred, the pay of 28 artificial limbfitters employed by Hanger's Ltd. After a go-slow, an increase of £2 a week from 2 January 1967 had been agreed. There were humanitarian reasons for settling the dispute; but if this were done by breaking the incomes policy rules, the political force of severe restraint would undoubtedly be weakened. In spite of the reference, the increases were paid, and an Order was made, reducing pay to the level of 20 July 1966. The PIB could not justify the increase, and recommended deferment until after the end of severe restraint. As the parties refused to postpone payment voluntarily, the Order continued until it automatically expired in August 1967 when the powers under the 1966 Act expired. Meantime the union put in a larger claim. The company would not respond, and another go-slow began. However pay negotiations were joined again, this time including proposals for increased efficiency and joint consultation as the PIB had recommended. The head-on clash with the policy died away.

The Electrical Trades Union came into conflict with the PIB, though it was a supporter of the policy in general. A three-year agreement for the electrical-contracting industry had been made a few days before the standstill began, escaping anything more than six months' freeze. But the agreement involved an increase of 13 per cent, and would apply to "trade-rated" electricians in many other industries as well.

Both the union and the employers believed the agreement had made a real breakthrough towards improved efficiency, as well as better industrial relations, in an industry notoriously bad in both respects, and were outraged to find that the PIB nevertheless could not agree that it was in accordance with the policy rules because the 13 per cent could not be justified by prospective cost saving. When the agreement was once more referred to the PIB two-and-a-half years later, the union refused to give any kind of evidence. But the PIB had mostly praise to shower on the way the later stages of the agreement had worked out.

For a few short months late in 1966, after the Act was passed, the administration suspended its discussion of powers while the application of the powers was sorted out. But Part IV of the Act lapsed in August 1967, and it had to be decided what was to be substituted. One body of opinion favoured repeating something similar, which would have required legislation, but it would not have been impossible. The short history of the voluntary policy was not encouraging. It had not been effective on either prices or incomes, for all the publicity and the PIB's efforts. Though both the CBI and TUC were campaigning for the end of powers and a return to a voluntary policy, they were on weak ground in face of the evidence. The CBI chiefly wanted to get rid of dividend restraint and a blanket restraint on prices. Costs were rising again and it was known that many firms were waiting for the end of restraint to put up prices. Opinion in the TUC had actually advanced somewhat in favour of an effective policy. But it remained vehemently attached to the voluntary principle to protect free collective bargaining.

However in administrative circles the argument about whether there should be powers got increasingly tangled up with the argument over what policy the powers should be used to enforce. It was quite clear that any realistic policy, judged by the forecasts of real income for 1967–68, could allow pay increases so small that powers of enforcement would be needed to get anywhere near what was required for economic management. The Government was anxious to get as near the TUC's view as it safely could. A new White Paper began by declaring the Government's continued attachment to a voluntary policy. But to make the policy credible, the powers of delay in Part II of the Act were to be substituted for Part IV. The Government accepted that "the availability of reserve powers cannot be a substitute for the voluntary co-operation of the majority". There would be further consultations about "a limited development of the reserve powers".

A second Prices and Incomes Act, 1967, was passed. The general requirement to give advance notice of price increases was dropped. Instead, the early-warning system for a list of named products returned. Dividend restraint was abandoned, though powers to require notice of increased distributions remained. The new powers of delay applied only to cases referred to the PIB. Pay or price increases would have to be deferred for three months while a report was prepared. If the PIB recommended against them they could be postponed for a further three months by an Order. Any increase could thus be postponed for a total of seven months.

The conflict with the busmen, led by the TGWU, continued under the new Act. The battle between the busmen and the employers had grown considerably fiercer since 1966. Industrial relations at national level were bad, deteriorating and soon to be broken off altogether. A number of local agreements were reported to the Ministry of Labour under the early-warning arrangements, in the late spring of 1967, as severe restraint was nearing its end. These were referred to the PIB. Before it could report, national negotiations ceased, and strikes and go-slows spread. The busmen were accused of "striking against the Government", or against the law. The union leaders were not sorry to make trouble for the policy; but they were in dispute with the employers, as they had a perfect right to be, incomes policy or no. Both sides did their best to defy the policy within the law. The first Standstill Orders under the 1967 Act were then made (see Appendix D2 for full list). The PIB advised the Government that the agreements referred were not in accord with the policy, and the Order was extended to the maximum of six months.

But turbulence in the bus industry was by no means at an end. One municipality after another reached alleged productivity agreements and many announced their intention of backdating the frozen increase as

THE POLITICAL FRAMEWORK: POWERS AND INFLUENCE

soon as the Standstill Orders expired. In all, the PIB reported on eight cases, followed by Orders.

Another, much smaller, union very ready to defy the policy was the then Draughtsmen's and Allied Technicians' Association, with members of similar status to ASSET. Four engineering firms reached agreements with DATA when strikes threatened. Standstill Orders were made under the 1967 Act, while the PIB reported, and were subsequently extended.

The only other Standstill Orders under the 1967 Act related to two cases where the PIB subsequently found that the increases proposed were justified. These related to clerks employed in Bristol docks (see p. 216), and sawyers and machinists in saw-milling (see p. 156). This was a very small tally for compulsion. The complete lack of resistance to the Orders and of demonstrations against them argues still more strongly for the general acceptability of the Act.

Once the Government had taken the decision in 1967 to reduce its powers to powers of delay only, it was virtually committed to returning indefinitely to a voluntary policy. But another balance of payments crisis was already on the way. This time the decision was finally taken to devalue. The devaluation of November 1967 imposed economic pressures once more, of a kind that should have made another prices and incomes standstill a policy to be seriously considered. But after the heated and protracted discussion of the preceding spring and its eventual conclusion in much-reduced powers, there was really no political hope of another standstill.

Yet it was clear that few resources would be available to increase consumption while the diversion to exports was going on, and that rising costs due to rising incomes would soon nullify the advantages gained by devaluation. A strict and restrictive prices and incomes policy was necessary to support the structural changes in the economy that would have to follow. Powers of some sort there ought to be; but it was the rules rather than the powers that were tightened (and these are discussed in the following chapter, see page 23).

The White Paper on the policy for 1968 and 1969 largely repeated the early-warning arrangements, though the list of goods and services to which early warning was to apply had been steadily extended by this time. (Additions to the list are shown in Appendix B, p. 278.) A new list of goods where "the trend of manufacturing prices" would be kept under review also appeared.

The Chancellor of the Exchequer announced in his Budget statement in April 1968 that the powers to require notification of dividend increases would be activated. Rent increases proposed by local authorities would be subject to early warning, and the Government would take powers to direct the local authorities to modify or phase them if they appeared "too high in present circumstances". Finally, the powers to delay proposed price or pay increases were extended to a total of twelve months. The third Prices and Incomes Act (1968) embodied all these additions.

The busmen and their employers were still embroiled with the policy, and the first Order under the 1968 Act applied to the same busmen's agreement, as the first Order under the 1967 Act had done. It extended the standstill to the total of eleven months provided for under the new Act. In two of the three cases, the parties agreed to withdraw and re-negotiate the agreements after the PIB report, rather than have a standstill extended. In the third, an Order extending the standstill had to be applied.

Apart from these relating to the busmen, only four Orders under the 1968 Act were made. One relating to the thermal-insulation industry was found to be justified, and the Order automatically expired. Two Orders extending the standstill to the full eleven months were made in respect of workers in electrical contracting in Scotland and workers in the exhibition industry (see p. 167 below). But in neither case was the Standstill Order the end of the story. While they were still in force, discussions were going on between the employers, th unions and officials of the DEP about productivity agreements on the lines recommended by the PIB. None of the Orders under either Act related to prices or to dividends or to rents.

What was to be done after 1969 remained a difficult problem, since it was still not considered politically possible to increase powers of enforcement. The politically practicable questions were whether the existing powers should be retained, and if not whether the powers to delay increases should merely be modified or suspended altogether. Powers of delay were reasonably important, since they did allow some possibility of cutting down the rate of increase of incomes, which was the whole purpose of the policy. But there were no powers to prevent employers paying delayed increases retrospectively, and this had increasingly been happening in 1969, especially in the case of the banks' and ICI staffs (see p. 166 below).

Perhaps general goodwill towards an incomes policy was running out too rapidly for delay to be effective. An important reason for disillusion with the policy was an accumulation of evidence that fairness to the lower-paid had not been achieved at all. Prices too seemed to be once again rising much more sharply, and to be more difficult to restrain, even where the policy rules were applied. It was not an encouraging background against which to ask the TUC to agree to another instalment of the policy on the same lines. The Government also had to bear in mind the decisive rejection of the policy at the Labour Party annual conference of 1969, and other evidence of party-workers' disaffection.

Moreover the argument about what the prices and incomes policy should be after 1969, and how it should be enforced, was increasingly sidetracked. Two other issues occupied the attention of the Government and the leading trades-union leaders and industrialists. One was the general reform of industrial relations. The other was the reform of over-lapping organisations. The Donovan Commission on employers' associations and trades unions had reported in June 1968. Consultations with the parties followed; and the Government's views and proposals were published early in 1969 in a White Paper, *In Place of Strife*. An Industrial Relations Bill followed, introduced into the House of Commons later in 1969. But the so-called "penal clauses", providing that trades unions could be fined, or even that their leaders might be imprisoned, led to a bitter controversy between the union leaders and the Government. Industrial relations, and the difference between Government and unions about them, had become a much more important issue than incomes policy. It was no longer possible to negotiate an effective policy while relations between Cabinet members and the TUC General Council were so hostile.

As a result of the Donovan report, the Commission on Industrial Relations was set up in 1969. This might or might not clash with the PIB's activities on wages, depending on the cases referred to each body, and the way each chose to treat them.

On prices there were two older institutions in the field and one contemporary: the Monopolies Commission, the Restrictive Practices Court, and the Industrial Reorganisation Corporation. Overlapping between them was an administrative inconvenience, since they were sponsored by different departments. The cases they handled, and what questions they were supposed to answer were matters of inter-departmental controversy and therefore on occasion of Ministerial controversy a time-wasting nuisance for the Government. It was also possible that the different bodies would adopt different policies on such issues as large-scale business versus competition. For the administrators the most awkward aspect of the problem was the PIB's competence in both prices and incomes. Had it been less successful than it was, there might not have been much difficulty about passing responsibility for either prices or incomes to another body. Given the PIB's relative success, and given also the danger that productivity would be fully investigated by no one if prices and incomes were put asunder, a solution was finally reached by proposing an amalgamation of the PIB and the Monopolies Commission. Responsibility for monopolies and restrictive practices (including the Restrictive Practices Court) was transferred to the DEP, and a Commission for Industry and Manpower (CIM) was to be set up to include the functions of the PIB and the Monopolies Commission.

The Government's view of the function of the CIM, as set out in the White Paper *Productivity, Prices and Incomes after 1969* (Cmnd 4237, December 1969) was then clearly that the function (though not the existence) of the PIB would continue. Proposals for price and income increases under the early-warning arrangements would continue to be referred to the CIM; general questions of pay structure and efficiency

B

studies of nationalised industries would also continue. But so would the work of the Monopolies Commission, as required by the relevant Acts. The PIB would cease to exist, though the CIM would acquire the PIB's chairman and some of the same members. The Government declared that it has always recognised that the full powers available under the 1968 and 1969 Prices and Incomes Act to delay the implementation of pay and price increases was called for only in exceptional circumstances and as a short-term measure. The delaying power under the 1967 and 1968 Acts had expired at the end of 1969 and would not be renewed. All that would remain would be the early-warning arrangements and powers to delay increases of pay and prices up to three months, while the PIB investigated and reported on the cases referred to it. The policy had almost come back to its voluntary form of the pre-freeze days.

3

The Development of the Policy

The prices and incomes policy can be divided into stages according to the successive White Papers about the detailed rules. All of these phases were associated with changes in the legislative framework described in the previous chapter. But there were also changes in the content of the policy, not resulting from changes in powers.

The first White Paper on prices and incomes (Cmnd 2639) was published on the same day on which the members and constitution of the PIB were also announced in the House of Commons. The rules meant to have most general effect were annual increases in incomes no greater than the "norm", and stability for prices.

The norm represented the annual average increase in incomes per head consistent with stability in prices. Output per head was expected to rise by about 3½ per cent from 1965 a year for the five years to 1970; but it would be lower in 1965. Shorter hours and longer holidays already agreed would reduce it further. Nevertheless, the norm was to be 3 to 3½ per cent from 1965.

The general rule for prices was to keep the general level stable. But, as the White Paper pointed out, changes in the price level are made up of movements of many individual prices; some prices fall even though the price level rises. So no rule governing all prices was given. Managements were to increase efficiency and avoid cost increases. Price increases should not be made—except:

1 where output per employee could not be increased without there being enough to pay wages and salaries consistent with the criteria for incomes;
2 where there were unavoidable increases in non-labour incomes such as materials, fuel, services or marketing costs;
3 where there were unavoidable increases in capital costs; or
4 where an enterprise was unable to secure the required capital to meet demand.

In all cases, possible productivity improvements or reductions in profit were to be allowed for before reckoning any price increase. Reductions would be expected where falling costs or rising productivity allowed, or where profits were based on excessive market power. But even these exceptions would not alone meet industry's needs. Squeezing unit costs could keep prices down; but so could squeezing profits. Administrative pressure on prices and profits fits uneasily into a modern market economy. High profits are the main incentive to invest more resources in sectors where demand is expanding. They are therefore necessary to promote the efficient working of the system, and some qualification of the rules was needed to make them less rigid. The rules were not intended to inhibit the structural changes necessary for faster growth. Competition had an important part to play in increasing efficiency, and should be a normal part of enterprising business behaviour. Profits were recognised to be a proper reward of successful competitors.

The same rules would apply equally to public enterprise. The Government regarded the nationalised industries as under the same obligations as private industry to contribute to stability, "while taking account of their financial and social obligations". As we shall see later, the qualifying clause virtually robbed the assurance of any force, though it looked straightforward enough at the time.

The general rule for incomes was that less weight than before should be given to changes in demand and supply for labour, trends in profits, comparisons with others, and changes in the cost of living. More weight should be given to the norm.

Exceptional increases would be justified:

1   where workers accepted "more exacting work" or a major change in working practice;
2   where a pay increase would be necessary and effective in securing a desirable redistribution of labour;
3   where there was "general recognition" that wages or salaries were too low to maintain a "reasonable standard of living";
4   where there was "widespread recognition" that pay had fallen "seriously out of line" with rewards for similar work elsewhere.

Exceptional increases would have to be kept to a minimum, "bearing in mind that they will need to be balanced by lower than average increases to other groups", if the national increase was to be kept within the norm. Shorter hours, higher overtime or shift pay, and improved fringe benefits would have to be taken into account since they all affected labour costs.

The first two criteria for exceptional increases were considerations arising from the efficient operation of the system, the third from considerations of social justice, and the last both from efficiency and equity depending on how the national interest was interpreted. The first, on productivity was the only one where above-average increases in income would not lead to lower real income being available elsewhere. But the national increase in productivity is only an aggregate of individual cases, including exceptional ones. By no means all increases in productivity arise from more exacting work or major changes in working practice. For instance increases in capital and improvements in management need not involve such changes. These would have to balance exceptional increases for the underpaid or low-paid.

The final thorny point was what more to say about profits. Distributed profits were after all an important kind of income. If other kinds of income were effectively restricted by the policy when profits were not, a worse distribution of income would result—an outcome which would lead to a serious withdrawal of support from the Labour side. The prices policy had been introduced as an alternative to trying in vain to get parallel treatment for profits and wages. Profits were not a close parallel to other incomes. Employment incomes are a contractual payment; profits are not. No alternative could be found on this occasion but a general proviso that monopoly profits would be looked to.

Such were the rules during the first voluntary period of prices and incomes policy. They were not greatly modified afterwards, apart from changes in the norm for incomes.

The second White Paper, *Prices and Incomes Standstill* (Cmnd 3073), recorded not only a nil norm for incomes but in effect suspended all the exceptions for six months. The only qualification related to what did or did not constitute "an increase in pay". The standstill did not apply to:

expense allowances; increases in pay resulting directly from increased output (piece-work earnings, commissions, overtime or profit-sharing); increases in pay resulting from promotion; and pay for age, or regular increments on pay scales.

Three additions to the general incomes policy were made at the same time. The first related to arbitration awards. Arbitrators operated in a way which was quite inconsistent with the policy. Their first duty was to settle disputes between employers and workers. Their awards need have little relation to the national interest (unless the national interest was taken to be merely the absence of industrial disputes). Yet unions found arbitration awards a useful means of getting employers to make wage increases they would otherwise resist, and which might be beyond the incomes policy requirements.

The standstill made a bigger difference to the policy on prices, since there was now a general rule that all prices were to be frozen. But there would still be exceptions, to the "limited extent that increases in prices or charges may be necessary because of marked increases which cannot be absorbed, in costs of important materials, or which arise from changes in supply for seasonal or other reasons, or which are due to action by the Government such as increased taxation". Any enterprise which felt compelled to propose an increase would receive "the most rigorous scrutiny in the light of national economic needs." The criteria were said to be much more stringent than the previous ones. The extra stringency lay in excluding increased capital cost or inability to secure the capital required from the circumstances justifying price increases. Increases of this kind are not made frequently and postponement for a few months was not likely to be very serious for most companies. After a period of rising profits, not many could be short of funds.

Specific reference to Government action as a reason for justifiable price increases was made. This was necessary because taxes imposed in the Budget of 1966 led to widespread protests from businessmen. There were increases in vehicle and petrol duty, and—most important of all— the Selective Employment Tax.

The standstill would also apply to distributed profits. All dividends were to be frozen, the only exception being "close-controlled companies" which might be penalised by tax laws if they could not do so. Any other increases could only be made if the Treasury gave permission after reviewing the case.

The third period White Paper, *Prices and Incomes Standstill—the Period of Severe Restraint* (Cmnd 3150), was published in November 1966, after more intensive bargaining between Government, trades unions and employers over the terms. These consultations resulted in a "wide measure of agreement" about national needs, though it could not be said that the detailed criteria were approved.

The general rule on prices was in the same form as in the first White Paper. All enterprises, private and public, should make as great an effort as possible to absorb cost increases. Reductions in unit costs ought to be reflected in reduced prices. It was hoped that the removal of the import surcharges, imposed in 1964 as a temporary support for the balance of payments, would offer scope for price reductions. The criteria for exceptional increases were relaxed, compared with the standstill, by allowing increases to "maintain efficiency and undertake necessary investment". During the first period some difficulty had arisen in the PIB's enquiries where one product of a multi-product firm had been referred. One product might be clearly unprofitable while others were just as clearly profitable. Naturally, price increases were only proposed for the unprofitable ones, and these were referred. Consequently it would be necessary in future to take into account particular increases in cost, the costs incurred by the whole enterprise, and the profitability of the whole enterprise.

Rent and rates could not be subject to a general rule. Rent in private housing was controlled by the Rent Acts, and could hardly be subjected to another control under another Act. Business premises and land were not controlled in any way; but it was difficult to think of an effective way of imposing any control. So the White Paper merely said that private landlords were "expected to have full regard to the need for severe restraint". Public authority rents were a different matter. Local authorities were expected to avoid any increase as far as possible; and where rent increases prove unavoidable, they were to "protect tenants of modest means" by rent rebates. Rates must still be restricted by economies in expenditure.

The criteria for exceptional increases in pay remained as in the standstill White Paper. That lowest-paid workers were to have special consideration was still a primary social objective. Any such pay increase should be confined to the lowest paid, and not passed on to others. Hours worked as well as wages were to be taken into account. This addition was in response to criticism from trades unions when the PIB seemed to them to take too little account of hourly earnings. Increases to correct a maldistribution of labour could not be left out; but only in the most exceptional cases should an increase be made. A shortage of labour should rather be met by a more effective use of the existing manpower.

Lastly, comparability was not an acceptable reason for increases; but there might be cases where a pay increase was "imperative" to correct a gross anomaly. Such cases should not be used as an excuse for "catching-up" elsewhere.

The real problem was how to get reasonably out of the standstill, rather than planning what rules to set for the period of severe restraint. The main objective was to set a limit to income increases in 1967. A widespread catching-up process would soon destroy any advantage gained by the standstill, and it would just as surely swamp any redistribution that had occurred to the advantage of the low-paid. But merely preventing catching-up was not enough. It was important to review more agreements at an earlier stage of bargaining.

An important addition was made under the heading of existing commitments, but only relating to agreements in the public sector. No increases would be made before the end of severe restraint. Thereafter substantial payments would be made in instalments.

Government salaries (and some others) were only reviewed at infrequent intervals; and although each revision only took into account the appropriate norms and criteria of the period since the last one, each award might be large. If the whole adjustment was made at once, expenditure took a large step upwards. Phasing could in general make an important contribution to stability. Employers would gain time to meet the cost; workers would gain the certainty of future increases without further negotiation.

Not much of this helped with the problem of getting out of severe restraint in an orderly way. Bargaining with the TUC and CBI was still going on, and no sort of agreement could yet be recorded. Yet guidance to negotiators was urgently needed for the period after 30 June 1967. So a paragraph was added in the name of the Government only, giving three ground rules and an earnest hope. The country could not afford shorter hours or longer holidays, and automatic cost-of-living sliding scales should be abolished. A more "co-ordinated approach" to wages and salaries was needed to determine the "relative economic and social priorities" of competing claims for different groups.

Dividend restraint was still to apply up to 30 June 1967.

But what was to come after 30 June? The arithmetic of prospective national output, minus prior commitments for improving the balance of payments, repaying international debts, and meeting public expenditure allowed nothing for wage increases. But no one believed that incomes would not rise, nor that there was an acceptable way of preventing a rise. The Government view was that a generous but effective norm was better than a severe but ineffective one. But even the generosity had to be limited to be at all credible in a national framework. The terms of the norm were also in question. A percentage norm gave a larger cash amount to the well-off than to the low-paid, who were still numerous. There was increasing evidence that the comparatively well-off were getting away with it, while the less privileged of wage-earners could not. The argument for a norm in money terms was persuasive on grounds of fairness, but not on grounds of efficiency. Changes of structure were still needed, and there were still differentials too small to encourage desirable supplies of skill.

The TUC took the view that as only a modest total increase was possible, social justice required a flat-rate sum for all. Having made its own calculation of the national product, it arrived at a norm of 14s a week, with anything more than this justified only by more overtime, bigger earnings from payments by results or productivity bargains.

The Government insisted that the TUC were too optimistic in their calculations (as indeed they were), and published their own conclusion in the fourth White Paper, *Prices and Incomes Policy after 30 June 1967* (Cmnd 3235). This urged continued moderation, and welcomed the undertakings given by the TUC and CBI to "play their full part" in the development of a voluntary policy. It avoided referring to the TUC's norm by not referring to a norm at all. This gave the appearance of continued severity, but whether it would act severely would depend on how the powers conferred by Part II of the Act were enforced.

The rules in the new White Paper were only slightly altered. Prices in manufacturing would need to fall in order to offset price increases in sectors where an increase was more difficult. Otherwise the criteria were the same as in the first White Paper.

Increases in rent and rates were outside the scope of the standstill and restraint policy, and had to remain so. Rising costs of housing (due to rising interest rates) and education because of the extra places required, made local authorities' expenditure and local rates march inevitably upwards. Short of being able to eliminate major inefficiencies quickly, local authorities would have to increase rents and rates soon. But nothing different could be said on rents. The effect of rate increases was reduced by discriminating between rates for households and commercial premises, and Exchequer grants were increased in an attempt to stabilise the rate poundage.

The incomes section pointed out that there was no justification for returning to the original norm, especially as it had been treated as the minimum entitlement. But now no one could expect a minimum increase. The criteria for exceptional increases were as in the first period. Comparisons were still not to be used to spread pay increases. The Government accepted the TUC's view that productivity agreements and the low-paid were the two groups deserving what increases could be afforded. A year was to be the minimum period between settlements, and there should be no making good ground lost during the standstill and severe restraint. The same rules should apply to arbitrators, independent review bodies and statutory wage-fixing bodies. The PIB itself had pointed out in its second annual report that the rules had not so applied, and this was bound to make the policy less effective.

The addition of what was in effect a separate rule for salaries was the more important from the PIB's point of view. Before this the same criteria were supposed to apply to salaries as to wages. But productivity bargaining was not possible in many salaried occupations; nor were many salary earners among the low-paid. It was difficult to justify any salary increase beyond the norm, using the same criteria as for wages. But salaries needed increases consistent with the aims of the incomes policy as much as wages. Therefore managements could now return to progressions based on added experience, increased responsibility or special effort. Also, it was in the interests of economic efficiency that there should be "a proper development of salary structures which provide incentives to improved performance".

The standstill on profits would end in July 1967 as the severe restraint White Paper had promised. Companies should "exercise moderation" in dividend distributions for the following year.

By the time the fifth White Paper *Productivity, Prices and Incomes Policy in 1968 and 1969* (Cmnd 3590) was being discussed, the Government and its advisers were preoccupied once more with the balance of payments, culminating in the devaluation of sterling in November 1967,

Once more the content of the prices and incomes policy had to be related to the strict requirements of economic management. What these ought to be was no less controversial than before. A fall in total personal consumption was coming and had indeed been induced by Government action. Prices would inevitably rise, this too due to Government policy. Some increases in incomes there would have to be if the fall in consumption was not to be greater than intended. Also the policy was again to be largely voluntary. It was a question of just how much the officially approved increases ought to be, in order to get an acceptable rate of increase in the event.

It was eventually decided to try to get more control over the total increase of incomes by putting a figure on the exceptional increases rather than having a norm with unspecified exceptions on the top of that. There would be a "ceiling" of $3\frac{1}{2}$ per cent.

The ceiling would be an annual rate, and higher increases could be given where more than a year had elapsed since the last. But such increases should be staged. The ceiling should include increases negotiated at national, local and plant level. However, it applied to a whole wage or salary bill, for the largest practicable group of workers, rather than to individuals. Changes in the structure making up the wage or salary bill would thereby be permitted. Efficiency overrode equity even more than before.

Finally, the $3\frac{1}{2}$ per cent ceiling was to apply also to dividends. All companies were asked not to increase dividends "without good reason", and to limit any increase they thought essential. In any case ordinary dividends should be limited to $3\frac{1}{2}$ per cent above those declared in the preceding year.

Increases in rent or rates were to be moderated. Though they were subject to the Rent Acts, sharp rises in private rents could occur as landlords took advantage of a new definition of "fair rents". What mattered for prices and incomes policy was the size or rate of increase rather than whether or not a new level was justified on some other standard. The fairest of fair rents could be increased too sharply for price stability. The Housing Minister was given powers to make Regulations for phasing increases above a stipulated minimum amount. Local authorities too were given more precise instructions and subjected to additional control, partly as a result of a PIB report completed shortly before. Early warning of rent increases would be required, and the Government would take powers to direct local authorities to moderate or phase rent increases.

Rates were not expected to rise further, partly as a result of the extra grants described in the previous prices and incomes White Paper. Rate rebate schemes were slowly spreading among authorities so that low-income families (including many pensioners) would pay less than before.

The first steps in reaching the rules for the sixth and last period came in October 1968. Mrs Barbara Castle, by then the Secretary of State for Employment and Productivity, invited the CBI and the TUC to begin discussions on the future of the policy. Little progress had been made with this by budget time in April 1969 however. Roy Jenkins, the Chancellor, then announced that "less emphasis" would be put on prices and incomes policy, and the powers would be relaxed. Discussions then continued, but understandably in a much less anxious way. The major attention of employers, unions and Government was diverted to industrial relations in general.

The sixth White Paper was *Productivity, Prices and Incomes Policy after 1969* (Cmnd 4237) published eventually in December 1969. By this time, it had been assumed for some months by management and unions alike that the policy was of declining usefulness or importance. Yet the White Paper was the longest and most elaborate of any. The aims of the policy were said to be:

"Establishing on a firm and continuing basis the principle of links between pay increases and the more effective use of labour;
securing fundamental improvements in the methods of pay negotiation and settlement;
creating wage and salary structures which will avoid successive leap-frogging settlements and eliminate friction;
improving the position of low-paid workers, particularly by re-organisations which will make better use of their efforts and by the introduction of equal pay for women;
raising the efficiency with which labour and capital equipment are used in all sectors of the economy—private industry, publicly owned industry, and the public services;
ensuring that the larger industrial units now being brought into existence use their resources efficiently and to the benefit of the consumer, and do not use their increased market power to operate pricing policies or pay policies which fail to take proper account of the wider public interest."

All this was very laudable, and mostly what the PIB had been aiming at all along, except for equal pay for women. But it had little to do with national management objectives.

Price stability would only be achieved if efficiency or competition required it. Restraint on incomes could only be achieved gradually as a result of a closer link between pay and performance.

The rest of the White Paper had a considerably different character from previous ones. Rules for the determination of prices and incomes and criteria justifying exceptions no longer applied. Instead there was "guidance" for pay negotiations, for determining prices and charges and in relation to dividends and rents and rates.

Money incomes should only rise at about the rate of productivity. This meant that most wage and salary settlements needed to come within the range of $2\frac{1}{2}$–$4\frac{1}{2}$ per cent annual increase. No single figure was given because none could be appropriate to the circumstances of all negotiations. There could still be exceptional cases where settlements would come above the guidance. The exceptions would now be six instead of four, as equal pay and public-service salaries had been added to the list. Reorganising pay structures still justified exceptional increases, if it opened the way to substantial improvements in efficiency. More rational structures, based on job evaluation would reduce the risk of leap-frogging claims and eliminate discontent.

The low-paid might be helped in some industries by negotiating higher minimum earnings levels. But the White Paper was at pains to point out that no technique would improve the position of the low-paid unless employers and unions willed it so. If every increase in minimum earnings levels became a floor above which all other rates moved, the only result would be inflation. Studies of particular situations would have to be made. The PIB (and later the CIM) would be asked to investigate in depth cases where low pay was a serious problem, and suggest particular means whereby improvements could be made Many of the low-paid were women—the Equal Pay Act (1970) would apply only in 1975. But instalments towards it should be made in some industries. This would involve changes in traditional differentials, and some bigger increase than the guidance.

Arguments for pay increases based on labour shortages had played too large a part in negotiations. Employers should consider whether efficiency agreements would reduce their labour requirements, or whether they had exhausted scope for internal transfers or training of their existing labour-force. Too much weight should not be given to comparisons, or supposed market rates. Comparisons were necessary in the right places, namely between one level and another internally.

Public service was distinguished because the jobs done by for instance, teachers, doctors and nurses, prevented measurement of their output, and there was no market price for it. Comparisons were important to them, in spite of all the efforts to find some other basis. The Government would continue to consult the PIB, and later the CIM on all public-service pay.

The net effect of applying all these rules and homilies would inevitably have been to increase the flow of incomes far above the four per cent guidance. The cases that would be exceptional in some respect, would be more than the Chancellor could seriously tolerate. Price stability—even assuming the incomes guidance was effective—would be something of a vain hope.

The guidance for determining prices was equally discursive, if not equally long. The criteria for price increases were still the same as in the first White Paper. The aim of the continuing policy was "to ensure in each enterprise that changes in prices genuinely reflect unavoidable costs and take account of the possibility of cost savings". Rents also should only be increased where there were unavoidable cost increases. Powers to require notification of dividend increases would remain, though moderation was the only rule suggested.

The elaborate guidance rang hollowly with no powers to back it. Hostility was growing to early warning, and there was little hope of general respect for the policy.

At all six stages of the policy, whatever the legislative framework, the rules had to be interpreted by the PIB. Its role was bound to be a minor one in terms of the number of cases dealt with. Its influence depended on the nature of the cases presented to it by Government Departments, as well as its advice.

The PIB has had 134 cases in $5\frac{1}{2}$ years, 72 on incomes and 58 on prices and four covering both. This was not unreasonable, and on the face of it a reasonably unbiased spread. However, the way references came and the type of reference made varied markedly at various stages of the policy. During the voluntary phase from April 1965 to June 1966, the DEA never referred more than three new cases in a month (after the initial four with which the PIB began). Then there was a complete gap of three months in the summer of 1965—while the Secretary of State, the Department of Economic Affairs and the leaders of the TUC and industry were preoccupied with discussions on the developments of the policy. There was throughout a reasonable spread between prices and wages.

The standstill and severe restraint caused a spurt of new activity as might be expected. But this only lifted the number of cases being examined at any one time to eight or nine a month, still more or less evenly spread between prices and pay.

After the end of the period of severe restraint (summer of 1967) the price and wage cases remained reasonably in balance. But in September the PIB had been given its special responsibility for reviewing public-sector price increases, and the first bunch of five cases were referred in October. By then the PIB was working much more on pay than prices in the private sector.

Throughout 1968 PIB were even busier than before. The total number of cases being investigated rose. At the peak of its activities in 1968, the PIB had 23 cases—eighteen were pay cases, four private-sector price cases and one public-sector price case. General responsibility for prices and incomes policy had been transferred to the Department of Employment and Productivity early in 1968. It was natural that pay cases should emerge quite readily. But price cases were dealt with in the first instance by many departments. By the autumn of 1968, price cases had dwindled to four and then three, the lowest since the statutory policy took effect. The imbalance between prices and incomes persisted throughout 1969, until pay cases dwindled too.

By the end of 1969, though the PIB was to continue for more than another year, the policy in effect had come to a halt. The PIB continued with its investigations; but little immediate effect on behaviour could be expected. The policy, if not the PIB, had come to need reappraisal and renewal well before the change of Government.

4

The PIB and its methods of work

The biggest step towards an acceptable and successful Board was taken when Aubrey Jones accepted the Chairmanship. But the Board was also to consist of "a number of independent members, a businessman and a trade unionist", the latter representing their respective interests, embodying the principle of the tripartite agreement on which the policy was founded. The other members were to have "collectively ... expertise in law, accountancy, economics, industrial relations and other relevant fields". As such, they would be more like expert assessors in cases put before them, than either judges or political decision-takers. In addition, the Board was to have its own staff, including specifically "accountants, experts on industrial relations, economists and statisticians".

Nevertheless, choosing the Board members was not merely a question of finding experts. The Board was to give its independent views on highly controversial and sensitive questions to both management and unions; and the recommendations it made would be accepted voluntarily —if at all. It was therefore necessary that an acceptably wide range of views and interests should be represented on it. There were to be two deputy Chairmen, and obviously they had to come one from each side in some sense. It would be necessary to preserve a political balance between left- and right-wing views, and it would be necessary to get some voices independent of the two sides in the industrial sense. And one would have to be a woman.

On the whole the balance was preserved and the more obvious pitfalls avoided. The Board was not ill-equipped to look actively for newer practices, and at radical ideas in whatever circumstances were presented to it. (A list of its members appears in Appendix E.)

The Board originally consisted of nine members, of which five were in George Brown's words "people whose past has been associated with our movement ... who know our experience, who have shared it, to ensure that they (trades unions) will get a fair judgement when they go there". In this respect it differed from "some previous bodies", like the

National Incomes Commission. In practice it was rare for party or political inclinations to determine the Board's specific conclusions, but it probably secured a Board less sensitive than usual to conventional wisdom and administrative needs, and more sensitive to the aims and needs of trades unions and consumers.

Assembling a staff for the PIB office was no less important than the members themselves. Constitutionally, this was a job for the Department of Economic Affairs, itself new, with no traditions, no conventions and no core of career staff. But, from the first, the Chairman of the PIB took a much more active part in choosing his staff than was usual in Government circles. The work was more demanding of professional skills than Government offices normally were, as the White Paper had recognised.

A combination of three fortunate circumstances enabled the PIB to build up an office with a distinctive momentum, philosophy and expertise rare if not unique in the environment of Whitehall. There was the intellectual bent of the Chairman, and his established interest in the policy. A few key appointments could be made by personal contact. Secondly, there was the unusual willingness of experts in relevant fields to come into Whitehall, if only for a short period, for the chance of participating in a new and promising project. Thirdly, there was the manifest shortage of relevant expertise already inside Whitehall offices.

The most obvious shortage within Whitehall was of accountants of any kind, and of economists, statisticians and industrial relations experts below the most senior levels. There was no alternative to employing outside firms to collect and analyse accounting data under the PIB's direction. Qualified accountants were not available anywhere in the civil service in sufficient numbers. One such firm was used continuously (beginning in June 1965) on PIB cases with all the advantages of continuity and personal contact between the firm's staff and the PIB and its staff. But it soon appeared that even this was not enough. Management practices were increasingly an area to be investigated carefully. Expertise in the management field was not then available inside the civil service, nor could it be assembled quickly. Again there was no alternative to using outside firms of consultants—though this time no continuing relation with any one outside firm developed, largely owing to the diversity of the projects to be done, and the diversity of consultants' experience and facilities. The general economic problems and prospects for an industry under review had to be assessed and presented to the PIB. This too was a job very often done by an outsider on commission to the PIB, usually an academic already having knowledge of the field in question.

From the first the PIB was fed with studies in many subjects, mostly of outstanding quality, far wider than any one Government Department could provide before this time. A routine of high-quality work was quickly established, and experience of working with a number of different kinds of expert on the same case helped to build up the PIB's characteristic style. Outside consultants were less used as the PIB's own staff was built up. The PIB's use of outsiders was often criticised from inside and outside the PIB. At first, the only alternative to commissioning outside consultants was to reduce the scope of the investigations. The intermittent nature of the case work also made it a more efficient user of scarce resources. Deliberate avoidance of outside consultants would have made some of the PIB's reports less persuasive, less comprehensive, and altogether more negative than they were. However there was still persistent imbalance in the advice and expertise to be got by any means. Experts on trade-union affairs were far more difficult to find in sufficient numbers than those on management, though they were often more important. It was fortunate for the PIB that it acquired a good staff of its own on the subject. Equally, experts on wage determination and structures were far scarcer than experts on price determination and structures, though reform of pay policy often gave far more rewarding practical results than reform of pricing policy. The PIB's own activities were probably responsible for restoring the balance a little.

In October 1966 the PIB's own enquiry team was set up, to undertake field enquiries into organisation and management practices. It was mainly composed of civil servants, many of whom had been on enquiry work in Organisation and Methods divisions, or the Customs and Excise Department. Direct recruitment of statisticians, accountants, economists, industrial relations experts and report secretaries independently of the normal civil-service procedures began in 1967. Also in 1967 a Management Operations section was established, with specialists in production, organisation, purchasing, marketing, information systems, corporate planning and operational research.

As the Government had no powers to do anything beyond referring appropriate cases for investigation, the credibility of the PIB would depend on a reasonable selection of cases, in the eyes of the public, being referred. The PIB itself had to establish a public reputation for competence, fairness and a modicum of common sense. Publicity and persuasion were the only weapons. This explains the importance it attached to independent enquiries, and the management tone of some of the reports.

The work consisted of establishing the facts, and formulating a conclusion in accordance with the letter and intentions of the policy. The Chairman decided from the beginning that the Board would do its own investigations, relying neither on the evidence submitted to it by the parties (as the National Incomes Commission and the Monopolies Commission did), nor on material available from departments or other official sources. Two characteristic features that contributed to the PIB's style of working and the prevailing atmosphere of its office were established on its first case. They were first, that significant results could be obtained in a very short time by concentrated, carefully directed enquiries covering a small sample of firms, the size of the sample being limited by the time available, rather than the determining the time necessary by the required size of the sample. That this should have been successful in so diffuse an industry as road haulage was something of a triumphant start. Second, it was amply demonstrated that there was great value in having the statisticians and accountants responsible for the factual material closely associated with the whole enquiry, not merely to defend their figures from unsupported conclusions or unwarranted neglect, but to take part in forming arguments and opinions about the problems as a whole.

The factual material had to cover the background to the claim or proposal referred to the PIB, and the general prospects for the industry or occupation concerned. In price cases, the core of the investigation was a statement of the extent of cost increases, reasons for the increases, and an analysis of the effect on unit costs. The extent to which costs could have been absorbed involved an assessment of profits, followed by possible changes in management to alter the make-up of costs, or reduce them relative to output. In labour-intensive activities, labour management, pay structures, and possibly negotiating arrangements were important areas for exploration. The PIB's interest in pay and labour questions in price cases sometimes took its clients by surprise, in spite of the fact that the purpose of the policy was to bring about a new relation between pay and prices. It was too readily assumed that pricing was a matter of cost movements, and establishing these was an accountancy exercise.

There was always a potential hazard to the accuracy of the results, in the necessity of drawing a sample from whatever list was easily available. Sometimes the only possibility was a list of trade-association members. These might well be a somewhat biased sample, especially where only a minority of firms belonged. But the PIB always tried to check its evidence from other sources, and to make use of its results with care. Conclusions were often stated negatively rather than put more weight on evidence that could not be shown to be entirely representative.

The PIB's most important pioneering work of a technical kind was the earnings surveys. In 1965 few industries knew what earnings in fact were. They knew details of wage rates, often dozens or hundreds of different ones. But total take-home pay was not known. Hence, the exact effect of negotiated changes on unit costs, or on the standard of living of the workers could not be estimated. The figures collected by the Ministry of Labour were seldom in a suitable form to be useful to negotiators, and in any case were too late for the purpose. It was directly due to the PIB's efforts and recommendations that better earnings information has been collected nationally, and that more negotiations are directly about pay, instead of a conventional base, the basic rate, from which uncontrolled and uncosted supplements were added.

Written and oral evidence from the trades associations, or other organisations involved in preliminary discussions with Government Departments, was naturally a main part of the material collected from industry. But the PIB also sought out evidence from other firms, from trades unions, from large customers, and possibly from the industry's or firm's main competitors. It thus had a commercial view of markets, as well as both sides of the case about labour costs, labour use or wage negotiations.

By the autumn of 1965, enough of a general pattern of work had emerged to be formalised into a set procedure. When a new case came in, the Chairman appointed a sub-committee of Board members (usually three), and the Secretary appointed a working party of the staff, consisting of a Chairman (an official at Assistant Secretary level), one or more report secretaries (Principals or equivalent), a statistician, an economist, an accountant and an industrial-relations adviser. The working party prepared a draft of questionnaires and the coverage for the various surveys within two or three days, which was then discussed by the sub-committee (including working-party members). At the same time background material of a general kind, and the views of Government Departments was collected. General problems that would have to be discussed in a report might also be discussed at this stage; but it was only when the statistical and accounting data were collated that the issues were discussed seriously, either by senior officials or by Board members. Only then could a draft report be prepared, containing anything like the final conclusions. The draft was then submitted to the full Board.

Occasionally differences of view at Board level, or total bafflement with acceptable proposals for intractable problems meant that a report had to be discussed a second time. Had there been persistent differences, the remedy while the PIB was still a Royal Commission would have been for dissenting members to produce a minority report. But this was never done. As far as possible the Board would argue itself into a conclusion all could support to some degree. When the PIB became a statutory Board, no minority reports could be submitted. The only course open to members disagreeing with majority recommendations would have been resignation. But by then, the Board was enough of a corporate entity to make major disagreements unlikely.

The most important change in the procedure came in 1969, when reports were discussed regularly twice at Board meetings, to give members rather more time to consider the implications of the evidence.

A skeleton of the PIB's procedure had been prescribed in the White

Paper on the *Machinery of Prices and Incomes Policy* (Cmnd 2577). It would work "in two separate divisions, to be known as the Prices Review Division and the Incomes Review Division respectively". The Chairman of the PIB would share the chairmanship of the two divisions with two of the full-time members. There would then be three potential chairmen for each division, so that "each division will be enabled to sit in two or more sections under an independent chairman". The Chairman of the PIB would allocate work to the divisions and to sections within the divisions.

Each Division would also decide its own procedure, even whether or not it was to sit in public. The divisions would "no doubt" take evidence from interested parties. Beyond that, reports should be made available with great speed. Two or three months should be the maximum "and if possible even more quickly" for pay claims.

In addition to the PIB itself, there were panels of special members, businessmen and trades unionists nominated by their organisations, who would be "appointed to assist ... the Divisions with the investigation of particular cases".

All this amounted to a definite structure for the PIB, if not a very definite procedure. But the PIB never operated in divisions, and never formally distinguished between members interested or practised in prices and in incomes. The panels of special members were occasionally used at first, even then intermittently, and soon not at all.

Why did the PIB adopt a procedure that failed to correspond in important respects with which had been set out in a document that had been agreed between the three parties responsible for establishing it? The immediate answer was that the Chairman chose not to operate like this. However this takes the matter but little further.

The Board did begin by dividing its staff, if not itself, into divisions specialising in prices and incomes. It also divided up into small groups on particular cases, led by one or other of the Deputy Chairmen. It might seem a small step to give one group income cases, and another price cases, the two Deputy Chairmen and the two full-time members specialising in the one or the other, with one of the part-time members attached to the prices group or the incomes group for particular cases.

The Board began by operating generally, mainly because it began with three price cases. Expeditious reports would have been hampered by perversely regarding them as the work of only one minority group of the Board (and the staff) while the others waited for work, even though the total volume of work to be done taxed the resources of the whole. Moreover, when the first incomes case came it concerned charges and costs as well. Having perforce begun to work on cases without attempting to specialise, Board members found that they could not carry out their responsibilities towards the policy by dealing with prices and wages separately. Government Departments had in the past suffered from just such a division.

There were other considerations against divisions. If the PIB was to have a reforming influence, it would have to propound some general principles in support of the policy. These might emerge from either price or pay cases. Consistency of attitude and thought, as well as the details of recommendations, was of prime importance, and was best achieved by the Chairman himself leading the discussion of issues arising from the investigations.

Equally, dividing the Board members into two specialist divisions by reference to their professional skills or experience would have ignored questions of political balance. Like the Chairman, all the original members came with a sense of commitment to the policy as a whole. If "prices policy" (price stability or cost absorption) was to apply, then "incomes policy" (orderliness if not restraint) had to apply—and vice versa. The prices and incomes policy, carefully though it was specified in the White Paper, could almost always be interpreted more or less harshly. A soft policy on one side, and a hard one on the other would not have been acceptable to any of the original members. Yet had they been restricted to one or other of the divisions, their influence on the balance of recommendations would have been minimal. When it came to final decisions on immediate recommendations the members acted as a Board, whichever side they might be on, according to individual experience or inclination.

Keeping a small board together to interpret the policy as a whole had other consequences, in respect of the PIB's own way of working, and probably in respect of its general influence as well. It undoubtedly added to the pressure of work, which a few found onerous but most found stimulating. It added also to the feeling of corporate loyalty to the aims of the policy. A chance to exercise a reforming zeal was to varying degrees welcome; and there was the wide range of interests and opinions to prevent it being too widely misplaced.

No special members could be appointed in the PIB's first case, because of the speed with which it began operations. However, pairs of special members were appointed on the next two cases—bread and flour prices, and soap and detergent prices. But difficulties arose. The White Paper on the machinery had clearly intended the special members to act as expert assessors; but this did not fit in with the PIB's procedure at all easily. In the first place, it was a most awkward arrangement for the administration. It was difficult enough to get part-time members of the PIB to commit themselves to meetings (usually lasting a whole morning or afternoon, and sometimes a whole day) at short notice. Getting two special members with full-time commitments elsewhere, as well as the industries being investigated, together at a days' notice was nearly impossible. The time and attention required for one PIB enquiry might not be a great deal, in relation to a year's work, but concentrated as it had to be into one month—as the interviewing-plus-analysing stages mostly had to be—was a very heavy commitment indeed while it lasted. Businessmen were not always impossible to find, but the trades unionists were nearly always too booked up to come at such short notice, and one without the other served no purpose.

There was a difficulty of function also. The PIB was working in anything but a legalistic way. In every case it was trying to frame its recommendations in such a form that whatever circumstance led to the problem referred to it, these circumstances were changed so that the same problem did not recur again later on. It was not just a case of applying the rules set out in the White Paper to the immediate proposal for increased incomes or charges. Each enquiry led to uncovering the most important reason for undesirable increases being proposed, followed by recommendations to alter the situation towards arrangements promoting better performance of some kind. Both of these operations were controversial. It was not easy for special members to have full part in either the interpretation of the problem or the recommendations, unless they became members of the PIB. This was not their function however. The PIB was already constituted as a balanced board, and empowered to make recommendations. The special members would have to make their final contributions in settling a report before the PIB as a whole reviewed the matter. In practice the final session in the sub-committee sometimes turned into an argument between the special members and the rest, not entirely about an important issue raised by the particular case, but about why the PIB had taken before, and wished to go on taking, a general attitude to certain questions. Since the Board members would in any case have the last word (whether that word were right or not), this particular exercise could be a monumental waste of time. In spite of all this, a few special members did contribute materially to the PIB's enquiries.

The general policy rules left a great many problems either open or uncovered, as they inevitably must. A formal or legalistic view of its functions would never have allowed the PIB to produce practical solutions to immediate deadlocks. Formal hearings of evidence would have been costly for the clients, and would have required much more time for reports. The clients might also feel obliged to have legal representation, a possibility the Board was anxious to avoid, since this would have pushed the arguments onto different and more arid ground. As far as possible, the PIB liked to appear sympathetic and reasonable to all the parties. That it achieved a measure of success in this was clear from the relaxed atmosphere at most interviews. Arguments might be fierce, but they were to convince and suggest, rather than to show force, or defend an entrenched interest or opinion against all attack. The PIB made a contribution to solving problems sometimes merely by providing a new and neutral forum for discussing well-known problems, or by putting old dilemmas into new forms.

The PIB rarely, and only reluctantly, ever heard the evidence of one side in a pay case in the presence of the other. This was also because its purpose was to get both to discuss their problems freely, unhampered by publicly declared positions. Sometimes there were nothing *but* publicly declared positions to hear; but at least these were less provocative and inflexible in form, behind discreetly closed doors.

Committees did not keep verbatim records of proceedings, though this was suggested from time to time. The PIB wanted a record of the issues arising, and the essence of opinions, rather than the precise route by which they were reached. Not infrequently, parties asked the PIB for copies of a committee's minutes, or to exchange minutes of meetings. These requests were almost always refused. Still less would the PIB agree to pass minutes of meetings with one side to the other, as was also sometimes demanded. Occasionally the evidence submitted in writing by one side was sent to the other, but this was always only done if the parties themselves wished to exchange evidence. Direct confrontation, the banging-heads-together technique, was the opposite of the PIB's intentions.

The most important characteristic of the PIB's work was its initiative in investigation. It could not rely solely on the evidence of the parties concerned in its own view. There was sometimes no agreement on what the facts were. In the absence of full information, especially about pay, the folk-wisdom about what labour-markets were like could flower. Similarly "competition" (undefined) could be invoked, in relation to prices or profits, to reach almost any convenient conclusion, while facts about costs, the behaviour of prices and the structure of markets were lacking. Having its own independent information, often superior to that of the parties, allowed the PIB to act independently. Without it the PIB would have been in much the same position as arbitrators, Wages Councils and Government Departments before its time, which were, as the PIB put it "obliged in the main to depend on the *ex parte* evidence of the people or organisations concerned". The result must be some compromise between the cases presented, regardless of whether either, or neither, were proposing something whose effects would be in the national interest. The prices and incomes policy had been formulated because the national interest required something different from considering only the interests of the parties directly involved, in either price or income increases. The PIB was determined that it should not be pushed into the position of just another arbitrator—as it might well have become, for all the policy rules.

The PIB's working methods had great advantages in the first period before the standstill. A high momentum of work was maintained.

Procedure was informal and concise enough to be quickly adapted to varying circumstances or time-tables. There was opportunity and inducement for ideas about the analysis of or remedy for problems to be pooled from outside the PIB's own resources (and outside the administration's normal resources) as well as within. By 1967 it consisted essentially of a relatively small staff, more highly skilled than most in its particular field, with more experience than any in case-work on prices or incomes, directed by a Board of experience, with relatively clear collective views on the policy and its application.

However, the method of work that had developed had its defects; with no strong formal arrangements for discussing ideas and conclusions significant points might appear at a late stage, and the volume of reports and supporting papers arriving shortly before meetings was impossible for the Board members to digest.

With a small Board, a small staff and a manageable volume of work, much of this tension was resolved by personal contact, usually through the Secretary. More closely in contact than anyone else with all parties, it was his constant task to consult, co-ordinate and conciliate. More than one attempt was made to formalise internal proceedings a little more, with the object of making consultation more effective at an earlier stage. But little came of these attempts, until circumstances forced the issue. More part-time members each devoting less time to the PIB's affairs, and more work in prospect (though this only materialised for a short time) made the old informal methods unworkable anyway.

From the autumn of 1967 to the summer of 1968, both Board and staff were growing rapidly in numbers. Moreover, there was an unusually rapid change of Board members and senior staff. In the autumn of 1967, seven of the original nine members of the PIB remained, together with the Secretary, most of his immediate subordinates and the senior industrial relations adviser. By the summer of 1968, there were already eight new members of the Board (and by the end of 1968, there were another three) and the original members had been reduced to five, three of whom were also soon to leave. Meanwhile, the Secretary had left, almost all the senior administrative staff appointed during the early periods had returned to other departments, and a number of the industrial relations staff had also left for other jobs.

The new Secretary, Mr Ken Clucas, came from a very different career, and was a very different character from Alex Jarratt. He was less required to join in the policy-making and more required to run the office in such a way that enquiries and reports were despatched in as orderly a way as possible, with more distinction of function between Board members and staff. In sum, the PIB was no longer a new, pioneering body, building up an institution as it went along. It had become a

second-generation, established institution. The time was now ripe for
modified procedure, and more formalised routine.

The PIB's problems were partly resolved by a method fashionable in
business: it appointed a consultant to report. Early in 1968 Professor
Joan Woodward became a part-time member of the Board, mainly, in
the first instance, to investigate the PIB's own procedure and report
to the Chairman. She duly found and documented all the weaknesses
that had emerged from the autumn of 1965 onwards, and reported. As
also happens elsewhere, some action was taken after this report, which
would not have been the case without the neutral imprimatur of a
consultant on it.

The Woodward report found the PIB's "basic task" had become "the
assembly and analysis of information". There was no question of Board
members specialising in one or other field of policy, nor in only a selection
of reports. In principle all Board members would still be concerned with
all references. But the number of reports going through by the time the
Woodward report was complete exacerbated the difficulties already
emerging from the increasing number of Board members requiring time
to see them. An established procedure was required to meet this; and
the chosen one overcame the problems by allowing "full participation"
to all members, should they so choose, at various key points of a case.
Three of these key points were selected: at the beginning, when enquiries
were designed; three-quarters of the way through when enquiry results
were available, and provisional conclusions could be reached; and at the
climax, when a draft report was considered.

This permissive system brought two great advantages to the harmonious
working of a Board of diverse interests. The first was that any member
with particular interests or strong views on any particular case could
only blame himself if he was not consulted enough, or not early enough,
in enquiries. Secondly, the onus for arranging time-tables for meetings
to allow participation by part-time members was put on the part-time
members. This allowed full-time members and staff to press on with
cases, and arrange time-tables with only the convenience of the office
and the outside parties in mind. It also meant that the full-time members
and the staff could carry out the collection and detailed analysis of
information in a more orderly way, as less now depended on personal
contact, and more on explicit procedure.

The PIB had now fashioned itself into an administrative machine
that could function indefinitely, as little dependent on the individuals
holding office on the staff or on the Board as Government Departments
usually are.

How all these changes affected the PIB's performance of its role
cannot now be fully assessed. The changes were not fully operative until
the spring of 1969. But the autumn of 1969 it was clear that the
Government was bowing to accumulating hostility to prices and incomes

policy, and hence to its previous view of the role of the PIB. Prolonged and powerful discussions about whether or not it should be merged with other institutions, and if so which ones, could not do other than weaken its influence in its former role, inside and outside the administration. The announcement early in 1970 of its prospective transformation into the CIM effectively halted any further development of its function. The Secretary and staff concentrated on the problems arising from its transition into a still more firmly established part of the Government machine.

But the unexpected change of Government in June 1970 put an abrupt and unexpected end to these developments, and cut off the PIB too soon after its maturity to leave much evidence about the success or otherwise of its new procedure. After the decision to transform the PIB, many members of the Board, especially the part-time members (none of whom had by then served for more than two years) felt less inclined to continue their work for it. In January 1970 it still mustered its full fifteen members. By the time the announcement of the general election put an end to preparing the way for the CIM, five members had resigned, and no new ones had been appointed. By the change of Government, it was down to ten members none of whom (apart from the Chairman) were industrial managers or employers.

The PIB's external relations were as important to the impact of its work as its internal workings. These existed at various levels. There were the contacts with interested parties on particular cases; there was the wider public, having no direct contact with PIB itself, but interested in particular cases; and there was the public in the widest sense, interested in a general way in the policy and its application.

As we have seen, contact between the PIB and its clients was relatively informal, and impressed itself as such on most of the clients. As time went on, these contacts became rather more between PIB officials and outside interests, than between Board members and outsiders. This was perhaps an inevitable result of increased work, more formal internal workings, and clearer distinctions between (a few) full-time members and part-time members. It was nevertheless a consequence to be regretted.

There was always some difference of attitude to these meetings between members of the Board and the staff, and between the Chairman and some members of the Board. The civil service is organised to take decisions, based on written evidence and opinion, largely generated within itself. Discussions with outsiders is a supplementary, and often dispensable activity. There is therefore too little appreciation very often of the importance of opinion, aims and beliefs among employers, unions, managers and so on, in shaping circumstances and prospects. Too little importance also was attached to those views being expressed personally to Board members. Many officials acted on the assumption that they had a duty to protect Board members from the public, as presumably they aim to protect their Ministers.

The Chairman did not share the prejudices of officials—as might be expected from a professional politician, and ex-Minister. Indeed, he was more aware than anyone else of the importance of continual contact with a wider public at various levels. But he disliked committee meetings and relatively formal interviews most of all. His dislike stemmed mainly from impatience with formal proceedings, received opinions and collective wisdom. His main endeavour was to get at the truth as it seemed to him; and only a very partial version of the truth emerged, sluggishly, from large representative bodies. The fact that his own views might have been put before the parties was of little importance to him, and that they should be discussed in such a forum was no part of his view of the PIB's and his own role. All this led sometimes to misunderstanding and even resentment. It happened that outside representative bodies expected to go to the PIB to hear and discuss the PIB's views and ideas, as well as to present their own, while the PIB met only to hear the outsiders' views.

The PIB's reticence partly arose from its whole function and procedure. It was always determined not to get itself into a position of negotiating its recommendations with the parties. Its job was quite clearly to apply the policy, whether the result was to support the claims of either or neither party to a case. Moreover, at the stage when most sub-committee meetings with outsiders took place, the PIB was often in no position to exchange ideas with outsiders, as its ideas (on that particular case) would not by then have been fully developed, nor exchanged within its own walls. Even where it did meet with the parties after its own ideas had crystallised, it was often in a position where even greater care had to be exercised not to suggest what its recommendations might be. Giving partial versions of the conclusions or immediate recommendations without the reasons might serve little purpose, or actively encourage opposition, where clients' hopes were to be somewhat disappointed. Often giving even hints of conclusions to one party, where others were involved would also have been (rightly) resented.

The PIB has been criticised in a more general way for the secrecy of its proceedings. Whether or not the PIB should sit in public to hear oral evidence was a question specifically referred (in the Machinery White Paper) to it to decide. It never did sit in public, in spite of criticism, and in spite of some requests from parties to be interviewed that it should do so. Again the PIB's own view was: "We have considered that discussions between ourselves and the interested parties would be freer and less inhibited if conducted in private; we have found this view shared by the interested parties themselves."

This view of things was consistent with its political-diplomatic inter-pretation of its role, as a general instrument of reform. Assessing what changes of practice represent progress and how these changes can be brought about depended on getting full and frank opinions on the matter, usually from both sides in incomes cases, and from the leaders of individual firms in price cases. These opinions would often not be given fully if they had to be made in the presence of the other side to a bargaining process, or a business rival, or if they had to be checked first as being suitable for general publication. In its early days especially, the PIB was always very conscious of the danger of adopting, or of being pushed into, the position of an arbitrator, or of a negotiator. Its role was to bring nationally desirable rules to bear on the limits or conventions within which bargaining or competition was carried on. Bargaining or negotiating is a different process. There was always also the difficult question of confidentiality. It would have been extremely difficult in price cases to discuss costs and profits freely in public, in the light of highly confidential information of obvious commercial value either to individual firms or to their competitors. Such commercial consideration did not so often offset the confidentiality of information on incomes cases. But even there either unions or employers might well have been reluctant to have it discussed in public.

Nevertheless, good reasons though there were for secrecy, the consequences of secrecy were probably not entirely favourable to the policy as a whole. Cases made in secret, necessarily by a few of the leaders of a union or industry, are secret from the other union members or firms as well. Where the PIB's recommendations were against a case, those who prepared or presented the case were obviously open to the suspicion that the failure was a failure of advocacy. Such suspicions might have been encouraged by the PIB's practice of trying to keep meetings and representations as small as possible. Again, this was for good reasons: to get orderly and productive discussions. It was usually only where interested parties insisted, that all the members of large committees would be encouraged to appear.

Secrecy was probably also more disadvantageous to trades unions than to firms. Trades unions are supported by far less research and information than firms or trades associations usually are. How well and fully their case can be put depends much more on the abilities of a few individuals than it does in firms of any size. Knowledge of the sort of questions asked by the PIB and the sort of point important to them would have been available through public hearings, and would probably have increased their understanding, if not sympathetic understanding, of what the PIB was trying to do. But equally trade-union leaders, often depending on periodic election for their job, might have been tempted to speak in public for the easy approval of their members, rather than to seek solutions to genuine problems.

For all the defects and difficulties the PIB was an institution with a definite purpose, with a procedure and style of working well adapted to achieving that purpose. Many people who worked there have commented favourably on the characteristic pace, level and content of its operations. The reasons for this were obvious enough in the early days: a small, new, well-regarded institution was being fashioned by a few determined and able individuals, as much attracted to it by belief in the policy, as to a technical job. But it was more significant that though the PIB's atmosphere inevitably changed, it never lost the momentum and general competence over a wide rage of normally separate functions with which it began. The source of this can only be guessed. That it started off with speed, efficiency and high standards must be part of the explanation. But its continuance was perhaps due to its having clear functions, leading to specific results, manifestly adding something to knowledge or understanding of the economy, without arbitrarily-defined departmental interests dividing up the full study of each case. Involvement in the case work, and possibly in the policy as well, was perhaps the remaining part of the explanation.

Part 2

Prices

5

The Private Sector: Labour-intensive Industries

The report on road haulage charges (No. 1) set the PIB's style fully in the spirit of the intention of the policy: its longest and most detailed recommendations related to incomes and their determination.

Early in 1965, the Road Haulage Association (RHA) recommended to its members a five per cent increase in all haulage rates after two previous ones, taking effect in September and November 1964. The PIB concerned itself with the practice of rate recommendation, more than the particular increase leading to the reference. The RHA had put forward two main arguments in favour of the practice. It "opened the door to negotiations" between the hauliers and their customers, and it informed the smaller hauliers of the extent of their cost increases. Imprudent operators, not fully covering costs, were considered to lower rates generally to the detriment of the industry. But the PIB found neither of the arguments valid. If there were no RHA recommendations, customers would not be so likely to accept hauliers' proposals automatically. The supposed disruptive activities of small firms were better counteracted either by absorbing small units into larger ones better able to use modern management techniques, or the RHA could organise inter-firm comparisons on costs, turnover, capital and profit margins. The practice of rate recommendation was undesirable from the national point of view. A new recommendation received wide publicity, and could be used to increase prices more than costs in firms with less than average increases. Moreover, the increase recommended was based on unchanged efficiency as costs increased. Rate recommendation should therefore cease, in favour of more efforts to improve efficiency.

If the latest recommendation was not withdrawn, it should not be accepted by the customers. The remedy was for the market to behave in a more competitive way, not for prices to be set administratively.

The most obvious result of the PIB's investigation of the industry was to show how greatly costs varied with the size and type of business, and the distance travelled. But some generalisations about cost increases

C

had to be made to assess the maximum increase in charges justified in accordance with the policy. Wages and salaries were universally the largest item of costs, accounting for just short of half the total in most firms. Vehicle running costs (fuel, repairs and maintenance, licenses and insurance) were the next largest item. Wage costs had increased steadily, owing to successive increases in wage rates. Vehicle costs had increased steadily, owing to tax increases and increased costs elsewhere. But the RHA had recommended increases in charges totalling 13 per cent, while costs had increased nine per cent.

Increases in minimum wage rates were determined by awards of a Wages Council, and had been closely followed by increased charges. There was plenty of scope for improved labour productivity; but the biggest obstacle was the negotiation of wages in isolation from working practices. Negotiations followed a traditional pattern, with the workers supporting their claim by reference to price increases and wage rises elsewhere, and the employers referring to the pressure of costs and competition. For this situation, the PIB considered the Wages Council system was to blame. Both employers and unions had already realised the defects of the situation and were discussing new negotiating machinery. Their efforts were to be welcomed, since only a closer link between wages and productivity was likely to enable a future wage increase to be absorbed. However, a uniform system of settlement was not likely to induce efficiency, since the scope for improving efficiency varied between sectors and firms. The new arrangements should therefore provide ways of removing general obstacles to efficiency, and encourage company or local agreements.

In spite of mounting charges, wages were still not high. Drivers had to make up for low basic rates by long overtime. More capital was employed in the industry than was needed, and the low returns perpetuated low wages. Increased earnings could be compatible with better returns on capital through increasing the haulage done per lorry, which could be done by different methods of work by men and management. The only way to get results quickly was for companies to negotiate agreements to finance extra wages out of higher productivity.

In its first case the PIB had established its primary interest in labour productivity. It had also established its inclination to rely on an active market to restrain prices and put pressure on costs.

In a second report on road haulage (No. 14), the PIB found that charges had actually risen by some three per cent in the second half of 1965, significantly less than the RHA had recommended. Fewer than half the firms had achieved increases as high as five per cent. They had experienced "considerably more resistance" from their customers than they had done before. The sequel was not entirely happy however. Two further references on pay (Nos. 48 and 94) were made, and it was found that although the RHA had ceased to recommend rate increases, little progress had been made with negotiating pay and productivity. By 1967, the Negotiating Committee had virtually ceased to function.

Costs, prices and wages in the printing industry (No. 2) were also referred to the PIB in 1965, after a new wage agreement. Once more a major issue was the determination of wages and their effect on prices. The case was also the first of many where a major problem was to establish what had in fact happened to prices. Many jobs were custom-designed, and even when repeated, there were commonly changes of format or quantity affecting costs and prices. However, the PIB found evidence to support the industry's claim that prices had been rising less than costs, with falling profits as a result.

Earnings had risen rapidly, while output per man-hour had risen slowly. The explanation was partly the structure of the industry, partly the quality of the management, and partly the attitudes of the unions. The structure of the industry contributed to its problems because printers of provincial newspapers, periodicals and general commercial printers all negotiated together, though they operated in radically different markets. Newspaper and periodical printers could not risk interruptions in production. Commercial printers were not so vulnerable; yet they followed the rates and practices established largely by the newspaper printers. Opportunities to improve productivity were being lost by failure to use modern management techniques. The employers' own estimates of the possibilities with existing equipment showed that no increase of price need be made, even after the latest wage increase. But stable prices would require a change of behaviour, and the responsibility for making the change rested clearly on the employers. They were not justified in passing on increases in cost to their customers because they could not get co-operation from the unions. As in road haulage, the customers too seldom questioned the prices they were asked, and this behaviour also contributed to the industry's insularity. The PIB relied on the customers to look more critically on prices in future; for the rest, changes in working practices would have to absorb further increases in wages (see p. 131).

Bread and flour (No. 3) were produced in an industry with a very different structure from either road haulage or printing, and prices were not competitively determined. Flour production was capital-intensive; but plant bread-baking was still relatively labour-intensive, and the PIB's report turned largely on labour use in the bakeries.

Bread-baking costs had increased 22 per cent between 1960 and 1964, and bread prices had increased in step almost exactly. The four national plant bakers had all suffered the same increases in the major items of cost; but their profits had not fallen equally, because of their varying efficiency, and varying shares in a falling market. The most important characteristic of the industry was the uniformity of cost increases. Two items, flour and wages, covered 70 per cent of the total. As the main cost of flour was the cost of wheat, flour price changes were uniform and affected the companies equally. Minimum wage rates, hours and allowances were all settled nationally by agreements that were strictly adhered to. With a standardised product and few producers, it was not surprising that prices went up together. Competition was not by price at all, but by multiplying outlets; far from restricting costs, it increased them. Virtually the only restraint on costs was the standard of management, kept up by slim and volatile profits. Each management felt itself under pressure, but the industry's structure could not prevent the linked wage and price increases it was the purpose of the policy to loosen.

Two-thirds of recent rises in costs were due to pay increases. Earlier in 1965, there had been new agreements with the distributive and bakery workers. Both of these contained an "element of unreality", namely an overt reduction in the working week, although it was merely a disguise for a wage increase. Both agreements had widened the gap between earnings and wage rates, though efficient working required it to be narrowed. Regular overtime of 14 hours a week was usual among bakery workers, as a means of maintaining earnings, thereby increasing operating costs further.

The PIB found that the industry was only proposing an increase in prices because it had conceded an increase in wages it could not match with increased productivity. (The employers were also anticipating a further increase and had taken them into account; but the PIB had "no hesitation" in excluding them from the calculations.) The PIB considered that the "approach envisaged by the Statement of Intent" and the gravity of the national situation both dictated that the price be held, it was suggested, for six months. During that time, proposals for the more effective deployment of labour should be prepared, and in the light of those, the Government should discuss prices again with the industry.

The case of bread prices turned out to be a case of bread wages. Soon after the report, the wage connections became only too evident, with strikes and threats of strikes. The Department of Economic Affairs had persuaded the bakery companies to defer a price increase for three months (instead of the six recommended). The unions continued to press their claims; but the employers felt unable to concede much, unless a worthwhile productivity improvement could be linked with the extra pay. While the industry was still in dispute the case was referred again to the PIB, this time to report on wages. The PIB itself had to look for the changes in practice that would allow higher wages to be absorbed. These it eventually found, as described further in Part III (see p. 135 below).

However, bread prices continued to increase, by 1d a large standard loaf in 1966 and 1967, 1½d in 1968, and another 1d in 1969. In 1970, the companies asked for 2d, on the grounds of low returns on capital. They got an interim 1d while the PIB reported on the other 1d. This time the same reference concerned pay and working conditions as well as prices; there would be no repetition of the earlier attempt to deal with prices in a labour-intensive activity in isolation from pay, followed by pay in isolation from prices. The companies' need for more revenue was urgent, and they had agreed with reluctance to wait for the PIB's report. An interim report on bread prices (No. 144) was therefore produced in the statutory three months, followed by a fuller account covering pay and conditions as well as costs.

Flour prices had become a less important cost (in spite of devaluation) as the steepest increases had occurred in pay and in discounts to distributors. Returns on capital were clearly low, as the most profitable firm had below average returns, and two firms were making losses. Forecasts for 1970 and 1971 showed that the average would become a loss, even with the 1d increase in price. The other 1d was clearly justified, and the PIB recommended it be allowed.

In the fuller report (No. 151) the PIB reported that its earlier recommendations for improving labour use had been carried out. Nevertheless, overtime working was even higher than before. The Government was advised to take into account progress in improving labour use when prices were reviewed. There was a case for continuing price reviews, in the PIB's view, just because neither market pressures nor negotiating procedures resulted in adequate restraint of costs. However the PIB was passing responsibility for putting on the pressure back to the Ministry of Agriculture, as it had not done in the early report. It had already agreed to the second 1d the industry wanted in its interim report. How much profits ought to be maintained by raising prices and how much scope there was for cost saving was postponed until the next review of prices, though by the time the report was published the Government had changed and it was clear there would be no such review.

Another labour-intensive activity that appeared among the PIB's early cases was breweries (No. 13). Some breweries gave notice of price increases for some brands of beer under the early-warning arrangements, and had drawn attention to their rising labour costs in doing so. Forty per cent of the total increase in unit costs was due to increased labour cost, 25 per cent to overhead costs, and 14 per cent to depreciation. Production labour costs had increased ten per cent and distribution labour costs seven per cent. But this time the PIB gave labour cost and industrial relations little attention; it merely recorded the facts. Hourly earnings had increased over 50 per cent in five years, compared with under 40 per cent in industry generally. Company agreements had provided bonuses which, on top of increases in basic rates, had brought earnings close to the national average, even though the work was not skilled. While labour costs had been increasing about ten per cent a year, the industry expected productivity to increase by two per cent a year. The PIB thought the industry ought not to pass on cost increases of such a size, but made no further analysis of working practices. It was more intent on the nature of the market and the efficient allocation of resources. It thought the industry "too closed" to restrain costs adequately. Therefore, no increase in wholesale prices should be made for six to nine months, and no increase in retail prices in public bars should be allowed. But the recommendation could not go unqualified. The case had been referred after some, but not all the breweries had increased prices, sometimes of only a few of many brands. Fairness between companies required that the round of price increases should be completed. The restriction was therefore to apply to companies which had increased their prices since the beginning of 1964.

The second report on beer prices (No. 136) appeared late in 1969. This time labour use and pay systems were investigated, and showed that payment-by-results schemes left much to be desired. The industry was commended to look at company productivity agreements as a remedy. Though the companies alleged that wages and salaries had risen 33 per cent in five years, the PIB found that unit costs had risen only five per cent. Increasing cost of labour and materials had been absorbed by better deployment of resources as amalgamations continued. Not all the potential savings had then been realised, and distribution could be further rationalised by operational research. The PIB's main argument on prices related to the adequacy of returns on capital. On the grounds that the brewers' returns had fallen below the level necessary to finance new investment in production and retailing, an increase of $2d$ a pint, as the industry wanted, was recommended. No pressure on labour costs would therefore have resulted.

The next labour-intensive industry referred to the PIB was bricks (No. 47). Labour costs were the largest single item, and wages accounted for the largest part of the increase in the industry's outgoings. Earnings had increased relatively fast, because of two recent wage awards. Less than half the increase in earnings had been offset by improvements in labour productivity. However, the PIB pursued the question of labour use no further. The labour-force changed relatively little with changes in output; hence labour cost per thousand bricks varied more closely with the capacity in use than with total labour costs. The industry had been able to absorb increasing wages without difficulty in the previous few years, because demand was increasing and capacity more fully used. But the standstill of 1966 hastened a recession of demand. Stocks were built up at brickworks, which itself added to costs, but surplus capacity nevertheless appeared. Profits fell, and increasing labour costs put up the unit cost of the smaller output even more sharply. Whether or not labour use improved, labour cost would increase still further, largely due to the effects of Government action. The PIB therefore had to decide the case on other grounds.

Though increasing costs and falling profits were a common experience, the industry was an extremely varied one with firms of all sizes, the market being dominated by the London Brick Company (LBC), which had been the price leader for a long time. An average price, cost or profit meant nothing, and certainly did not indicate whether a price was justified. The opinions of the companies about the size of the increase that would meet their needs was as varied as the firms, and ranged from nil to double figures. But demand was already recovering (by autumn 1967), and there was no convincing evidence that it would again contract, apart from the cyclical fluctuations usual in this industry.

The market situation could not be ignored. Whatever the PIB recommended for prices, the market price would be determined by what LBC charged. The PIB therefore recommended that the price-policy rules should be applied to the LBC alone. No other company of any size would be able to increase its prices appreciably more than LBC, and the hundreds of small firms could not be effectively supervised anyway. There remained only one test of the right price, namely returns to capital in the light of the investment needs and profits of LBC. The result was to suggest a further increase of $1\frac{1}{2}$ per cent, on top of the temporary increase of three per cent agreed with the Ministry of Works, while the PIB investigated. The case marked a development in the PIB's attitude, since it was the first time the recommendations applied to one firm, where prices in a whole in industry had been referred. It was also the first case where low capacity use had forced up costs and prices, in spite of the prices policy, and in spite of it being relatively labour-intensive.

The second reference of bricks prices (No. 150) followed the pattern of the second reference of bread prices, in being referred after a wage settlement, and after a Government Department had already agreed to a price increase. Pay and conditions of work were included in the reference. The case covered LBC alone, as it alone was subject to early warning, following the PIB's recommendation.

Process and maintenance workers had both gained five per cent more pay, but there was no proposal to increase productivity. The PIB found that work study had been little used, even though the union (the TGWU) had agreed to it. Labour management was weak, especially for an industry so dependent on labour.

Costs had risen 27s per thousand bricks, while revenue had risen by 19s 6d since the previous investigation. Returns had consequently fallen, due more to the continued under-use of capacity than to increases in cost. A price increase of about 13s per thousand would be needed to bring

returns back to the average level of the previous three years. But the
PIB thought this would discourage demand and still further depress the
use of capacity. There was, concluded the PIB, a case for a "very
modest" increase. But the situation had been transformed meanwhile. In
June 1970, before the PIB had reported, and a few days after the Conservative Government had taken office, the industry had made another
agreement for a 20 per cent increase in pay, nine months after the
referred agreement. The Minister had promptly agreed to the LBC's
proposal to increase all prices by 20s per thousand, far above any
previous increase, and far above anything justified before the settlement,
and more than was needed to cover even that. The PIB could only point
out the implications. LBC had no reason to resist any wage increase,
or to negotiate any reform of pay structure when it could so easily pass
on price increases with Government approval. Equally the unions had
no reason to agree to productivity improvements to get extra pay. "The
Government has made its choice and no recommendation on our part is
called for", concluded the affronted PIB.

Shortly after the first brick report came another labour-intensive
industry dominated by a price leader, national daily newspapers (No.
43). A proposal to increase prices had been put to the Government by
the price leader only, the *Daily Mirror* (published by the International
Publishing Corporation). It was also like bricks, in that a high proportion
of its costs were fixed in relation to small changes in its output.

The problems of the industry were reviewed by the PIB in the light of
its use of labour. As it had observed before in the printing case,
newspapers were vulnerable to pressure for wage increases, because of
the very perishable nature of its product. The result had been lax labour
practices. An independent survey had recently been made of the possible
savings in production costs, and this had been estimated at £3 million
for the industry. The *Daily Mirror*'s share was the largest and amounted
to £¾ million, in spite of its having been relatively successful in cutting
down labour already by some thirty per cent. The IPC itself estimated
that further savings of 25 to 30 per cent could be made. It also seemed
likely to the PIB that editorial costs could be cut, since the popular
papers spent far more annually than the qualities for less editorial
matter.

The *Daily Mirror* wanted a price increase to cover the increased
price of newsprint and to improve the size and quality of the newspaper.
It had already increased its charges to advertisers (which did not
come within the early-warning arrangements). The PIB concluded that
the increased cost of newsprint could not be recovered while costs could
obviously be reduced elsewhere. Changes in size and quality it found
not to be relevant, as it was tantamount to changing the product.

After discussions with the Board of Trade, IPC agreed to hold prices for six months. But devaluation intervened, and newsprint costs rose so rapidly that there was no alternative to allowing the 1*d* increase three months afterwards. Negotiations to reduce manning were proceeding, with the unions showing a growing awareness of the long-term problems of their industry.

A further round of price increase was notified by all the national dailies in 1969, and their costs and revenues were again referred to the PIB (No. 141). The competitive strength of the papers varied greatly, but all had falling profits or were making losses. Newsprint prices had gone on rising and another rise was expected (rightly) later in the year. There was still scope for reducing labour costs. However, the PIB decided this time that major economies could only be made in the course of years. Meanwhile the need for more revenue was urgent. Consequently, the increase was approved on the grounds that without it, inadequate cash flows would prevent necessary investment. The PIB went on to recommend plant productivity agreements, within a national framework agreement on wage structures; but these were not a condition for the price increase.

The last private-sector labour-intensive manufacturing industry reviewed by the PIB was bright steel bars (No. 118). But increased raw material costs rather than labour costs directly brought it for investigation. The PIB enquired into labour use in the firm that had given notice of the proposal to increase prices, and found there was scope to improve efficiency. It therefore interpreted the policy as not allowing the firms to recover anything more than the bare costs of raw materials, which was about half the firm's proposed increase. The PIB also recommended that other producers should be allowed to increase their prices to the same extent, if they wished, and if competition allowed it.

The PIB's general strategy to remove inflation of costs and prices in labour-intensive industries was to make use of market pressures where they existed. In road haulage and printing and perhaps steel bars, customers had enough choice and influence to keep price increases below pay increases. But price rises were more likely to follow pay rises where industries negotiated pay collectively at national level. An outstanding feature was that not a single one of them was found to negotiate pay and productivity together, with a coherent policy so that labour costs could be restrained, let alone minimised. Prices and incomes policy clearly had to be part of a single strategy, as it was supposed to be, to change these conditions.

Reports

No. 1 Road haulage rates (Cmnd 2695)

No. 14 Road haulage charges (Cmnd 2968)

No. 48 Charges, costs and wages in the road haulage industry (Cmnd 3482)

No. 94 Productivity agreements in the road haulage industry (Cmnd 3847)

No. 2 Wages, costs and prices in the printing industry (Cmnd 2750)

No. 3 Prices of bread and flour (Cmnd 2760)

No. 144 Bread prices and pay in the baking industry (Cmnd 43)

No. 13 Coal prices (Cmnd 2919)

No. 136 Beer prices (Cmnd 4227)

No. 47 Prices of Fletton and non-Fletton bricks (Cmnd 3480)

No. 150 Pay in the Fletton brick industry and the prices charged by the London Brick Company (Cmnd 4422)

No. 43 Costs and revenue of national daily newspapers (Cmnd 3435)

No. 141 Costs and revenue of national newspapers (Cmnd 4277)

No. 118 Prices of non-alloy bright steel bars (Cmnd 4093)

6

Distribution and other Services

Distribution and service industries are all comparatively labour-intensive but they have some other characteristics rather different from manufacturing. The bulk of the capital involved is often the premises, the costs of which are as inflexible as their uses are flexible. Though their markets were extremely varied, the PIB's attitude to them had some common features, as efficiency always involved making better use of given premises, and usually of skilled or experienced staff.

The first of the PIB's distribution cases came at its own request. Try as it might, it had found no alternative to recommending an increase in the pit-head price of coal in February 1966 (No. 12, see p. 109). But it asked to examine distribution costs, and the extent to which the price increase should be reflected in retail prices, in the hope that the increase to domestic consumers might be mitigated.

The cost of transport from pit to depots accounted for one-third (average) of the margin; and this had not increased substantially for some years, the net result of increases in the price of rail transport, offset by the economies of large-scale operation. But labour costs were the biggest item, and were increasing as wages rose. Labour productivity had been falling on balance, though costs showed great variation from firm to firm. Domestic sales had also been falling, and merchants had been extending their services to customers in an attempt to maintain them. This also had caused costs to rise rapidly. Some large firms had managed to increase productivity and reduce unit costs in spite of this, by mechanising larger depots. Further amalgamations would clearly make the containment of costs easier.

The immediate issue was the incidence of SET. The standstill had been imposed during the investigation, and increased costs due to Government action could be passed on if they could not be absorbed. SET would cost 2s per ton on average, with considerable variation between firms. It could eventually be absorbed by further mechanisation. Meanwhile, the PIB found that price increases would be justified to cover it.

But some merchants had already raised prices (many on 18 or 19 July), in anticipation of the standstill and the coming incidence of SET. Prices increase was only justified when SET had to be paid (September 1966) and when the increased pit-head price came into force (November 1966). The PIB recommended that further price increases should be less than costs where such increases had been made. It could find no other prospect of restraining costs, other than further concentration of the industry. Despite this, a number of firms did raise their prices more than the pit-head price, which naturally caused more complaints to Government Departments. But no further action was taken.

The incidence of SET was also a major issue concerning the charges made by laundries and dry-cleaners (No. 20). The case was originally referred because of public complaints, before SET had been announced. But it had clearly to be taken into account in the PIB's report.

The most obvious result of the PIB's enquiries into both the industries was the variation in charges, costs and profits between firms. Both industries were highly competitive, and their customers relatively discriminating, resulting in a wide range of services and prices.

In laundries, unit costs could only be measured indirectly as the customers responded to changing prices by altering the size and make-up of the laundry bundles. But it was clear that prices had risen generally, and that the main reason was increasing labour costs. As increased wages were followed by increased prices, the customers responded by sending less laundry. Unit costs were then further increased because capacity was underused. Prices increased again, followed by another contraction in demand. This process would continue unless capacity could be more fully used, a development that would only come with further amalgamations of firms.

Prices for dry-cleaning had also been increasing, also largely because of rising wages and salaries. There was also under-used capacity, this time due to too many entrants in an expanding market. Greater price competition might help to induce the withdrawal of outdated equipment; and to this end the PIB recommended that price-lists should be displayed in the shops (a practice that was then uncommon).

Like coal merchants, laundries and dry-cleaners would be liable to SET. Firms would be able to absorb the tax to different degrees by reducing their labour-force. Where this could not be done, the average increase ought to be $4\frac{1}{2}$ per cent for laundry and four per cent for dry-cleaning. Charges went on increasing while the PIB investigated, and there were increases in anticipation of SET, as among the coal merchants. Public complaints continued, and eventually a Standstill Order under the Prices and Incomes Act (1966) was made. But most applications to increase prices were still allowed by Government Departments.

Charges made by garages for repairs and servicing were another subject of public complaint, before they were referred to the PIB (No. 37). SET had by then been announced but had not come into operation. The industry was labour-intensive (though considerably less so than laundries or dry-cleaning) with few large firms. The reference concerned only part of the normal activities of garages, and much effort was expended on disentangling repairs and servicing costs from other costs. Labour charges had increased by no less than 24 per cent in three years, four per cent being the equivalent of the industry's liability for SET and the remainder due to increased wages, overheads and profits. Charges were lowest in small firms and highest in large ones, and increases had also been highest in the large firms. The earnings of garage workers had increased by somewhat less than 20 per cent, and overheads and profits (per job done) more. Profits appeared to have increased more than either costs or prices. Profits on repairs and servicing (so far as they could be distinguished) were low in relation to capital employed, but were increasing rapidly; while profits on other activities were high but falling. Small firms appeared to be making losses on repairs and servicing, and large firms a modest profit.

Garages had reacted to SET in different ways. Some did not intend to recover it in charges for repairs; some had increased charges for repairs to cover the tax on work in all departments. The trade had every appearance of a high degree of competition with plenty of consumer choice. But the PIB decided this was not the case. The system of limited franchises to sell new cars, granted by the manufacturers, seriously limited competition between large and small. Location was more than usually important; and the customers' ignorance about the proper price or quality of work prevented much discrimination. Consequently competition could not be relied on to improve performance or restrain charges. Pressure would have to come instead from the car manufacturers and the insurance companies. The PIB thought that the manufacturers should restrict the franchises to large firms, award them for longer than one year at a time, see that proper accounting procedures were used, and recommend standard prices for the replacement of parts instead of recommending standard times. The insurance companies should use their weight with the trade to ensure that repairs were carried out with the maximum efficiency. In addition, the customers' associations, the AA and RAC could do more to raise standards in the non-franchise garages by introducing a grading system (which did not then exist).

A follow-up report, in reply to a reference just before the General Election in 1970 gave some evidence of the response to a PIB report in a diffuse and competitive industry. The then Ministry of Technology had set up a committee representing the trade and the Department, to consider the recommendations. Of six recommendations for changes by the trade, two had been carried out three years later. These were, to improve accounting procedures and to provide franchise dealers with proper management information. The committee had decided against manufacturers recommending maximum prices for replacing parts. Neither the manufacturers nor the trade had welcomed the suggestion of longer franchises and neither wanted Government interference on the matter. Prices for warranty repairs was another bone of contention between manufacturers and the trade where neither wanted the Government to intervene. Improving stock control was found by the committee to be a more complex problem than the PIB thought, and nothing had come of it. Where progress had been made it had clearly been extremely slow.

Meanwhile labour costs had continued to increase, for the same reasons as before. The industry had made its own situation worse by offering wages in excess of the nationally negotiated rates, and by introducing inadequately controlled incentive schemes (in spite of the PIB's advice on how to do it). However, the PIB's second enquiry stimulated some improvement in that the Economic Development Council for the trade was asked by the trade association to study incentive schemes and their effects on standards of workmanship.

The British Insurers' Association had started garage pricing schemes, by which certain garages agreed to carry out specified repair jobs at an agreed low price in return for a steady flow of work. Secondly, some inspection units had been established to report on damage and estimate repair costs for any insurance company wishing to use them. In addition, the AA and RAC had started a grading scheme for garages. This was not in the right form, since it merely distinguished facilities rather than the efficiency with which the facilities were used. The PIB could only urge once more that they do more to protect their members against poor workmanship, whose existence had again recently been demonstrated by the Consumers' Association.

Competition in the garage trade had resulted in neither good service to the customers, nor keen prices, nor operating efficiency, and certainly not in the economic use of its main resource, labour. With little Government influence, pressure could only be provided by organised consumer interests.

The distribution costs of the fresh fruit and vegetables trade was referred soon afterwards, as a direct result of SET (No. 31). The wholesalers' association recommended its members to introduce a "surcharge" of 2d in the £ to cover SET, and (as an afterthought) other costs. The retailers protested to the Ministry of Agriculture, who supported them, persuaded the trade to reduce the surcharge to a temporary 1d in the £, and referred the case.

The trade had reacted very like the garages. Some wholesalers had no intention of charging the tax, and vehemently objected to their association's policy. Some seized on the chance to pass on a cost increase, backed by a collective policy. The PIB could not condone so blatant a restrictive practice. As SET was not a tax on sales but only one component of costs, any wholesaler who was unable to absorb it by increasing turnover per head of his employees (especially salesman) should not pass it on by means of a surcharge, as this would be a temptation to other traders to collect the same amount.

It was probably unlikely that the surcharge could have been effective, in the face of competitive pressures. Large suppliers and customers were both also exerting pressure against it. But market responses might have been slower than the Government was able to secure, using the PIB. Some small part of public resentment of the effect of SET was thereby avoided.

A trade's hasty reaction to the Government's anti-inflation policy brought another case after public complaint, the rents for TV sets and TV relay (No. 52). One of the measures to restrict credit, a part of the squeeze to accompany the freeze, was a new Control of Hiring Order by which new contracts to rent equipment had to begin with 42 weeks' advance rent. SET was also due at the same time. Some firms had responded by charging higher rents on existing contracts as well as on new ones. The complaints had not unnaturally come from these latter customers, who felt helpless in the face of exploitation (like the hirers of data-processing equipment [see p. 89]).

SET had certainly increased costs, and labour costs were inflexible in relation to the rental companies' shops. But some had contained labour costs by increasing the number of sets rented per shop, partly by concentrating their own business, partly by amalgamation. However, some firms with high profits had been among those increasing charges, a misguided reaction in a competitive market. A slight relaxation of the Control of Hiring Order early in 1967 gave them the oppportunity to reverse their mistake, and charges were put down again.

The PIB could only observe that the lower charges might have applied in 1966 as well and attracted more business, if only more firms had held their rents steady, as they could well have afforded.

The situation on relay was fundamentally different in that each relay network was a local monopoly, where reception on bought or rented sets was poor. It was from such areas that the complaints had come. The costs were mostly the cost of equipment, and the return was consequently extra-sensitive to the consumer density of the network. The remedy for the low returns was therefore to increase the density. The customers seemed to the PIB to need protection; but provision for this was already available in the licenses granted to the companies by local authorities. There were invariably powers to approve charges as a condition of the license, and local authorities should use their powers (which they had not previously done), to insist that adequate costings were produced whenever they were asked to approve an increase.

Another case referred to the PIB partly as a result of the customers' resentment of price increase imposed by a monopoly was the fares and freight charges of the North of Scotland Orkney and Shetland Shipping Company (No. 67). Their costs had been increasing for five or six years, partly due to increased fuel costs (for diesel and other oil), and partly due to increased wages. Increased dockers' wages had led to a steep increase in dock charges, and crew wages had also increased (at a slower rate). The surcharge of 2d a gallon on oil, imposed by the Ministry of Power in June 1967, to cover the extra costs due to the six-day war in the Middle East, had also increased costs steeply.

The PIB could not find much scope for cost saving with the existing services. The proposed increases in fares and charges had therefore to be allowed. For the future, it could only suggest altering the services provided; and to this end it discussed various ways of altering price structure, between freight and passenger charges, between in and out of season charges, in some detail, an increasing preoccupation of the PIB in later years.

The only other case involving passenger transport privately provided was that of London taxi-cabs (No. 87). Fares were prescribed statutorily, on a scale relating mainly to the distance travelled. There was evidence that more cabs were needed, and that a fare increase would induce more drivers to enter the trade. The PIB concluded that the increase of 11 per cent asked for should be allowed, and then went on to consider the structure of fares. Costs were not related to time and distance in the same way, distance-related costs being far less in proportion to total cost than distance charges to total income. A time charge plus a much lower distance charge would more nearly represent the costs. But as this would mean changing the meters, the PIB recommended meanwhile a bigger increase in the time charge, and a smaller increase in the distance charge than the trade had asked for.

The charges made by London employment agencies for office staff were referred early in 1968 (No. 89). The case was sent to the PIB because the Government itself was a major customer of the agencies, and had come to believe that the charges for temporary office staff were inflating office salaries generally. Since the Government itself operated employment agencies, it might well be asked why departments, if not other employers, were making use of them at all. Moreover, the Government had already committed itself to controlling the agencies as an alternative to abolishing them, as the International Labour Organisation wanted, and as many other other countries had done. The reason for the agencies' expansion was that employees seeking work appeared more readily in private agencies than in labour exchanges; and that the agencies organised the market for temporary or part-time workers in the absence of a Government service.

Many of the agencies' customers besides the Government were dissatisfied with the service they received. But the PIB did not find that the fault lay mainly with the agencies. Some of the agencies were as ready to complain about their customers, principally about their vagueness as to their own needs. Job description was perfunctory, and office managers often failed to make effective use of their staff. The PIB largely confirmed this, and pointed out that many more employers could improve matters in the same ways as a few large firms had done, by better supervision, systematic audio-typing, and work or method study.

Large agencies were more profitable than small and had been more successful in keeping their income up in line with increasing costs; indeed their returns were exceptionally large. Competition was restricted more than it need be by the customers' lack of knowledge of the charges and what services ought to be rendered for them. To improve the market in this respect the PIB recommended that charges should be expressed as a sum of cash, instead of as a percentage of the salary of the employee. If customers considered they got a bad or costly service, they should bargain more carefully among the many competing agencies. Large employers, especially the Government, should negotiate centrally about the supply of temporary staff, and about placement fees for permanent staff (which was then left to each department, including the PIB itself). But for all the imperfections, it did not appear that the pay of the "temps" exerted any great influence on the pay of permanent staff, when the great difference in conditions, like holiday and sickness pay, was taken into account.

In 1968, after SET had been in operation for some time, and after responsibility for prices policy had been transferred to the DEP, a group of cases concerning the distributive margin on certain goods were referred. They were: the distribution costs and margins on furniture, domestic electrical appliances and footwear (No. 97); distribution margins in relation to manufacturers' recommended prices (No. 55); distributive margins on paint, children's clothing, household textiles and proprietary medicines (No. 80). The PIB was also asked to report generally on how distributive margins ought to change after devaluation.

These references covered a group of goods whose prices gave a good deal of concern to those who still wanted pressure on prices (including the DEP), because it was known that margins were high enough to play a major part in determining the retail price. It was also widely believed (probably with some foundation) that gross profit margins on some of them were unusually high. But the PIB could make little of any of them, in the form in which the references were made. All the goods were sold widely, in shops ranging from large stores and national chains of specialist shops, down to single local enterprises. All except furniture and footwear were sold among many other goods not referred. The report on furniture, domestic electrical goods and footwear was the nearest to a suitable form for a thorough study to be made of the three wholesale trades, with some reasonable general conclusions. The PIB found that mail-order firms earned a high return and could afford to reduce their margins. Other traders (wholesale and retail) were not making large profits at the expense of the consumers, for the usual reason: rising labour costs.

The sum of the evidence on all the cases was that increasing productivity was a matter of increasing turnover per head. The PIB suggested three ways to achieve it: more training for retail managers; relaxing the regulations on opening hours; and allowing more general freedom to experiment. Apart from these, there was only the usual remedy, amalgamation.

The PIB was eventually given the opportunity in food distribution costs (No. 165) to generalise its findings about efficiency rather more, very late in the day, May 1970, when its demise was imminent, and when as it turned out it was no longer in a position to complete the necessary enquiries. The trades not unnaturally took the PIB's efforts less seriously than had earlier been the case, without (mostly) being positively obstructive. Nevertheless, the PIB finally produced a reasonably weighty report, mostly putting the trade in a more favourable light than was probably expected. The reason for the reference was the steep rise in food prices late in 1969 and early 1970, which brought to the surface the suspicions of consumers, small-shopkeepers and food manufacturers alike, that the large chains of retail grocers were dominating the market to the detriment of all of them.

The PIB concentrated its efforts on grocery, fresh meat and fruit and vegetables. It found that margins had nowhere increased, and had sometimes been reduced, in the previous three years. Labour and transport costs had both been rising faster than food prices; but these had been offset by major changes in the structure and practices of the trades, such as the development of cash-and-carry wholesaling, and the rapid spread of supermarkets. The food distributors could not therefore be accused of contributing unduly to the rise in food prices.

This welcome result had been derived largely from economies of scale, which were considerable. Both increasing size of shop and of the parent organisation had contributed to the economies. But the very increase in size was the root of the suspicion that the large firms were beginning to exploit something of a monopoly situation. The PIB decided that this was not so. To keep up their profits they needed to attract the consumers by keen prices. Part of this was due to their ability to bargain with the suppliers from a much stronger position than ever before; but their activities had not worked to the detriment of the consumers. The multiples had themselves become more efficient in their use of resources, and had induced more efficiency in others. The PIB believed that competition was still effective in keeping costs down and profits at a level which was not excessive.

But how far the process of amalgamation could go without the break-down of competitive pressure on prices and costs was a question left open. This was one of the major pieces of unfinished business the PIB left behind. Having advocated larger, fewer firms as the means of con-centrating trade in the hands of fewer, more expensive staff, it never really dealt with the problem of what was to take the place of competition to keep either costs or profit margins from rising again in the end.

Financial and commercial services are also large users of premises and labour, where the concentration of business on each office helps to determine costs. However, the two PIB cases concerning charges and profits in building societies and banks involved the cost of their "raw material", borrowed money, to an important extent.

The building societies case (No. 22) concerned a proposal by the Building Societies Association (BSA) to raise its recommended mortgage rates following the Budget of 1966. The increase was said to be needed to maintain the growth of business without an "undue reduction" in reserves, as the Budget had introduced Corporation Tax and SET, both increasing the societies' tax liabilities.

The BSA had only recently adopted the practice of recommending rates of interest for money lent to mortgagees, and for funds borrowed from investors; and most societies followed the recommendations. The rates charged to mortgagees depended ultimately on the rates which attracted investors to subscribe the necessary funds. As borrowers, the societies were only one of a number of competitors for funds borrowed on similar conditions. The market rate for funds was rising, owing to rising Bank rate, (increased to seven per cent in November 1964), and competition from a new issue of Savings Certificates. However, two other important factors determined mortgage rates, the margin main-tained between borrowing and lending rates, and the rate of expansion of the societies' business. The immediate issue of the reference related to the margin, which had been three per cent in 1965, the difference between $3\frac{3}{4}$ per cent for borrowed money and $6\frac{3}{4}$ per cent charged to mortgagees. But the borrowing rate had been raised to four per cent in June 1965, and the societies considered the remaining margin too low. It was proposed to raise the morgage rate to $7\frac{1}{8}$ per cent, making the margin $3\frac{1}{8}$ per cent.

The case for increasing the margin turned on the building societies' need to accumulate reserves. Part of the margin was held to meet tax liability; the rest covered management expenses and additions to reserves. Though the societies were important as employers of staff and premises from the national point of view, these were of minor importance to the industry. Even a 10 per cent reduction in staff costs would be too small to affect the mortgage rate. However, as any reduction here would have the effect of increasing allocations to reserves, from which the growth of business could be financed, the PIB investigated the matter. The workers employed per 1,000 accounts had increased by 17 per cent in 10 years, possibly partly due to accounts being used more actively. But the PIB believed it was also the result of the larger societies' policy of expanding the network of branch offices, so far that they could not realise the economies of scale fully. It even appeared that some endured diseconomies. The remedy was to be found in further amalgamations among the middle-sized societies (in spite of the evidence that management costs had not then been contained in large societies), because the PIB thought it most important to spread the costs of premises over a larger volume of business.

The Chief Registrar of building societies subsequently announced changes in administrative practice, whereby his consent would be easier to come by than before for the amalgamation of societies.

The minimum reserve ratio required by statute was $2\frac{1}{2}$ per cent of assets below £100 million, and two per cent above it. But many societies had reserves well above the minimum, and although reserves had been falling, they were still likely to remain above four per cent in aggregate by the end of 1966. The PIB considered the minimum ratio itself too high in relation to the risks (of mortgage or investment loss) actually incurred, and actual reserves were even higher. A difference of opinion appeared between the societies and the Chief Registrar about how the ratio should be regarded. The societies treated it as an irreducible minimum, while the Registrar assured the PIB that he would regard a temporary fall below the statutory figure with equanimity, and societies would have time to re-establish it. The PIB felt that a minimum ratio should be based on a statistical analysis of the risks, and recommended the BSA to commission a study. The result should be a normal operational aim only, and should be reviewed from time to time. The BSA commissioned an independent committee to advise in the matter; but this proved abortive, as the committee reported that the reserve was in the end, a matter of commercial judgment.

The PIB decided it could not recommend a mortgage rate, since it depended on the market-determined rate to investors. But the margin should be maintained at the 1966 level.

The issues raised by the case relating to bank charges (No. 34) were similar in some respects to the building societies' case. The banks were also lavish users of premises and staff, but costs were overwhelmed by the cost of money. The PIB was asked to investigate the system and level of charges to customers, in the light of the banks' profit and dividend records, the only time a dividend was ever referred to the PIB. Banks' profits were then still only partially disclosed, and dividends bore an uncertain relationship to true profits and to the banks' assets, since their reserves were also only partly disclosed.

Banks were unlike building societies in that the cost of their borrowed money was decided as much by convention as by market forces. Also their money-transmitting function provided them with unique access to money. They were similar in that rates of interest to borrowers depended substantially on the rates offered to lenders, the margin between the two covering management expenses, additions to reserves and profits (unlike building societies which are non-profit-making). The adequacy of the margin depended on the prospects for management costs, the need for reserves and the reasonableness of profits.

Profits in absolute terms had increased substantially, and for some years dividends had increased faster than profits. But reserves had also been increasing with expanding business. Profits were unusually difficult for the PIB to judge, since the nearest approximation to capital employed was the sum of shareholders' capital plus reserves. But if reserves were in some sense too high, the rate of profit would appear to be lower than it was in relation to the resources needed. The banks themselves had no "concerted views" about appropriate reserves, nor about the right principles to use. Like building societies, reserves were mainly to safeguard them against loss. The reserves could not be shown to be unreasonably high, so profits had to be related to them, and the PIB could not recommend charges that implied a reduction.

Apart from reserves, profits depended on income from commissions and interest charges on loans, minus the costs incurred. The banks had enjoyed windfall profits on a considerable scale as a consequence of high interest rates, and might do so again. Advances had increased and these were the most profitable business. There were also handicaps, because the demand for loans was inhibited by the high rates, and the risk of bad debts was somewhat increased. But there was a substantial gain on balance. The PIB could only conclude that profits had been excessive in the sense that they had accrued simply from high bank rate. The banks' dividend distributions had also been excessive, though since July 1966 they had not increased them any further. However, in spite of the probability of Bank rate remaining high, there were reasons for expecting profits to decline. Though the banks had previously had little difficulty in passing on increases in operating costs, more competition for banking was likely in future, and it would be difficult to increase the proportion of the most profitable assets any more (so long as the minimum ratios required by the monetary authorities remained the same). A contraction of profit margins could be expected, except for the gratuitous "endowment" of higher profits when Bank rate increased. The PIB considered whether the banks could somehow be deprived of this "endowment" element, by a levy when Bank rate rose, and a rebate when it fell. But after much deliberation, decided not to recommend it, as windfall profits were virtually impossible to distinguish from earned profits derived from extra efficiency or enterprise. Moreover, if the banks were more competitive, they would be less able to maintain profits and reserves unconnected with efficiency or enterprise, and more able to employ their resources fully.

Competition should be encouraged by changing practices and conventions, before any remaining problem of unearned profits was dealt with.

The banks' heavy use of clerical labour was obvious; equally obvious was the extravagant use of branch offices, which were a permanent advertisement of their services. More branches added considerably to costs; and decisions to expand the network were difficult to reverse. Competition had produced an excessive number of banks, especially in small towns. The only way to have fewer branches would be to have fewer banks. It was still then assumed by the banks that the Treasury would not allow further amalgamations. However, having been asked (and consequently having had to review the question), the authorities were found to have no such objections; and the PIB urged the banks to bear this in mind in considering their future development. It was shortly after this that the first of the recent amalgamations among clearing banks was announced.

Increasing turnover per branch by new business would also help to counteract inflexible costs. The banks' outstanding advantage was their knowledge of their customers' creditworthiness, and they should exploit this in considering an "entire spectrum" of new business. To some extent they were already diversifying, by acquiring interests in hire purchase companies; but it was not necessarily making the best use of their resources to keep these activities separate from banking. Any impediments to competition between banks or with other financial institutions, such as the cartel arrangement on interest rates and some of the monetary regulations, should be removed. Radically different behaviour by banks depended on how their activities were circumscribed by the monetary authorities.

The PIB thought that the banks should not charge their account-holders less than the cost of managing the accounts. But equally the customers should have the opportunity to choose rationally between the alternatives open to them. Tariffs of charges should be published, and the banks should end their agreements on commissions. Existing charges were not too high in relation to existing costs; but too little discipline exercised managements in controlling their operating costs.

The PIB had found both its monetary-sector cases to have strong analogies with other institutions in the commercial sector. Both operated in a partly competitive market. Both operated on rules and conventions that reduced competition, without much advantage to the authorities or the customers. Both were using increasing amounts of scarce resources, and neither was expanding fast enough for extra business to counteract rising costs. The only general remedy was amalgamation.

Providing professional services is usually thought of as a different activity from service industries. Some of their charges are commonly subject to regulation, either by statute or maintained by professional organisations. Yet there is competition in their markets; and their costs are as dependent on the volume of business done by each enterprise as industry. The PIB investigated two such cases, solicitors (who were made the subject of a standing reference in 1969) and architects.

The immediate cause of the first reference of solicitors (No. 54) was a proposal by the Law Society to increase charges for leases and for work done in County Courts, both being determined by a statutory scale. The PIB set about investigating solicitors' incomes from all sources, and found two-thirds subject to statutory control. A large part of most solicitors' work was conveyancing, most of this being subject to scale charges.

The PIB's view was that the "proper criteria" were similar to those applying to any other activity: whether price covered reasonable costs, and produced a profit which allowed adequate investment and the efficient allocation of resources, the main resource being trained manpower. The relationship between charges and the costs of each type of business would show whether fees were reasonable.

In fact, charges were not related in a way to encourage the most effective use of manpower among solicitors, or, the PIB reported, the most desirable distribution of work between solicitors and "adjacent and contiguous professions". Conveyancing was profitable, and the scale charge was in practice the minimum. Solicitors charged on the basis of time spent if they thought a case would be abnormally costly; but they did not abate their charges when it was abnormally cheap. The PIB recommended that solicitors should be able to cut charges below the scale if they chose, and that there should be some supervision of actual charges. It also considered whether competition from outside the profession might be encouraged, to protect the customers from overcharging. But it concluded that the time had not yet come for such a development. The reason being the continual possibility that legal problems might arise, rarely though they might actually occur. The scale would also have to continue, though the structure needed modification; work at the top end was exceptionally profitable, and at the bottom end so unprofitable that there was a danger that some solicitors would refuse the work. Therefore increase in charges on transactions of low value were recommended, balanced by a reduction elsewhere.

Court work was much less profitable than conveyancing, and a considerable number of solicitors refused certain types of litigation altogether. The balance between the income derived from the two kinds of work ought to be rectified, by increasing County Court charges. The increase was eventually put at 55 per cent (the last increase having been in 1956). The net effect of both recommendations was to leave income unchanged in total, while altering its main sources to correspond more closely to costs, with the intention of altering the effort devoted by the profession to the different types of work.

The Government accepted the PIB's report after four months' consideration. But a year later it had not been implemented by the profession. The case was referred again as a standing reference (No. 134). An impasse had been reached over charges. The Non-Contentious Costs Committee, which dealt with conveyancing charges, had no powers to act on County Court charges; and the County Court Law Committee had no powers on conveyancing. So no change was possible in the profession's view.

The PIB again reviewed costs and profits, especially the incidence of SET, which had added three to four per cent to total expenditure. But revenue had also increased, because of increased volume of work and increased charges. Profits still came mainly from conveyancing. As the same unbalance of costs and profits persisted, the PIB repeated its previous recommendation.

By the time of a third report (No. 164), scale charges for conveyancing had been increased for small properties, but no reductions had been made in the middle of the scale. Instead of income from conveyancing being reduced, it had been increased. By now the PIB had collected detailed information of the costs of various types of work, the first such information available. Conveyancing was still extremely profitable. But the PIB concluded this time that lower fees were only likely in response to lower costs, through simplifying procedures. Meanwhile the statutory orders should be amended to make it clear that the scale was a maximum, and that any solicitor could if he chose, charge less. In future charges should generally be brought into closer relationship with the costs; and it would be fairer to solicitors and their clients if scales were based on objective, properly quantified estimates of costs. However the previous recommendation to reduce some charges was not again repeated.

As statutory control of fees had not resulted in any particularly desirable scales, some independent review body ought to advise on them after the PIB had gone out of existence. The Office of Manpower Economics (by now announced as the PIB's only successor), would be suitable, as it would inherit some of the necessary expertise. The matter was eventually taken up by the Lord Chancellor's office, whose policy was to abolish the scale altogether.

When the PIB came to investigate architects' costs and fees (No. 71), it found a marked difference in the profitability of large and small firms. The distribution of earnings and the range of profits was larger than for solicitors, probably because the larger and more profitable jobs went to the large firms, and they were able to maintain a more continuous work flow. They were less well rewarded for their services than solicitors; but the profession was over-manned.

Fees were related to the expected cost of building projects, on a scale which the PIB thought needed modification to bring the fees into closer relationship with the costs incurred. The scale consisted mainly of charging six per cent of construction costs, and most customers and some architects considered this too crude a measure. But the PIB eventually recommended a comparatively minor amendment to the system. Percentage fees should be tapered for the most expensive projects (beginning at £100,000), while fees for small projects should be increased. Like the solicitors, individual architects should be free to charge less than the scale, if they chose, to encourage competition.

The PIB's views on distribution and services might be summarised as follows. Where competition was fully operative, there was little the PIB could say about prices. The containment of costs, in face of the universal increase in labour costs, was to be achieved by the concentration of business in fewer hands. Its function in respect of these was to confirm that competition indeed existed. Where some degree of monopoly was exercised, as was common in services other than the distributive trades, prices (or fees) needed review, and could usefully be commented on, as the customers could not otherwise know whether increases were justified or not. But as far as possible, competition should be increased to allow more business to go to the relatively efficient firms. In almost all the reports in this group the PIB was breaking new ground, since prices and other charges in these very important fields were not commonly investigated before.

Reports

No. 21   Coal distribution costs (Cmnd 3094)

No. 20   Laundry and dry-cleaning charges (Cmnd 3093)

No. 37   Costs and charges in the motor repairing and servicing industry (Cmnd 3368)

No. 163 Costs and charges in the motor repairing and servicing industry (Cmnd 4590)

No. 31   Distribution costs of fresh fruit and vegetables (Cmnd 3265)

No. 52   Costs and charges in the radio and television relay industry (Cmnd 3520)

No. 67   Passenger fares and freight charges of the North of Scotland Orkney and Sheltand Shipping Company Limited (Cmnd 3631)

No. 87   Proposed increases in London taxi-cab fares (Cmnd 3796)

No. 89   Office Staff Employment Agencies Charges and Salaries (Cmnd 3828)

No. 55   Distributors' margins in relation to manufacturers recommended prices (Cmnd 3546)

No. 80   Distributors' margins on paint, childrens' clothing, household textiles and proprietary medicines (Cmnd 3737)

No. 97   Distributors' costs and margins on furniture, domestic electrical appliances and footwear (Cmnd 3858)

No. 126 Smithfield Market (Cmnd 4171)

No. 165 Prices, profits and costs in food distribution (Cmnd 4645)

No. 22   Rate of interest on Building Society mortgages (Cmnd 3136)

No. 34   Bank charges (Cmnd 3292)

No. 54   Remuneration of solicitors (Cmnd 3529)

No. 134 Standing reference on the remuneration of solicitors (Cmnd 4217)

No. 71   Architects costs and fees (Cmnd 3653)

7

Other Private-sector Industries

Where labour costs were not the most important influence, prices had to be assessed by the PIB in other ways. In all of them returns to capital, with or without price increases, was the criterion for approval or disapproval (as it was also in many of the labour-intensive industries). Nevertheless there were distinct groups of cases involving other issues. These were the manufacturers of highly advertised products and multi-national companies often concerned more with international price-structure than with UK policy.

The heavy spenders on advertising often attract public suspicion when they raise prices, probably as much due to the industrial structure which gives rise to the advertising, as to the advertising itself. A few large manufacturers, controlling most of the market for a frequently-purchased consumer good, are clearly not subject to the same sort of competitive pressures as an industry of many small ones. Hence it was no accident that one of the heaviest spenders was among the PIB's cases referred on its first day, namely soap and detergents (No. 4). It also gave the PIB its first encounter with giant international companies, operating in UK markets of very limited competition.

Lever Brothers (a subsidiary of Unilever) and Proctor & Gamble shared between them 85 per cent of the market for household soap, over 95 per cent of the market for soap-flakes, soap-powder and synthetic powders, and over half the market for synthetic liquids. The markets for toilet soap and liquid detergents were more competitive, the two international companies having substantial market shares but not complete dominance.

Public criticism was caused by a succession of price increases for household soap and detergents during 1964 and 1965, after a relatively long period of price stability, from 1960 to 1964. The PIB found it impossible to quantify the increase since prices were subject to various special offers (by the manufacturers) and to spasmodic price cutting below recommended prices (by retailers). But there was no doubt about the trend of increase. World prices of vegetable oil and tallow, the main raw material for soap, had actually been falling before 1963, but thereafter began to rise at an increasing rate. Increased raw material costs accounted for three-quarters of the rise in manufacturer's selling prices. The manufacturers responded by increasing prices less than the increase in costs. Small reductions were made in advertising and promotion costs; but the main impact was allowed to fall on profit margins.

Raw materials for detergents were a home-produced by-product of oil refining. Raw material costs had increased somewhat since the manufacturers had agreed with a Government Standing Committee to alter the constituents of detergents to reduce the foam remaining in sewage; more expensive packaging was then necessary. But prices had increased considerably more than costs. One company was making profits high enough to absorb the increased costs comfortably. But a price difference would merely have reduced its revenue without increasing its market share, since demand would not change much in response to price changes. Prices were more likely to move upwards in response to changing costs than downwards.

The competitive situation also explained the parallel movement of soap prices with detergent prices. The companies could not be accused of collusion over prices; but it was in the interests of neither to risk disturbing market shares. Hence, competition took the form of advertising and sales promotions, so that advertising and selling expenses were a large part of total costs. The companies already achieved what economies of scale in marketing there were. Minimum effective expenditure was very large and unit costs of selling fell markedly as the volume of sales increased.

The problem for the PIB lay in the structure of the industry. Manufacturing costs had less impact on profits than promotion costs, and were insignificant given the nature of the competition. The prospects for restraining prices depended on either changing the market structure, or inducing the two companies to stabilise prices. The prospects for changing the structure were slender. It would be no easy task for a newcomer to break into the market because of the large minimum expenditure on advertising necessary to launch a new brand. The prospects for stabilising prices depended to a large extent on stabilising advertising expenditure. Surprisingly enough, an agreement to this effect had been made by the two companies in 1961, because of "signs of public concern at the apparently wasteful element in the selling effort". Both companies had then reduced their prices by similar amounts, on the same day. But the agreement had broken down within a year, due to the uncertainty of each about the intentions of the other, particularly about new products. There were two formidable obstacles to another such agreement. One was the problem of accommodating a possible newcomer, the other, the concern expressed by Proctor &

Gamble that the agreement might be held to run counter to the US anti-trust laws. All the PIB felt able to do, therefore, was to "expect that the companies will exercise restraint over the whole of their expenditure on advertising and promotion". Further cost increases in raw materials for soap making were not expected to be as steep as in the past, and increases in productivity (in manufacturing) would enable them to be absorbed. The companies should not therefore raise their prices before the end of the following year (1966). A significant decrease ought to lead to lower prices. Synthetic liquid was not likely to increase in price anyway because of price competition. On detergents the PIB eventually concluded that the White Paper rules would be satisfied if prices of synthetic powders were also kept stable for 1966.

Chocolate and sugar confectionery was also the subject of heavy marketing expenditure, much of it for advertising (No. 75). The industry had as much interest as the soap and detergent manufacturers in attracting and maintaining as many retail outlets as possible for their products. But there was more competition, and many more firms. When the reference was made, the Minister of Agriculture had already allowed some price increases, but it was thought desirable for the PIB to examine the industry "with special regard to the need to finance new investment".

Ten large national firms (out of over 200) produced most of the chocolate and half the other sweets sold; and were steadily increasing their share of a static market by absorbing the business of smaller firms. The average value per ton of confectionery sold (the nearest concept to "price" to the manufacturers), had increased more than either retail prices or food prices between 1961 and 1967. This was partly due to purchase tax, but also to a significant increase in distribution margins. The Ministry of Agriculture had allowed another three per cent increase in price in 1967, followed by another one per cent for the effects of devaluation.

Unit costs in the large firms had risen by some $8\frac{1}{2}$ per cent in six years due to increased packaging and labour costs, while raw material costs had actually fallen. Direct production costs had been reduced but indirect costs had risen by nearly 30 per cent on average, with the largest firms showing the largest increases. Wages and salaries of indirect (non-production) employees had risen twice as fast as the tonnage sold. Other marketing and selling expenses per ton had also increased steeply, part of the price the largest companies had paid for increasing sales volume against market trends.

The large companies maintained that profits had been reduced, and that "it should be permissible to restore these to reasonable commercial levels". The PIB found that the rate of return had certainly fallen, but remained "neither particularly high nor low". The PIB could find no ground for regarding the industry's profitability as below "reasonable commercial levels", and indeed there was scope for absorbing further cost increases by reducing profits. As the market was static, there was no need for new investment to expand production. There was no case for a price increase. As competition took the form of intense marketing efforts, which had increased costs, and the customers were insensitive to price changes (especially when they were concealed by changes in weight), the PIB concluded that the largest firms at least ought to be "subject to the restraints of the early warning system".

More than a year later, another case involving highly advertised products came the PIB's way, manufacturers' prices of toilet preparations (No. 113). There had been no particular price increase and no early warning. The PIB therefore investigated costs, prices and profits. There was the familiar wide range of sizes and firms from large multi-product firms, supplying the bulk of the market, to small specialist firms. The market as a whole was very fast-growing, while amalgamations were still reducing the number of firms. Prices had increased by about 11 per cent in three years, though such varied products were included, that the average was even less meaningful than usual. However, prices appeared to have increased fastest in the fastest growing markets, and least in the static markets. All costs had increased in relation to output; but a really rapid increase (of the order of 25 to 50 per cent in three years) was shown in indirect factory costs, namely selling and distribution and other overheads. Profits had fallen because prices had risen less than costs. But both the cosmetics and toiletries sides of the industry showed high returns on capital employed, and seemed to be "particularly high" for medium-priced cosmetics and specialist hair preparations. Moreover, profits had been remarkably stable over a longer period, which was consistent with the industry being at low risk. High profits seemed to "flow mainly from the special attitude of the consumers to these products and their prices". But the evidence for the nature of this special attitude was perfunctory to say the least: it was "exemplified by the fact that the cheapest products account for only a small share of the market". The PIB was unable to recommend anything to increase competition, other than communally provided information, by commending the efforts of the Consumer Council and the Consumers' Association. Profits were "high enough to enable manufacturers generally to absorb some further cost increases", unless circumstances changed. As "the nature of the markets makes for high profits", the Government had already done the right thing in imposing tax (but only "right" in the sense of being reasonably sure that the tax would be passed on in higher prices—an odd view for the PIB to take).

A final group of heavily advertised foods was referred to the PIB late in its history, beginning with margarine and cooking fats (No. 147). The market structure was similar to chocolate, with four large firms and a number of much smaller ones. Early-warning arrangements included the large companies, but none of the small ones. All four had notified their intention of raising prices towards the end of 1969, the main reasons being increases in the cost of raw materials and packaging. Having considered the cases separately, the Minister of Agriculture accepted proposals made by the CWS, Kraft, and Bibbys, but not from the largest, Van den Bergh and Jurgen (another subsidiary of Unilever) on the grounds that more information was required. But the three companies did not increase their prices until VBJ did so early in January 1970, the increases then averaging 11 per cent. The PIB concentrated its attention on VBJ because of its obvious price leadership. It was increasing its market share in a static market. But new varieties, particularly soft margarines made with vegetable oils, were expanding sales. Significant savings in production cost had been made, and the PIB could not find much scope for any more. Advertising and promotion expenses were "a significant item", at 11 per cent of total costs, and the industry considered itself dependent on this to maintain the volume of sales and keep down production costs. But it was not clear that advertising had actually reduced costs, certainly not to the extent necessary to give the customers more stable prices.

VJB as a whole had made "clearly high" profits in the past few years, ranging from 23 to 29 per cent. However raw materials accounted for about two-thirds of unit costs, and sterling prices had increased early in 1968 due to devaluation. VBJ had then been allowed by the Ministry of Agriculture to increase its prices. But prices had fallen again in the autumn of 1968, and VBJ had gone back to pre-devaluation prices. Oil prices had begun to climb again in 1969, mostly due to difficulties of supply. The climb had grown steadily steeper late in 1969 and early in 1970 (while the investigation was going on). Though the return on capital was still high, profits were declining as oil prices rose. They would probably increase further, and with no savings to be made in production (and not much discussion by the PIB of marketing costs), the price increases had to be allowed—though it was nearer the time of the PIB's report (May 1970) that the case was fully justified by actual cost increases, than at the time of the price increases (January 1970).

The level of advertising and other market expenses was again a central issue in the tea trade's case for a price increase. In the early months of 1970, the food manufacturers had notified the Ministry of Agriculture that they would no longer abide by the early-warning arrangements. The Government replied by referring costs and profits in food distribution generally to the PIB. But a few weeks later, the price leader among tea companies, Brooke Bond Oxo Ltd, took the opportunity to announce a 10 per cent price increase. The Government referred it to the PIB for examination "in the light of the trend of costs, prices and profitability" (No. 154).

Brooke Bond's price increase had been exactly matched by the other three major suppliers: Typhoo, Lyons and the Co-operative Tea Society. All three companies had considered holding their prices below Brooke Bond, but rejected this policy on the grounds that consumers would consider the cheaper teas were of poor quality. The fact that the trade's recommended price was widely cut by retailers was not thought to invalidate the argument, since the recommended price was printed on the packets, and it was this that consumers were supposed to accept as an indication of quality. If so, it was a bad indicator, since the blend in a 1s 9d tea (per ¼lb packet) varied quite substantially from one brand to another, and from time to time within the same brand.

The PIB forebore to make any comment on the companies' pricing policy, except to recommend the companies to increase their promotions to increase competition. It then concentrated on Brooke Bond's costs. By far the larger part was the cost of the tea, which was determined competitively at public auctions. Prices had been rising modestly, after a long trend of decline. But the cost was to some extent within the control of the companies, by substituting cheaper teas for expensive ones in blending. Apart from the cost of the tea, one-third of costs was for production (blending and packaging), one-third distribution, and one-third advertising and marketing. Distribution and selling costs were increasing, a supplementary reason for the price increase. Brooke Bond's costs were relatively high, and seemed not to reflect any economies from the large and increasing volume of sales. Increasing expenditure on distribution and advertising was no doubt in the company's own interest, but the PIB found no evidence to suggest that lower unit costs or lower prices for the consumer would follow. Short term at least, costs and prices were being pushed up.

As Brooke Bond was clearly profitable, prices should not have been increased at all as there was no need for new investment, the only other reason consistent with the policy. Now that the companies had done so, however, the PIB could only recommend that price cutting by retailers should be encouraged. Once more the PIB had found that in a trade with every appearance of price competition at the retail end, there was no pressure on the price leader to restrict marketing expenses.

When the Food Manufacturers' Federation recommended the cessation of the early-warning arrangements in early 1970, the Ice-Cream

Federation passed on the recommendation to its members. As a result, T. Wall & Sons (another subsidiary of Unilever) and Lyons Maid, accounting for over three-quarters of ice-cream sales, announced price increases, the third in six months. Costs, prices and profits were thereupon referred to the PIB (No. 160).

Prices were some 20 per cent higher than a year before, after a period when they had risen less than other foods in spite of an increase in purchase tax. Raw materials, packaging and wages and salaries had all been pushing up costs, with wages and salaries accounting for about one-third of costs, materials one-third and distribution one-third.

The PIB did not discover much scope for cost-saving in production. The main reason for the cost and price increases was the proliferation of varieties. To market a wide range of ice-cream "confectionery" and "desserts" to compete with other packaged desserts (like yoghurt, frozen mousses and so on), higher costs had been incurred. But profits had not risen, and normal capital requirements would only be financed with difficulty. Returns on capital did not compare badly with other food manufacturing; but extra revenue was needed to finance investment. The price increases must therefore be allowed.

The only means the PIB found for counteracting the cost-inflating multiplication of varieties was market pressure. "Own label" ice-cream would materially add to the degree of competition from retailers. Meanwhile more competition on price and discounts to retailers between the companies was highly desirable.

All the PIB's cases where advertising and marketing expenses were considerable involved industries appearing competitive but where competition took forms not particularly conducive to price or cost restraint. Most of the trade was done by a few very large firms, and most of these were relatively well-managed, and efficient in a technical way. But the result was not necessarily price stability or good value for the customers. Efforts to defend market shares of established products, and to expand business by marketing new ones were increasingly costly, counteracting the economies in production that should have contributed to a more stable price level.

More large manufacturing companies, or industries dominated by them, were referred to the PIB as a result of changes in international markets, either for raw materials or for finished goods. Rises in raw material costs were included as an exception to the policy rules, from the start. However, in 1965 and 1966 such increases were not much of a problem, as world prices of many materials were stable. Import prices did not rise fast enough to put much pressure on UK prices, until devaluation in November 1967. Immediately after this a spate of early warnings were given to Government Departments, and a few cases were passed to the PIB.

The first substantial post-devaluation case concerned the prices of secondary (rechargeable) batteries, such as car batteries (No. 61). There had been reductions in prices in previous years; but following devaluation some manufacturers gave early warning that they wished to increase them "to take account of increases in costs, including increases due to devaluation". The Ministry of Technology had raised no objection to proposals from one manufacturer to increase prices by $7\frac{1}{2}$ per cent. But the firm was unable to do it in face of competition from five other large manufacturers and some two hundred small ones. Because the small firms made only a few fast-selling lines with no national distribution, their costs and prices were lower than the larger manufacturers making a full range, and they determined prices. None of the small firms had notified any intention of raising prices. There had been reductions in battery prices in 1967 because the price of lead was lower than in the previous three years. Now both lead and antimony prices were rising. The PIB found the price increases now proposed were about right in relation to the increase in cost due to devaluation.

To assess the possibility of absorbing any of this, the PIB tried to examine profits and the return on capital. But secondary batteries for the replacement market was not the only output of any of the firms, as they were supplied in large quantities to vehicle manufacturers and others. The PIB could therefore only reply negatively that the rate of return on capital without the proposed increases was "not so high that these increases could be absorbed without depressing the rate of return to an unreasonably low level". It concluded that an increase was justified, up to four per cent overall; though, as Oldham's had already discovered, market conditions might make it impossible to increase revenue by raising prices.

On the same day as the secondary-battery reference, two other post-devaluation cases came to the PIB from the Ministry of Technology. They were mercury hearing-aid batteries (No. 64) and Hoover domestic appliances (No. 73). Both were made by UK subsidiaries of large international companies, having their headquarters in the USA. Both had reported their intention of increasing prices very soon after devaluation, as they were required to do under the early-warning arrangements. Both were now proposing to raise their prices, after some years of stability in the case of the batteries, and price reductions in the case of Hoover products.

Mallory Batteries Ltd, the makers of the hearing-aid batteries, had a monopoly in the UK market. They were used in hearing aids bought privately but not in those supplied by the NHS. There was only indirect competition from NHS hearing-aids, which used other types of battery. However, those who already had a privately bought hearing-aid needing mercury batteries were effectively locked in by their previous "investment". The cash increases in price were not great, as the battery in greatest demand cost only 2s 9d. But the increase was no less than 50 per cent, the biggest increase ever referred to the PIB. The Ministry of Technology had actually let the increase be made on 1 January 1968. But, as might have been expected, there was widespread protest from the customers; and the PIB itself received more complaints in this than in any other case.

The company justified the price rise on two grounds: that rising costs could not be absorbed without jeopardising profits needed to finance new investment; and that prices in the home market needed to be increased to the same level as export prices. The first was a familiar argument, covered by the current White Paper; but the second question touched on aspects of pricing policy not covered by any of the White Papers.

The rise was not justified by cost increases. The firm expected that costs would increase between 1967 and 1968 by some 14 per cent, due to increased cost of mercury, extra expenditure on research and development, and on marketing. The PIB could not find reason to dispute this. But the value of sales was expected to increase more than costs, profits and the return on capital would rise. The PIB considered that, bearing in mind the company had no competitor, the prospective rate of return was already high enough to finance future investment. Within the terms of the prices and incomes policy, there was no case for an increase in prices at all.

However there was the second consideration, not covered by the policy White Paper. The UK export price had been below the US price, and dealers could sell UK-produced batteries in the US at lower prices than US production. The result was that the firm's long-term investment decisions might be quickly undermined. The UK export price was, therefore, gradually approaching the US price. Hence the UK export price had become higher than the UK domestic price. The effect of devaluation had been to widen the gap still further. Dealers could buy from Mallorys at the domestic price and undercut Mallory's own export prices at a profit. Mallorys reacted by raising the UK domestic price to the same level as the export price. If the gap was closed by reducing export prices again, Mallory's US market would once more be undermined. This was obviously against the company's interest, because export earnings would be reduced. But there were other aspects of the national interest. The steepness of the price increase had "dealt a blow" to the prices policy. It would also increase a high rate of profit, and possibly attract new competitors. The company's action was clearly against the national interest, and arguably also against its own. The company would have been prudent to "seek a third and middle course", namely to put a restrictive covenant preventing resale, on sales to wholesalers at the domestic price. The gap between the home and export price should then be discussed with the Government, with the company recognising that gross anomalies should be remedied gradually, and the Government conceding that the anomaly must indeed be removed ultimately.

Another PIB case where international price structures contributed to an increase in UK prices concerned butyl rubber (No. 66). Like mercury batteries, there was only one UK producer, Esso Chemical Ltd. Also, like mercury batteries, devaluation had been seized on by the company as an opportunity to raise UK prices to the same level as those already charged elsewhere. Again, prices had been stable for some years before devaluation. But unlike mercury batteries, butyl rubber production was not profitable.

The company had kept the UK price at the same level as the US price. When sterling was devalued, the export price was raised to the same extent as the devaluation, to keep UK and US export prices in line. The proposals referred to the PIB was to increase UK home prices to the same extent, so that UK domestic and export prices were once again the same. The company did not justify its action in relation to the international price structure, nor to increased costs following on devaluation: it had taken the opportunity to improve profitability.

The plant had been plagued by production problems. The process had proved unreliable technically; and both the capital cost and running costs were higher than expected. In addition, continued production losses had raised unit costs even more. The company clearly had no incentive for new investment, but none was needed. However, the plant would need replacing as world demand was increasing. Costs could not be offset by reductions in profits, so an increase in price was justified.

Like Mallory Batteries and Esso Chemicals, Hoover Ltd was also part of a large international company with headquarters in the USA (No. 73). It also made an application to raise prices after devaluation, alleging that there had been general increases in costs since prices had previously been raised, as well as the extra costs directly due to devaluation. But it was not a monopoly seller, either in the UK or other markets. Transactions between it and associated overseas companies were at the prices which would rule between independent buyers and sellers. The PIB therefore treated the UK company as though it was a separate enterprise, and investigated its case in the same way as any other UK company.

The case turned partly on the proper return on capital, and partly on the market situation. Unit costs were very sensitive to the utilisation of capacity. The firm had absorbed much of the rising costs of raw materials and labour for five years past, by substituting one material for another, and by improving labour productivity. Increasing efficiency had itself required additional investment; and returns to capital had fallen faster than profits. Another credit squeeze had been imposed after devaluation, and demand fell. The result was that unit costs rose faster, as fixed costs were spread over smaller production.

The company had made great efforts to contain costs. But profits depended on the prospect for using capacity more fully. Hoover's had been more profitable than its competitors with "floor care" equipment (mostly vacuum cleaners). There had been a high level of capacity working in 1967, and a higher level still might be achieved in 1968. Unit costs would tend to fall, but not quite enough to offset the effect of devaluation. This and other Government action had increased costs by about three per cent. Hoover could not absorb the cost increases here, so prices could be increased by three per cent.

For laundry and other equipment (mostly washing machines), capacity was underused, and the level was unlikely to improve. Little profit was being earned, and some price increase seemed justified. Competition would decide how much was possible. The PIB would not put itself in the position of price leadership which no company could assume by suggesting a figure. Hoover must decide its own prices "in the light of competition".

Soon afterwards a bigger international company, IBM, also with headquarters in the USA, was referred to the PIB. This time the reference related only to rental charges for data-processing equipment (No. 76). Prices for data-processing (and other) equipment sold outright, had already been increased by 10 per cent (on 1 January 1968), and this increase had neither been stopped by the Ministry of Technology nor referred to the PIB. But users already renting equipment had to be given three month's notice of increased rents. Protests were made to the Ministry, and the increased rentals referred to the PIB. It was alleged by IBM that devaluation had been, among other things, the reason for the increase. The company was in competition with a number of others offering equipment for rent. However IBM's customers were in a weaker position than the market structure would suggest. Once the decision to instal an IBM computer had been made, IBM data-processing equipment was necessary. It would be difficult, and costly, to switch to another supplier in response to the increased rent.

The case could only be approached by relating rents to the price of the same equipment for sale, since the PIB had no access to the parent company's books. A year earlier, IBM prices had been increased by five per cent everywhere except in the UK. Now the company argued that this fact, plus devaluation, justified an increase of 20 per cent in prices, though they had only in fact increased them by 10 per cent. Their reason for their moderation was "the climate of opinion ... in the light of the prices and incomes policy". The PIB considered that increasing competition also explained it.

The PIB found two arguments to support the case for an increase on old contracts. First, part of the rents covered the suppliers' costs (for instance, for maintenance) and these had undoubtedly risen. Secondly, the cost to IBM of continuing to rent a machine to an existing customer was the revenue the machine would yield if transferred to a new customer. But neither of these arguments would support a 10 per cent increase on all contracts. The case had been made out only for newer machines, which had a higher value to new customers. There should be no increase in that part of existing rents meant to cover extra costs, and rising value in alternative uses, should apply only to newer systems. The increase in rents should be seven per cent instead of 10 per cent for the new systems and five per cent for the old ones. The "feeling of helplessness" suffered by the complainants might soon be mitigated by a wider variety of rental contracts, possibly to be offered by new entrants to the market.

Early in 1970, the Ever Ready Company proposed to increase the price of primary batteries by varying amounts, to yield 14 per cent more revenue (No. 148). It did not have a monopoly in the sense of being a sole supplier, but it dominated the UK market. The company's case for increased prices rested on rapid increases in raw material costs, mostly due to increases in world prices of non-ferrous metals. Devaluation had steepened the increase, and future reductions seemed unlikely in the near future.

The company had been offsetting wage increases by higher productivity for some years past, and it was now more difficult to continue the same process. Direct labour had been reduced in a major way, partly by automation, though the full benefits were yet to come, in the new plant only partly in operation.

The PIB found profits to be "inadequate and falling" as the company submitted; but more important was the company's need for extra cash to maintain the investment programme already planned. It had been borrowing as well as running down its cash reserves, and should be allowed to build up more funds to complete its investment.

The PIB's analysis of prices turned as much on marketing policy as on raw material costs, and more on returns to capital in the light of that policy. But it was the prospect in each case of continuing increases in world prices of materials that prevented a recommendation that the price increases should be reversed or even modified, in spite of high profits. The PIB's attitude to the companies suffering rising costs as world prices rose, especially in 1969 and 1970, depended partly on the nature of competition, and companies' marketing policy, and—increasingly—on returns to capital in the light of the policy.

To reach an adequate rate of return on capital was a reason given in all the policy White Papers for allowing exceptional increases in price. The reasons for concentrating on the return to capital in the private sector were compelling: it is a standard by which resources are attracted or repelled to and from one product, firm or process to another; and it contributes to the fund from which new investment is financed. It was in practice a far more important criterion for the PIB than any other. It was the reason finally used to justify the PIB's price recommendations on breweries and bricks, in spite of the relative importance of labour; and in all cases, including other labour-intensive ones, adequate returns to capital was used as a guide to the feasibility of the recommendations.

The earliest case to show the difficulties for price stability posed by looking for a proper return to capital was breweries (No. 13). The problem was depreciation which had increased by no less than 13 per cent in one year, between 1965 and 1966. Amalgamations and re-organisations had led to more accurate valuation of assets, replacement of long-lived equipment and additions to capital. Increased charges had been incurred before much benefit from rationalisation had accrued. As brewery companies owned pubs, hotels and off-licences, their assets were like those of property companies. Unless such assets are frequently revalued, returns to the (under-valued) capital look deceptively large. But prices ought generally to be based on current valuation of the assets involved, to allow a proper comparison with the costs and returns of alternative investments. With a high proportion of assets in property, prospective economies in production were only too likely to be swallowed up by increasing capital charges. Relating prices to long-term costs, in an industry owning properties and subject to rapid structural change, was only too likely to lead to the conclusion that profits were far too low rather than too high.

Aggregate demand and output were increasing during 1965 and early 1966, and most capital-intensive industries had little difficulty in containing unit costs while the utilisation of capacity was high. But when the deflationary measures of 1966 reduced demand, they were quickly in difficulties in avoiding price increases as capacity utilisation fell. Four products of highly capital-intensive industries were referred to the PIB in quick succession after the standstill had begun: aluminium semi-manufacturers, standard newsprint, compound fertilisers and Portland Cement.

The PIB was invited to consider the prices of standard newsprint and whether the proposed increases should apply during the period of severe restraint (No. 26). All four UK manufacturers had notified their desire to increase prices. They operated in competition with overseas producers having natural advantages in the availability of raw materials.

All U.K. producers sold newsprint at the same delivered price, unchanged since 1963. Scandinavian supplies were meanwhile available at £2 to £3 a ton less than UK supplies. They proposed to increase prices by £2 a ton, the equivalent of the $5 a ton increase in the world price made shortly before.

As UK producers only supplied half UK consumption, and as the rest could easily be supplied by overseas producers, the PIB felt obliged to consider not only the national interest in price stability but also the national interest in the continued existence of the UK industry at all. The main reason the industry survived was better service by quick delivery, a range of sizes, and less risk of interrupted supplies through dock strikes. Newsprint machines had a long life; adapting existing machines was much cheaper than equipping a new mill. The PIB was not entirely convinced by the arguments, but the balance of payments advantage also helped to tilt the balance in favour of the industry.

Returns on capital were low. UK producers sold two-thirds of their output on long-term contracts (running for as long as ten years), and these contracts actually prevented an increase in the share of the market. UK mills allowed *pro rata* reductions of contract tonnages when demand fell. The contracts gave a stable market share to the UK industry, instead of stable output and more stable costs. But if a British newsprint industry was of value to newspaper companies, they ought to help it to work to as full capacity as possible, so long as it could sell at competitive prices. This could be achieved either by further integration of newsprint and newspaper companies, or by both agreeing the desirable level of capacity, and the tonnages to be delivered. Producing and consuming industries would both gain from this, and the national interest would be served by import saving.

This in itself still did not settle the question of whether or not an immediate increase of £2 a ton was justified. Process costs had remained stable before 1965, because of increasing capacity use and technical improvements. After 1965, unit costs rose as demand and capacity utilisation fell.

The PIB considered that the pertinent question to be the adequacy of profits in the light of investment needs. The most profitable firm had earned less than nine per cent on newsprint alone and the others considerably less up to 1965; but in 1966 the most profitable firm had made less than five per cent, and two others had made losses. While returns from the UK mills would always be below those for overseas mills, and the issue was whether incentive existed for investment in cost-saving improvements to existing equipment (such as handling equipment, processes for de-inking waste paper, and increasing machine speeds). As profits were not sufficient to encourage such projects, the price increase should be allowed.

The standstill White Paper had invited the PIB to consider "the overall profitability of an enterprise". The companies themselves had found more profitable uses for their money, and the PIB did not consider they could now finance investment from revenue on other production. The price increase was therefore justified on three of the criteria. Raw material costs had increased and could no longer be offset because of the fall in demand. Profits were inadequate to maintain efficiency and cover investment in ancillary equipment. The capacity of the more profitable parts of the business to carry the less profitable was not such that investment "would or should come from the profits earned in other fields".

Major manufacturers of compound fertilisers also gave warning that they proposed to raise prices. In particular, the PIB were asked to examine whether the increase should be made in the period of severe restraint. Once more the PIB had to deal with only one product of large multi-product firms (No. 28). The industry was dominated by three large producers, Fisons, ICI and Shell Star, each producing other things in different markets. The smallest of the three had the largest share of the market, a situation giving rise to fierce competition. The home market had recently stabilised after a period of strong expansion. At the same time rapid technical changes were taking place in production processes, and great economies of scale were expected when the new processes were in full operation. But anticipated cost reductions had not occurred because of unexpected delays and failures in the new plants. Prices fell with expectations of falling cost, and small producers were being driven out of the market, while profits in the large ones had gone steadily down. Fisons had previously been the price leader. After six or seven years of steady reductions, it had increased prices in 1965, partly to compensate for the increased price of sulphur. Unit costs were kept down by technical improvements but the increase of sulphur prices coincided with the failure of demand to rise. The unexpectedly costly new plant was running at less than capacity and returns on capital fell.

The PIB considered that the needs of the industry, the risks involved, and the state of competition would all affect the size of an adequate rate of return, and therefore prices. The case for a price increase had to be judged in this light. Changing technology had considerably increased the risks as well as investment needs. Fisons had already borrowed so much that more capital would have to be raised in the form of equity, and this would not be forthcoming unless there was an acceptable return to equity capital already issued. ICI had also had to borrow heavily. In deciding whether to devote borrowed money and their own accumulated funds to fertilisers, it had rightly been mindful of the comparative profitability of compound fertilisers. The only difference between the two firms was that ICI could afford to take a longer view. If it was necessary to raise additional capital in the market, the companies would have to have the market rate of return. The market rate was high, partly because of high interest rates, and partly because of credit restriction, both the result of Government action. A higher rate of return would be needed to compensate for risk. Both companies had produced details of cost-saving investment that had been or would be postponed because of low rates of profit.

Fisons had asked for a price increase of six per cent, but it was not certain that ICI would follow this lead. In the PIB's view of its function, it ought not to take a view about what would or ought to happen so far as competitive response was concerned. A six per cent price increase was on the face of it reasonable, even if different firms might have different views about price policy.

The possibility of cross-subsidisation had also to be considered. But neither would be justified in diverting resources to fertilisers when profits were so much lower than the interest charges on new money and these latter rates were up to seven per cent. Also, there were still nearly 50 smaller manufacturers whose rates of return on capital were low as well, and where cross-subsidisation was not possible. The mere fact that they specialised, and so had no access to self-financing from other products should not be the reason for small firms, and price competition, disappearing.

A price increase of the order originally proposed by Fisons was therefore justified, even in the period of severe restraint. But whether that increase was actually made or not depended on the precise response of the main producers to market pressures.

Portland Cement was also referred in the period of severe restraint, and had also been affected by falling demand. The PIB was asked to report on the price and the appropriate rate of return on capital investment in new works (No. 38). The industry was well organised, and its practices had been reviewed by the Restrictive Practices Court. Seven manufacturers were banded together in the Cement Makers Federation (CMF). There was a common pricing system throughout the industry, by which a "base price" was fixed for each works, with delivery zones around them attracting higher prices. The base prices were fixed by the CMF through a Costs Committee consisting of two members independent of constituent companies. The price arrived at was said to be voluntary but it was never in fact broken. The Restrictive Practices Court had decided in 1961 that the agreement did not operate against the public interest, since it considered that prices were lower than they would have been to attract investment under competitive conditions. (New entrants might want a return of 15 to 20 per cent assuming the risks applying to a competitive industry; whereas members of the Federation had accepted about 10 per cent from new works.) The Court had recommended that the agreement stand so long as the pricing methods remained unaltered.

The industry notified the Government in January 1967 that costs had increased, and profits would be lower than the Restrictive Practices Court had approved unless prices increased. At the same time, the manufacturers questioned the adequacy of the level of profit approved by the Court "to maintain the momentum of investment". Whether the Restrictive Practices Court judgment was any longer in the public interest or consistent with prices policy was a question not referred to the PIB; and the industry objected vehemently when it was suggested that the issue might be raised, an objection sustained by the Government. The PIB could therefore only accept the Court's ruling, and refrain from discussing whether or not freer prices would be preferable to the existing system.

Home demand for cement had been rising steadily, with two very good years in 1964 and 1965. But it failed to rise in 1966, as a result of the cuts in Government expenditure and credit restriction. In 1966, therefore, exceptional surplus capacity appeared. Direct costs had also increased, due mainly to higher wages and higher prices for electricity. The proposal was to increase prices by $5s$ a ton, the price then being about $110s$ a ton.

While the industry had been working at high capacity levels it had offset direct cost increases to a considerable extent. The estimates for 1966 made by the industry's Cost Committee had taken into account further absorption of cost, mostly due to more efficient capacity coming into production.

No new official estimate of demand had been made for 1970, after the National Plan estimates had been put awry by the standstill. Assuming that demand again rose excess capacity would be eliminated. But when this would happen, the PIB could not tell in the absence of forecasts of Government and other demand for construction. After the two good years in 1964 and 1965, the subsequent two years were not likely to be so good, but equally not abnormally bad. If the bad years could be shown to persist for a long time, there might be a case for a price increase, with low capacity utilisation. But taking 1965, 1966 and 1967 together, the average level of utilisation might not be low.

In a competitive market, prices would fall with demand. The CMF was proposing to do the opposite. But since the CMF did not reduce prices in good years, the request for a price increase in less good ones must be examined on the assumption of a normal level of activity. The cost increases alone did not therefore make the case for a price increase.

The Cost Committee estimated prices to give a return between nine and $11\frac{1}{2}$ per cent; a price increase of $5s$ a ton would increase the return to over 11 per cent. It also fixed a base price for new works, and it was this the industry considered too low. Investment would be maintained if the expected returns over the life of the investment were greater than the costs involved. The PIB recommended that the required return should be calculated by discounting back to present values the expected flow of revenue and costs (taking taxes and grants into account) over the lifetime of the project. (In other words, the industry ought to use discounted cash flow methods of appraising investment.) From this point of view, the cost of capital in various forms, and the possible mix of these forms had to be considered. The rate of return required would depend on the mix of capital of various sources that could be chosen. The cement industry was in a relatively favourable position, since it then only had $11\frac{1}{2}$ per cent of its capital in the form of loan finance. Furthermore the low risk involved, given its price agreement, would enable it to raise rather more than usual in this form. If the industry met as much as possible of its requirements from retained earnings, and raised the rest on loan, the cost would be eight or nine per cent overall. But the proposed price increase would give a discounted return on new investment of the order of 12 per cent. It was not reasonable to suppose that a gap so wide was the "modest margin of profit" approved by the Restrictive Practices Court. A discounted return of over 10 per cent would be sufficient to allow for some risk. The "momentum of investment" would be maintained on this criterion by an increase of $2s$ a ton, rather than the $5s$ proposed. But a further temporary increase might be allowed to take account of the extra, temporary (it was then thought) increase in oil prices.

The cement industry was referred again to the PIB two years afterward (No. 133). This time it did much better. The CMF proposed at the time of the reference to increase prices by $12s$ a ton (about 10 per cent) and the PIB recommended no less than $13s$ $6d$ (about 11 to 12 per cent).

The recommended $2s$ a ton increase in August 1967 had been implemented, followed by another $2s$ a ton to meet the cost of the surcharge on fuel oil. The second $2s$ a ton remained when the oil surcharge was removed, to offset other increases in costs. Prices had therefore risen by $4s$ a ton during the two years between the references. Shortly after the second reference the CMF raised its proposed price increase to no less than $22s$ $4d$ a ton (subsequently increased to $23s$ $4d$ and then $28s$ $5d$ a ton), because of new calculations of the value of the assets employed.

The industry had calculated that its current return on capital would soon fall to about two per cent compared with the 12 per cent claimed to be a reasonable target. But the PIB considered that the right price would be given by comparing the discounted cash flow on new investment with the cost of capital, as had been done previously. New investment would be needed when demand recovered. Since the previous report the industry had financed investment by issuing more debentures as the PIB had recommended. The required return was about 11½ per cent, higher than before due to the continued rise of interest rates and to a higher proportion of equity finance. This time, taking a lower average level of capacity than the industry had done, the PIB found that current prices fell below what was required by no less than 13s 6d a ton. It then recommended the increase without further qualification.

Another capital-intensive industry, aluminium semi-manufactures, also suffering from inadequate demand, came under review early in 1966. "In view of the scope that appears to exist in this industry for increasing productivity", the PIB was asked to examine their case (No. 39). Large firms supplied a competitive world market, where the UK manufacturers (partly US and Canadian-owned) were at a disadvantage compared with overseas producers, with about a dozen much smaller competitors. Competition was fierce but not openly on price. All the firms bargained with their customers over discounts from list prices; but the most important form of competition was in service: speedy delivery, a wide range of sizes and finishes, almost any specification to suit the customer. They had gone in for ambitious investment programmes; but all had over estimated the size of their market and their share in it. In spite of concentration, capacity was too great for existing or foreseeable demand. Competition by service had only aggravated the problems, since providing a complete range of products meant installing a complete range of machinery.

Returns on capital were low. There were only two remedies (assuming the industry was viable at all): either to reduce costs or raise prices. Costs could be reduced by increasing productivity or increasing capacity utilisation. The long-term prospect for an increase in demand was thought by the PIB to be good, providing the national income grew at a reasonable rate; and rising demand would automatically mean rising profits. Increased prices in the circumstances would be "tantamount to asking the consumer to pay for the extra capacity created by the industry". All it could, and should, do meanwhile therefore, was to look to its productivity and expand throughout, as soon as the market allowed.

The remaining reference concerning profits in the standstill–severe restraint period was the remuneration of milk distributors. The dairymen's remuneration was a "guaranteed target rate of profit", fixed by the Government and reviewed from time to time. A decision about 1965 had still not been taken a year later when the standstill began, and it was then deferred during the standstill. After this, the Government asked the PIB to examine it. The questions actually put to the

PIB were two: what the remuneration for 1965–66 should have been; and what the future method should be.

The PIB's answer was uncommonly brief in an interim report (No. 33). It was impossible to comment reasonably on what was due on an existing system, without reviewing the system itself, as a reasonable remuneration depended on what consequences flowed in the way of improved efficiency or contained costs.

The PIB's general conclusion in a further report (No. 46) was that the system was "inherently objectionable". The so-called target rate of profit was the cash sum per gallon of milk, changing with changes in the value of money. It should be related to the returns on capital employed. An appropriate rate of return could not be based on the discounted return on new investment, since there was little new investment. Moreover, "capital employed" by the dairy industry (though not the Co-operative Societies' dairies) included goodwill. Though this was necessary for the individual firm, the industry as a whole could not be said to have it. What the rate should be could only be a matter of judgment. At one extreme, the current cost of finance set a lower limit. At the other, the rate should not exceed what was obtained elsewhere in distribution, at greater risk. Having surveyed the trading results of a hundred other firms in distribution, and considering the low risk resulting from the Government guarantees, the PIB recommended a rate of 11 per cent on net assets (including goodwill).

In September 1968, an early-warning application was made to increase prices of synthetic organic dyes and organic pigments (No. 100). The industry was dominated by two large firms, ICI and the Swiss-owned Clayton Aniline Dye Company. The international market was highly competitive, though buoyant and expanding. All important producing countries had a price leader, invariably the main home producer. Competition was more on service than on price, as it was feared that an "aggressive" price policy would bring loss of revenue. In the UK market, the PIB found two discernible trends in price formation. ICI acted as price leader when general increases were made. But competition then undermined the new price level, the extent varying for different products. Smaller manufacturers might follow larger firms in putting prices up, but to a lower extent. However, the smaller firms were at a disadvantage since they were less able to develop and exploit novelties or new qualities of colour or fastness, which were highly profitable for a short time.

The PIB tried to answer its now routine question in such cases: whether the return on capital employed was adequate in the light of investment needs. It analysed the costs, profits and prices of the price-leader. By 1968, ICI's capacity was fully used and would need to be extended to allow the company to export more, or to expand its share of the home market. Though exports were expected to increase, their profitability was not expected to grow; new investment could not therefore be financed from export profits. But increased revenue would only follow if ICI could increase its prices effectively, that is if other producers followed suit. Overseas producers had raised their prices by eight per cent the year before, and it seemed likely that ICI could raise theirs to the same extent in the UK. The PIB had to decide whether the return would then be "excessive". The proposed price increase would yield return on proposed investment which seemed not to be excessive in relation to the cost of raising capital. The national interest, as well as the company's interest, required extended investment in production for export, and to avoid imports. The increase was therefore approved. Finally, as a mild safeguard, a rider was added that the Government should "expect that investment and research would be undertaken on a sufficient scale to help improve the balance of payments".

The prices of man-made fibres and cotton yarn were referred later still, in February 1969. The PIB reported separately on viscose yarn (No. 110), a small part of the total supply of man-made fibres for which Courtaulds was the only UK producer. Courtaulds had informed the Board of Trade that they wanted an increase of 6d a pound, equivalent to nine per cent, to apply uniformly to all kinds of viscose yarn. But the existing structure of prices represented neither current costs nor relative value to consumers. The PIB told the company that the uniform increase would not improve matters, and might well make it worse. New proposals were then produced. Some increases would now be more than 6d a pound, a few less, resulting in an increase of only five per cent on average. These the PIB then proceeded to investigate.

The market for the product had been declining with fierce competition from newer products all over the world. Courtaulds' total sales had been declining up to 1967, but the decline had halted from 1968. Of the four factories still making viscose yarn, one was just breaking even, and three were making small losses. If no price increase was approved, one factory at least would stop production. Imports would be more likely to increase if home prices were held down than if they were allowed to increase, since there might be an abrupt reduction in production if a factory closed. Moreover, it might be difficult to find alternative work for the employees (and the factories). There was a case for employing them on viscose yarn, rather than not at all.

There was no question here of a need for new investment, merely of a national interest in a slightly better balance of payments and slightly higher employment. The PIB concluded, therefore, that the increase proposed was no more than what was needed to "provide the necessary inducement to remain in production". The price increase as amended was therefore approved.

When the PIB came to deal with the rest of the reference in its second report on man-made fibres and cotton yarn prices (No. 127) it was dealing with very different problems. Acetate filament yarn was, like viscose yarn, made by Courtaulds virtually as a monopoly producer. Cellulosic fibre in general (viscose and acetate yarns) had been investigated only recently by the Monopolies Commission, which had had no doubt that a monopoly existed to the detriment of the public interest. A number of remedies had been suggested, including a reduction in import duties and a ban by the Board of Trade on further acquisitions. The only other producer, Lansil, could not charge prices different from Courtaulds; so the PIB report was concerned solely with Courtaulds' costs and profits.

Unit costs had been falling, due to improvements in productivity, and the effect of increasing output. The question was whether prices should be reduced, as they ought to be according to the policy rules if costs were falling, or if there were excessive profits due to "excessive market power". The case could not be entirely proven since staple fibre, chemicals and plastics were produced as well as acetate yarns by the same process, and had not been referred. Profits were fluctuating, but on a rising trend. The company maintained that most of this was due to chemicals and plastics, and that profits would be reduced in 1969 to 1970 because of the fall in the demand for acetate yarns. The PIB pointed out that Courtaulds seemed to have confidence in the future, since a 25 per cent increase in capacity was planned. Courtaulds argued that their profits were not excessive because their list prices in the UK were below overseas producers' list prices in their home market, and because it could export yarn and sell it at above the UK prices (net of transport costs and import duties). But the PIB was not impressed. That prices were not as high as they might be, nor as high as elsewhere did not mean either that Courtaulds prices should be raised, or that it ought to be absolved from a reduction. Productivity was increasing at more than the national average; and the prices and incomes policy required that such increases should be remitted to the consumer by lower prices. The case was the stronger since the Board of Trade had decided not to reduce import duties for the time being. A "modest reduction" was required. If the trend of productivity continued upwards, there should be further price reductions as well as higher earnings for Courtauld workers and higher profits for Courtauld shareholders. The Government should keep the case under review.

Cotton yarns were a different case again. There was much competition among a hundred different companies of varying size and structure. Moreover, they were producing for a falling market, subject to cyclical recessions of demand, to orders from weavers or knitters often larger than themselves. The PIB concentrated on profits, which had been "low to average"; modern mills working with a reasonable use of capacity had remained profitable, though there had been losses elsewhere in the industry.

Many mills remained far behind the best technical standards. The Textile Committee report had suggested that this was due to an "insufficiently aggressive price policy", that is not reducing prices readily enough when demand failed to keep up with output. But the PIB found that there was less opportunity for mills to increase sales quickly by price-cutting than was commonly supposed. What appeared to be the market for a homogeneous product was in fact divided into many sections, dealing in particular finenesses or types of yarn. Price competition was practicable only within narrow limits. On balance, margins were always likely to be reduced during cyclical recessions of demand. Intervention to reduce prices might discourage investment. So the PIB advised the Government to "refrain from action to reduce the rate of return", by means of reduced prices.

Another monopoly producer was reviewed by the PIB later in 1969, when plasterboard prices were referred (No. 130). British Plasterboard Limited had notified a proposal to increase prices, by differing amounts on different products, averaging 5.9 per cent. After the reference the company, like Courtaulds, revised its proposals, to a flat-rate increase on all products, giving a slightly higher average increase. Costs had risen and it was no longer possible to absorb them, and, it was said, planned investment would not receive an adequate return without the increase in price. Both these contentions were borne out by the investigations.

The case rested on the rate of return on new investment. The company was already installing new capacity, and the PIB confirmed that the prospects justified it. Though the PIB thought the company's own calculation of the expected return too low, their own reworking of the estimate showed that the probable rate of return was not above the cost of capital, even with the proposed price increase. It should there-fore be allowed, on the grounds of providing necessary new investment.

In the last phase of the policy, after the publication of the last White Paper, electric motor prices (No. 139) were referred. The (small) motors concerned were produced mainly by four manufacturers, three of whom had given early warning of price increases of five per cent (subsequently raised to $6\frac{1}{2}$, 7 and $7\frac{1}{2}$ per cent). The fourth had had an increase of six per cent the year previously.

This was another industry subject to cycles of demand, not closely related directly to general movements of demand or investment. It was also an outstanding example of industries where list prices concealed rather than revealed the charges actually made. Discounts against list price had been growing, in spite of apparently uniform increases in price. What had been happening to prices properly speaking, the PIB could not discover. Costs proved equally intractable. Even illustrative figures could only be given in relation to one popular motor. The PIB commented glumly that only "broad conclusions" could therefore be reached.

The case had to be resolved negatively by reference to returns on capital. Profits were not so high that they could be reduced without prejudicing new investment. The companies were entitled to increase prices—if they could. Competition would clearly determine what actually happened. The PIB concerned itself with the structure of discounts. The system had the virtue of simplicity of operation; but it should be "subject to more vigorous question than in the past", and without so much tradition and custom about it. The manufacturers should relate prices more strictly to costs. But there was still the question of the increase in list prices to be recommended. Each company should be allowed to raise prices by up to four per cent (weighted average of list prices), and prices should then remain unchanged for at least a year.

Among the last clutch of cases sent to the PIB in the spring of 1970, was one relating to the costs and revenues of independent television companies (No. 156). The programme contractors had been complaining of falling profits; and some pressure had built up to relieve them of the Government levy on advertising revenue. The Government then used the PIB to examine not the levy itself, but any other scope there might be for improving matters.

The circumstances were peculiar, in that the companies came into being and were dissolved again as a result of administrative decisions, taken by the Independent Television Authority (ITA). Once installed, their activities and their revenue were strongly influenced by the ITA's rules. Many other companies suffered reductions in profits in 1969, but there were few industries showing as spectacular a fall, since theirs had fallen from a remarkably high level. The companies were pessimistic about future trends in advertising; the PIB thought them unjustifiably gloomy, though it could not persuade them otherwise. All calculations had therefore to be made twice, allowing for the two forecasts. But the PIB's estimate only showed a likely return of $6\frac{1}{2}$ per cent or $9\frac{1}{2}$ per cent, on capital employed.

The industry would need finance for more investment, even though capital requirements would tend to be low towards the end of a contract period (ending in 1974). The cost of finance would be relatively high, because of the peculiar risks involved. The pre-tax return required was estimated to be 22 per cent, the after-tax return $13\frac{1}{2}$ per cent. In spite of the doubt about the estimates, and the notions behind them, the conclusion was not to be resisted: present returns were inadequate.

The PIB went on to observe that there were changes of operation which could reduce costs or increase revenues, since there were large and unexplained variations in the use of resources by different companies for similar programmes, and an experimental rescheduling of production done by the PIB staff, but within the companies' conventions of operation, showed considerable saving. It appeared that existing resources were used only to 65 or 70 per cent of their capacity. Their activities were relatively labour intensive; and the wage and salary bill had increased by 36 per cent in four years, considerably more than the average rise in earnings. Negotiations were badly conducted, mostly because of weak and divided managements. No less than 123 job grades and 30 basic salaries prevented proper use of labour and invited drift by pressure for up-grading. Even marketing, which must be a major concern of management in an industry whose income depended entirely on advertisements, seemed not to be as well-directed to long-term aims as it could be.

But no change within the control of companies would be enough to improve returns to an adequate level. Apart from the levy, which the PIB was directed not to discuss, there were only three ways to do it: to allow longer hours of broadcasting, which would cut unit costs by using capacity more fully; to enlarge the companies, with the same end in view (both of which would change the relationship between costs and revenue); or to reduce risks and so reduce the cost of capital profits must cover. The PIB's general view of the case was that in a market where it was not at all clear that total revenue could be much increased, the national interest required returns to be raised by reducing unit costs. This was more a matter of increased capacity use than anything, even though improvements in labour use (and management) could be made within it. But with major indivisibilities in transmitters, as well as studios and their equipment, and with the distribution of the population between regions imposing a major constraint on markets, fewer companies with fewer overheads was the only obvious way to achieve it. There was no competition between companies anyway, of the kind that might restrain costs (though there might be between them and potential new entrants over new contracts). Companies could not put up prices (advertising rates) or reduce the quality of the service to the viewers freely because of ITA's powers of supervision. The usual disadvantage of concentrating production into fewer units did not therefore apply.

Maintaining returns on capital employed at a level adequate to finance necessary investment grew more difficult after 1966, partly as a result of restraining demand, partly as a result of high interest rates. Price increases to improve returns were the more likely. The PIB's contribution lay in two areas, to see that the returns on which prices were to be based were the proper ones; and to see that forecast costs made due allowance for improvements in efficiency. In the first, its contribution was to insist that the proper return was on new investment, in the form or quantity justified by expected demand and market structure. This in itself allowed some modification of proposals for price increases, notably in respect of cement. But it could not approach anything like what was necessary for price stability owing to high interest rates and little prospect of growth of output and income. In the second, it had less than full opportunity to find possible long-term opportunities, partly because so many references related to only one of the products of multi-product firms, partly because prices and not pay, costs or productivity were referred. Some useful comments on the use of resources occur in this group of reports, though scope for major changes was not found here.

Reports

No.   4   Prices of soaps, soap powders, soap flakes and soapless detergents (Cmnd 2791)

No. 75   Costs and prices of the chocolate and sugar confectionery industries (Cmnd 3694)

No. 113   Manufacturers' prices of toilet preparations (Cmnd 4066)

No. 147   Margarine and compound cooking fats (Cmnd 4368)

No. 154   Tea prices (Cmnd 4456)

No. 160   Costs, prices and profitability in the ice-cream manufacturing industry (Cmnd 4548)

No. 61   Prices of secondary batteries (Cmnd 3597)

No. 64   Prices of mercury hearing-aid batteries manufactured by Mallory Batteries Ltd (Cmnd 3625)

No. 66   Price of butyl rubber (Cmnd 3626)

No. 73   Prices of Hoover Domestic Appliances (Cmnd 3671)

No. 76   Increases in rental charges for the equipment hired from IBM (UK) Ltd (Cmnd 3699)

No. 148   Prices of primary batteries proposed by the Ever Ready Company (GB) Limited (Cmnd 4370)

No. 13   Costs, prices and profits in the brewing industry (Cmnd 2965)

No. 26   Prices of standard newsprint (Cmnd 3210)

No. 28   Prices of compound fertilizers (Cmnd 3228)

No. 38   Portland Cement prices (Cmnd 3381)

No. 133   Portland Cement prices (Cmnd 4215)

No. 39   Costs and prices of aluminium semi-manufactures (Cmnd 3370)

No. 33   The remuneration of milk distributors (Cmnd 3294)

No. 46   The remuneration of milk distributors (Cmnd 3477)

No. 100   Manufacturers prices of synthetic organic dyestuffs and organic pigments (Cmnd 3895)

No. 119   Man-made fibre and cotton yarn prices (Cmnd 4092)

No. 130   Plasterboard prices (Cmnd 4184)

No. 139   Electric motor prices (Cmnd 4285)

No. 156   Costs and revenues of the ITV Companies (Cmnd 4524)

8

The Public Sector

At first, the prices policy applied to public and private sectors in much the same way. The price increases by public enterprises inevitably received more publicity than private enterprise, partly because they provided basic services, and partly because making a significant change in their prices was a long-drawn-out and semi-public affair. After the standstill and severe restraint, public-sector increases attracted even more public protest. In September 1967, the Prime Minister attempted to meet the mounting criticism by announcing that all proposals for major price increases by nationalised industries would be referred to the PIB. It would at the same time make "all the necessary enquiries into the efficiency of the industries", an extra function not before exercised. But at all periods of the policy, there was a more important difference between private and public sectors: nationalised industries were obliged to operate to stricter standards, in particular concerning the returns to capital.

In the early period of the PIB's investigations, the nationalised industries were still operating on the principles laid down in the 1961 White Paper, *The Financial and Economic Obligations of the Nationalised Industries* (Cmnd 1337). At the time of the Prime Minister's statement, a new White Paper was being prepared, and was eventually published as *Nationalised Industries: a Review of Economic and Financial Objectives* (Cmnd 3437) in November 1967. According to the 1961 White Paper, each industry was to earn a specified return, taking the quinquennium 1962–67 as a whole. This return was to cover depreciation, interest, and additions to reserves to finance investment. There were no explicit pricing principles, except that revenue was to cover full cost and the target returns. While these rules still applied, the PIB had to report on gas and electricity tariffs, and coal prices.

London Electricity Board (LEB) tariffs were the first to be referred. The LEB proposed to increase prices by over 10 per cent from 1 July 1965, a proposal which had given rise to a dispute between the LEB and the London Electricity Consumer Council. Proposals by three Gas

Boards to increase charges were referred four months later. The two cases were pursued separately; but when it came to compiling the reports each was found to turn on similar general questions. Similar financial obligations rested on each, and the question of avoidable and unavoidable costs concerned each. They were therefore finally dealt with in one report (No. 7).

Both references showed the conflict of Government policy between the financial obligations of the nationalised industries and their price-stability obligations. The LEB case ostensibly concerned costs. However, by far the largest item of direct cost was purchased electricity, the price charged by the Central Electricity Generating Board (CEGB) for bulk supplies to the Area Boards. The CEGB's costs had risen fast, mainly due to higher capital charges and "surplus". Capital charges comprised provision for depreciation and interest on borrowed money; the surplus was supposed to add to reserves, so that over half the industry's investment could be self-financed. Capital charges had risen by 15 per cent a year; this increase alone had raised total costs by five per cent a year. This was due in particular to the large amount of plant under construction but not yet operating. The CEGB was trying to increase plant in commission by 100 per cent in five years to provide more spare capacity, and to meet extra demand, as forecast in the National Plan of 1964.

The PIB addressed itself to considering whether the target rate of return (of 11.9 per cent) should have been eased, at least to the extent of the unexpected increase in plant under construction. The CEGB was obliged to earn 5 per cent of sales revenue on plant under construction alone and this would rise further. The PIB could not question the target return as such, but asked whether it had forced the industry into undesirable pricing policy. It would be undesirable to raise prices at the very time when unit costs were being reduced as a result of the new investment. But in spite of major innovation, and larger scale production, capital costs would not fall, and might well rise because of increased construction costs. Hence it was unlikely that total costs would fall. This conclusion in turn meant that the price increases proposed by the LEB were largely justified, since so large a part of their costs, and of the prospective increases in cost, were charges for bulk supplies.

The PIB related gas prices to the trend of costs and demand. The increase proposed was based partly on extra costs already incurred, partly on prospective increases. Though the PIB disapproved of anticipating cost increases on the grounds that it was inflationary, it nevertheless had to allow some firm prospective increases to be included, if only because cost increases occur frequently in small steps, and prices cannot reasonably follow exactly or so often. But it was important that pay increases should not be reflected in prices until they had been settled and the precise amount involved was known. The 1961 White Paper on the obligations of the nationalised industries did not define costs, other than those arising from capital charges: the prices and incomes White Paper required that all costs were to be examined before cost increases could justifiably lead to increases in price. Anticipating cost increases in price increases was an inflationary process that the prices and incomes policy was to avoid.

However, it was not enough to relate gas prices to costs. Prices influence demand as much as supply and there ought to be some reasonably stable relationship between them. Otherwise consumers might be induced to buy equipment they afterwards regretted, or use extra gas only available at inordinate cost, or fail to use cheap gas. Whatever other obligations public enterprises had, their prices ought to be "in the direction of long-run costs".

All the Gas Boards had a number of tariffs, and the three Boards referred proposed to raise the extra revenue they needed in various ways. In Scotland, consumers using large amounts for space heating would have to pay most of the increase (up to $26\frac{1}{2}$ per cent more). So many consumers had taken advantage of the low running rate on a two-part tariff that the Board's revenue per therm would still be less than three years earlier. The tariff had been an error of judgement, and the Board's losses had been increased when new plants were unexpectedly late and unexpectedly costly. But charges sufficient to make good the deficits would not reflect long-run costs. The special once-for-all costs had to be met, and this should be done by a temporary surcharge on the standing charges. Prices should in general be in line with long-run costs, and running rates should only be increased in line with costs, assuming the new plant had worked as expected, which would mean a smaller increase than the Board proposed.

The South-Western Gas Board was also failing to meet its target return on capital; and without an increase in charges, revenue would be insufficient to cover outgoings. The Board proposed to increase its charges because of unforeseen increases in costs, the largest single item being wages and salaries. Labour productivity could not be increased because the plant was old and soon to be replaced. On the other hand, sales had increased more slowly than anywhere else, and prices were the highest in the country. To charge a still higher price might discourage the use of gas in new housing, and therefore deprive consumers in the South-West of the advantages of the cheaper gas soon to be available. The PIB concluded therefore that charges should be increased by only three per cent, to cover extra operating costs but not the target return on capital.

The Minister of Power had been urging price increases on the reluctant Wales Gas Board to ensure that its surplus was nearer the target. The PIB saw the conflict of policy over price and return on capital as a conflict of authority between the Government and the Board. The PIB had no doubt that, "since the ultimate responsibility for finding the capital falls on the Government", the Government's authority should prevail; but only "provided the resulting prices broadly meet our criterion of being in line with longer-term costs". Costs were rising because of high distribution costs and high interest charges, as an enthusiastic Board extended its operations to more and more remote areas. That consumers in towns with low costs should to some extent subsidise the extension of gas to consumers in high-cost rural areas was an obligation laid on all Gas Boards; but this could clearly be done too extravagantly. The PIB decided that this must be left to the judgement of Boards, influenced or directed by the parent Ministry. But the price increases were not out of line with long-term costs, nor would they inhibit demand. The proposals must therefore stand. The PIB had reached its conclusion by reference to costs, and not to the financial obligations; but it did not suggest they be altogether ignored, as they imposed some "discipline" on management that market constraints did not provide. But rates of return would not be enough by themselves. In spite of competition between fuels each still had enough monopoly to make it relatively easy to raise prices to meet their financial obligations. The Boards were actually under every inducement to do so as the end of each planning period approached. The target rates of return should be combined with some requirement with regard to costs, if upward pressure on prices was to be mitigated.

Coal prices were first referred to the PIB in December 1965 (No. 12). The PIB was asked to examine the case for a price increase to bring £80 million more revenue in 1966–67 "against the statutory financial and other obligations" of the National Coal Board, as well as in the light of the prices and incomes White Paper.

As coal was a labour-intensive industry, it appeared that labour use and wages would be the major issues. But the effect of a declining market was far more important. Labour productivity had been increasing, and was expected to increase. Labour costs however might well increase as wages rose. But the possible increases in operating costs were trivial beside the increase in overhead costs, as they were spread over a declining total output, and the decrease in unit revenue, as a greater proportion of low-grade, cheaper coal was sold. There was no alternative to approving the proposed price increase unless it could be shown that it was out of line with longer-term costs. However, the prospect was that all the underlying causes of increasing cost and falling revenue would continue. The price increase necessary to increase revenue by £80 million would not only meet the current deficit, but would bring prices closer to long-run costs. It must therefore be recommended.

Reports Nos. 7 and 12 were the only public-sector price cases the PIB was given to review under the 1961 rules about the financial obligations of nationalised industries, and the only ones before the Prime Minister's statement about the PIB's own special interests in their efficiency. All the subsequent cases were reported on in the light of new financial obligations, set out in a new White Paper, still to be taken as having prior importance over the prices and incomes policy as before.

All nationalised industries were to earn a target rate of return on their capital; and the relevant value of the capital employed had to be agreed between the industry and the Treasury. The rate to be earned was set taking into account the return expected on any low-risk enterprise. This rate was influenced by the current rate of interest and by actual returns elsewhere. But this time new investment was to be examined in relation to a "test rate of discount" set at eight per cent, and the discounted cash-flow method was to be used to calculate the yield. The appropriate price needed to give the right rate of return would not necessarily be the same as the right price in relation to long-run marginal ¦cost. But exactly what relationship there would be between the two would depend on the circumstances of the case. The target rates of return would be more or less crucial in determining prices according to whether the industries needed more or less capital.

The announcement of the efficiency reviews was shortly followed by a bunch of four public-sector references to the PIB, which allowed it to redefine its attitude in a general way to public-sector pricing. Two of them, on the bulk supply tariff of the CEGB (No. 59), and gas prices (No. 57) raised again issues that the PIB had dealt with in No. 7, but now interpreted in the light of revised financial obligations. The other two were London Transport Board's fares, and British Railways' fares and charges.

The Prime Minister's statement was the response to continued public protest over the increased prices which all the Area Electricity Boards had announced in April 1967, to apply immediately after severe restraint ended. But the LEB case had shown that it was no use referring a proposal by a supplying Board, when the CEGB controlled major costs for the entire industry. It was the bulk supply tariff that was referred therefore, rather than electricity prices.

The Government had relieved the electricity industry of its financial obligations in 1966–67 in the interests of price stability, in spite of increased costs. But in the absence of new targets for the period after 1967 (as the new White Paper was not then ready), the Government had requested it to get back to its previous target in 1968–69. The PIB clearly disapproved of so strict a requirement, in spite of its inability to alter it. Capital charges were again a major issue. Operating costs per unit were expected to fall in 1968–69 as more efficient stations came into operation. But capital costs had risen (as the PIB had expected in No. 7). Indeed the industry's problems had grown worse than expected, mainly because of lower demand than expected. The gap between estimated and actual sales was so great that, had the building programme in fact been completed on time, surplus capacity of over a third would have appeared. The higher capital charges would then have been offset to some degree by falling operating costs. But the backlog of plant planned or under construction, but not yet operating, had grown even faster. Nothing could be done to increase capital use, or speed up building in 1968–69. The only question was whether the CEGB's finances might be improved by a different treatment of work-in-progress in the accounts. But the PIB eventually rejected this argument because it amounted to a reduction in the target rate of return. The Government's financial targets had been calculated including work-in-progress, and the PIB's terms of reference required it to take account of the financial targets. The capital charges as stated would therefore have to be met.

There remained the CEGB's surplus. On this issue the PIB was not quite so narrowly confined as at first appeared. The target for the whole electricity industry would not be achieved merely by approving an increase in the BST, to enable the CEGB to meet its required 11.9 per cent. The Area Boards had already fixed their prices for the current year, taking into account the increased BST. But they had also overestimated their sales, and their surpluses would be too low to meet their target. If their costs increased further because of the BST increase, they would be still further from meeting their financial obligation, unless they could squeeze other costs to compensate. The PIB therefore did not consider it consistent with the terms of reference to "place the CEGB in a position to fulfil its financial obligation by prejudicing ... the ability of the Area Boards to fulfil theirs". This was the more undesirable since the pricing policies of the CEGB "render it entirely immune to the consequences of a fall in demand", and this was not a situation to encourage efficiency. Both parts of the industry should be under pressure to reduce costs. Therefore the PIB considered that the effect of the gap between actual sales and forecast level of sales should be evenly distributed between the CEGB and the Area Boards. This would mean that both could achieve their target if renewed efforts were made to squeeze costs.

The only issue involving general efficiency discussed in the report was the structure of the bulk supply tariff. This was not in a form best suited to reflecting long-run costs. Changes in the tariff should therefore also change the structure towards this end.

The next report to be published was the case of railway fares in London (No. 56), which involved the structure of prices as much as the financial obligations. Like the NCB, the London Transport Board was a labour-intensive activity faced with a declining market. But its problems were greater, since opportunities for improving labour productivity were limited. Moreover it was obliged by statute to provide a costly service, namely "an adequate and properly co-ordinated system of passenger transport".

Given that the LTB had to cover its outgoings, the fare increase was obviously justified as running costs would not be covered otherwise, and no quick-acting way of reducing costs could be found. But fare increases would increase social costs elsewhere. Demand was likely to fall if fares were increased and much of this would be transferred to private transport, giving rise to all the costs of extra congestion. But the data were lacking to make proper calculation of them. Hence the PIB could not convincingly argue either that the fare increase was un-justified or that it should be modified. It urged that social costs be examined by the Greater London Council (to which LTB was soon to be transferred) or by the Ministry of Transport.

The LTBW as still required to submit price increases to the independent Transport Tribunal. Operating with different terms of reference and using different (much more legalistic) arguments, the Tribunal reached a different conclusion. It allowed only part of the proposed increase, mainly on the grounds that it could not take the transfer to the GLC into account before it was actually embodied in legislation. Instead of fare increases estimated to yield £8.6 million, which the PIB had reluctantly recommended, the Transport Tribunal allowed increases designed to yield only £5.8 million.

Six months later the case was once more referred to the PIB, when the LTB sought to raise another £8 million (No. 112). The Minister of Transport had agreed that the LTB should be transferred in a "clearly viable" state, meaning that revenue covered prospective costs and pro-vided £2 million for reserves in the first year. The LTB had no option but to seek more fare increases.

The PIB in turn had no option but to agree. Nevertheless, it repeated its general misgivings about the wisdom of raising fares, bearing in mind the likely reduction in fare-paying passengers as a result.

The LTB duly became the London Transport Executive, and a creature of the GLC, on 1 January 1970, the recommendations for increased fares in No. 112 having been implemented in the autumn of 1969. The LTE then got GLC approval for further increases in May 1970. These were referred to the PIB but nevertheless implemented in August 1970, before the case had been completed owing, it was said, to the urgency of the case (No. 159).

The previous fare increases had given LTE extra revenue, but this had been more than counter-balanced by increased operating expenses, due to pay increases. These were not out of line with pay increases elsewhere, and as it endured a chronic shortage of labour the LTE could not avoid them. The PIB this time accepted the argument (unlike its conclusions in its first encounter with London buses, over busmen's pay, see p. 145), and also that no improvements in productivity were open to it in the immediate future. The new fare increases only could be allowed. The problem of financing public transport was not to be solved by reviewing the technical pricing or management problems of the enterprises.

Passenger fares and freight charges of British Railways had been referred to the PIB in the autumn of 1967 (No. 72). The British Railways Board (BRB) had already announced some months previously that it wanted to raise fares and freight charges, by amounts varying from 4 to 10 per cent. Railway transport was another labour-intensive industry, in a declining market and subject to increasingly fierce competition. The BRB had, like the NCB, increased labour productivity while rapidly reducing its labour-force in the past five years or more. But unit costs were rising while average revenue stagnated. The inevitable results were deficits and prospective deficits. The industry's financial obligation was to cover expenses, and make some provision for replacements. As in the case of the LTB buses, there was no doubt about the BRB's need for extra revenue. The question was whether their proposals would in fact yield the extra revenue, and whether they were consistent with the prices and incomes policy. BRB's own estimates showed that it was not likely to cover costs without increased revenue, let alone provide for replacement of assets; though it was not clear what assets would need renewal in a system still being run down rapidly. The only conclusion the PIB could reach was that the extra revenue needed was certainly greater than the BRB had asked for. But it recommended a change in pricing policy nevertheless. The BRB proposed a uniform percentage increase on all charges as in the past. National industries were required to price according to long-run marginal costs where possible. This was a difficult concept for the railways; but costs must still be relevant to determining prices. BRB should therefore relate prices to cost by setting the minimum level of all charges at the avoidable cost incurred for each particular type of business. The BRB would have to exploit its competitive advantage wherever it was to be found (the orthodox prescription for maximising revenue), so that fixed costs were covered and the financial target achieved. The PIB considered that a justifiable policy for the railways, since it clearly under-priced some of its services. The BRB should not therefore be allowed to impose a general increase in fares and freight charges. There should instead be a new structure of fares, discriminating between routes and classes. Freight contracts should be negotiated individually, taking circumstances, especially the competition, into account in each case.

The BRB was back again in August 1969, this time with a proposal to increase London fares only (No. 137). Like the LTB, when the GLC took over its transport functions, BRB had been given new financial obligations. The principle (set out in the White Paper on *Transport in London* [Cmnd 3686]) was that the London commuter services should be "treated as a network", viable in itself. (This principle was thought to be desirable for BRB since the GLC insisted that the LTB was viable.) BRB was then to determine the appropriate London fares, when a financial obligation for the network had been agreed.

Costs were persistently rising against static revenue in London as elsewhere. Either fares must increase or Government grants must increase (instead of disappearing, as the White Paper proposed). The BRB proposals would raise revenue to cover only a minor part of a wide gap. The Minister of Transport had subsequently increased the grant, because of the extra social cost of more road congestion. But as social costs could still not be calculated with any accuracy, the PIB still could not comment on the amount of extra revenue really appropriate. The PIB could find little prospect of stabilising the level of fares or freight charges except to the extent that extra social costs elsewhere justified some subsidy.

With the report on the gas industry (No. 57), the PIB returned to another expanding, and therefore heavily investing, nationalised industry. By 1967, the industry had fast falling operating costs counter-balanced by increasing capital charges. New plants were being installed, partly (like electricity) to increase the plant margin; and the rate of interest had increased, making the charges proportionately higher. This time, all twelve Area Gas Boards were proposing to increase their prices.

War in the Middle East (and in particular, the closing of the Suez Canal) had made oil more expensive and naphtha difficult to obtain. Moreover, the Gas Boards (like the CEGB) were required to get back to their target returns in 1968–69, after temporary release from them during the standstill and severe restraint. Larger financial commitments accounted for half the extra revenue they were seeking; the other half was necessary because of falling unit revenue. Most extra gas was used for space-heating by existing consumers on two-part tariffs, on which running rates for large quantities were much lower than other charges, so increasing consumption meant falling average revenue. If unit costs had fallen in line, no difficulties would have arisen. But demand at peak times had increased, requiring increasing investment in new capacity. Consumers were probably not paying enough to cover the extra costs of supplying gas at peak times; and the PIB strongly recommended Boards "to consider basing their tariffs, where possible, on the incremental costs of providing extra capacity and extra therms and on the incremental costs associated with new consumers."

As the financial target obligations had to be accepted, the extra revenue the Gas Boards wanted was necessary, given all the Government's prior conditions, and little change in the price increases proposed was possible.

The PIB also began enquiries into efficiency, the first of the investigations in its new role, and the result was published later (No. 102).

Problems of planning capital investment, pricing policy and tariff structure, the use of manpower and some aspects of consumer services were considered generally. In the nature of the report it threw more light inwards on the gas industry than outwards on the PIB's principles or prices policy. It all amounted to a favourable report on the management of the industry. The review of management practices was continued and supplemented a year later, in No. 155, on costs and efficiency in the gas industry. This reference was one of the more carefully formulated group that appeared in the last stages. A set of pay agreements, covering first manual workers (January 1970), then craft workers (March 1970), and finally staff workers (May 1970), had been negotiated nationally. (Senior staff were subsequently also given rises, but these were not referred, although they were clearly at least as high proportionately as those for the workers under their control.) The PIB was to examine the prospects for absorbing the pay increases by cost saving, so that prices should not rise in consequence. This allowed much more scope for making effective recommendations to stabilise prices than before. The PIB had mostly been faced with recommending a price increase simply because there was no time to implement cost-saving changes without abandoning the financial obligations while they were made. Now the circumstances were very favourable. The industry was strongly expanding, meanwhile taking advantage of a long-term capital-saving innovation, the arrival of natural gas. There were also signs of an improvement in the Government's financial control imposed on the industry; the Gas Council was trying to get its target for the current quinquennium applied to the whole period and not to each year separately, a change the PIB had recommended five years before.

The PIB concentrated on investigating possible reductions in labour cost. The new pay agreements included undertakings that the workers would co-operate with changes to improve productivity. But no specific improvements to cover the increases were proposed. However, the PIB showed that improvements in labour management could secure savings large enough to do so. If best practices among the Area Boards were adopted generally, the savings would compensate for the pay increases. The net effect of its recommendations would be to keep prices stable, to meet the financial target over the quinquennium (though not in the early years), while paying wage and salary agreements in full. However, even while the case was being investigated, other cost increases had occurred. There had been extra pay for contractor's labour (following on the gas industry's own settlement), extra pay for senior staff, and price increases for steel and coal. Meanwhile, also, the industry had reduced its forecasts of revenue. Some increases in the price of gas and other charges were only too clearly in prospect. But the PIB could not take these into account as they were not referred. It concluded that the cost saving proposed was not easy, but "given the will", the savings could and should be made.

The fifth of the five nationalised industries to appear before the PIB in September 1967 under the special review procedures for proposed increases in charges, was the Post Office, which had notified the Government of general increases in many of its charges in the summer of 1967, for implementation in 1968 (No. 58). The PIB regarded it as two enterprises, postal services and telecommunications, run by a single administration. The two enterprises were subject to very different market conditions. The postal service was labour-intensive, and served a market that was then expanding, though more slowly than the national income. Its costs were very sensitive to the service provided, and the quality of service had increasing effect on revenue, as there was growing competition for parcels traffic and money remittance. Telecommunications was a capital-intensive industry, in a rapidly growing market enjoying technological advance to ease cost problems. The immediate problem bringing both sides' activities before the PIB was a common one: failure to reach the Government's financial targets in face of rising costs. Both sides had earned their targets in the past. But both faced increased costs due to increased wages and salaries and telecommunications had also to meet increased capital charges from an accelerated investment programme. Postal staff costs were virtually fixed in the short term; consequently the expected level of business determined expected "productivity" (output per man), expected profits and the price increases necessary to reach the target. Some extra costs would be incurred in handling extra business, for overtime payments and transport. This would partly offset the extra revenue earned thereby. But the Post Office was unable to estimate the balance between them.

Prospective demand for telecommunications governed investment and staffing as well as productivity.

Estimated costs and profits in both services depended on the current costing system. Costing was done with great care; but the system of analysis was not appropriate. Prices ought to be based on either long-run avoidable cost, or marginal cost, as the White Paper on nationalised industries had laid down. The PIB recommended the Post Office to commission the studies necessary to calculate them.

The PIB was in a difficult position over wages and labour productivity. In spite of the Post Office as a whole being so labour-intensive an activity, and so large an employer of labour, it did not examine labour use in any detail. The Post Office needed extra revenue for the usual reasons. Increases in postal charges were needed to meet the financial objective, and to "maintain the grade of service by introducing a two-tier postal service". As labour costs in the post service were rising faster than could be offset by increased productivity or were likely to be absorbed by bigger turnover, extra revenue was needed, though the PIB estimated the need at rather less than the Post Office. Generally speaking, the PIB accepted the Post Office's proposals for raising the revenue, with modifications as to timing. For telecommunications, though labour costs could be held, capital charges would inevitably increase. Extra revenue was needed to meet its target. Some changes in the detailed proposals for increased telephone charges were recommended, on the grounds that prices needed to be related more closely to marginal costs.

The Government did not wholly accept the recommendations about timing. Increased postal charges (and the two-tier service differentiating between first- and second-class mail), were introduced in September 1968; while the increased charges for parcels and remittance services were postponed until the spring of 1969. By this time the prospects of the postal services had declined compared with both the Post Office's and the PIB forecasts. The question whether and when the increase in charges for parcels and remittances should be introduced was therefore sent back to the PIB in May 1969 (No. 121).

The Post Office was now facing considerable losses on postal services. Costs had turned out to be higher than estimated; but overwhelmingly the reason for the short-fall against so recent a forecast was a short-fall of revenue. Letter traffic had fallen instead of rising, under the impact of the new two-tier system, which was very unpopular. A new forecast assumed that the volume of letter traffic would recover by 1970–71, but would still be $5\frac{1}{2}$ per cent below the earlier forecast. Parcels traffic was also falling instead of rising, as previously forecast. The Giro was making slower progress than expected, and was not yet adding to revenue. Major increases in cost had been incurred due to higher interest charges and extra depreciation. The interest charges were much bigger than expected, partly because more had to be borrowed to meet the unexpected deficit of 1968–69, itself partly due to the decline in business. They were also partly due to higher capital expenditure and to a revised method of working out depreciation charges.

The PIB considered there was still "considerable scope for increasing the responsiveness of costs to changing traffic levels". Control of direct costs based on better management information would enable savings to be made. The Post Office had already developed a suitable system, and the PIB urged that it be extended as rapidly as possible.

E

There was no doubt about the losses involved in the parcel and remittance services, due to the decline in traffic, and increased costs.

In the course of the two enquiries the PIB had reviewed a number of aspects of Post Office management, covering forecasting, marketing and costing methods in general, and planning investment in the parcels service in some detail. The results were on the whole favourable to the Post Office. Modern management techniques had long been used, and the Post Office seemed to be generally efficiency conscious. Some criticisms were justified, but "the very substantial merits of the Post Office should be recognised. In spite of its defects we have been favourably impressed with its efficiency and with its high regard for the public interest."

The Post Office had been drawn into a series of steep increases in charges on the postal side for similar reasons to the National Coal Board. Relatively declining industries with large labour costs, they were both vulnerable to rising costs, if productivity failed to offset wage increases. Both managements had persistently made over-optimistic forecasts of their prospects, with the result that their income and prospective income declined seriously, and only a series of price rises could quickly provide the necessary funds to meet their expenses. At the same time, the apparent frequency of the rises, and the publicity accompanying them drove some business towards their thriving competitors, and making another round of rising unit cost, rising prices and falling business the more inevitable. The telecommunications side was more similar to electricity or gas, needing to earn more to cover steeply increased investment, while operating costs and unit revenue declined as a result of past investment, so that charges were more and more sensitive to capital charges—and the targets that determined them.

The case of steel prices (No. 111) referred in December 1968 belongs here, in that it concerned a public-sector industry, and the reference specifically mentioned the Government's decision to refer all major price increases to the PIB. But it was unlike the preceding ones in that the British Steel Corporation had only recently been formed, and had not then got far with the reorganisation of the industry from its shape under private enterprise. It was also unlike the rest as it had not then been given a financial target, nor had the precise amount of its capital been agreed with the Government. Nevertheless, to the PIB it was another public-sector pricing case.

In the absence of an agreed target rate of return, the BSC had set itself one in calculating a price increase. The average rate of all assets employed was about 13 per cent, including a substantial margin for risk and a higher provision for depreciation than before, mainly due to shortening the imputed life of fixed assets.

But nationalised industries were supposed to relate prices to marginal costs as well as to earning an appropriate rate of return. The BSC had ostensibly tried to assess long-run marginal costs by "updating a formula used by the former Iron and Steel Board to estimate the cost of operating new plans on 'greenfield' sites". This comparison was of dubious relevance as no greenfield development was proposed or needed. A 1965 estimate had been revised for subsequent cost increases. The PIB found this ill-founded in principle, and resulting in too high an estimate, as it did not take account of any changes in the structure of costs due to technical improvements. But the BSC had merely used the figures to support its case for proposals formulated on the other grounds. Study groups had been set up for each of 28 main products to estimate costs and required prices. There had been uniform assumptions about capacity utilisation, but as there had been no such uniformity about what a "representative" (average) cost might be, there was no real uniform pricing principle either. Even the capacity figure might be inconsistent with the cost and price calculations of the groups.

These "required selling prices" were then modified in the light of what the market would bear. Most of the price differences between products did not appear to be consistently defined, and taking the proposals altogether, the changes were so comprehensive that the new prices and extras could not readily be related to the existing schedules. It was extremely difficult therefore for the PIB to judge whether they were or were not too high in relation to the Government's general principles for pricing in the public sector.

But the PIB was also concerned with the national effect of a rise in steel prices. Its own estimate of the consequent increase in prices elsewhere was that the costs of the output of the metal manufacturing and engineering industries would rise by about three per cent. Since these two sectors covered 40 per cent of UK exports, the increase proposed by BSC would perceptibly erode the advantages gained by devaluation. The PIB concluded therefore that the level of prices required "deeper consideration" than that concerned with the revenue of BSC alone. There was on national grounds a strong case for abating the proposed increases, if only this could reasonably be done in the particular circumstances of the steel industry.

The most important part of the solution lay in the usual place—on the possibility of cost saving. Because of the urgency of the case on the one hand, and the complexities of the industry on the other, the PIB was not able to make a comprehensive review of the industry's efficiency. But consultants were employed to visit a representative (small) sample of works. As a result, the PIB was not satisfied that the BSC had made proper allowance for cost saving in its forecasts. Though the BSC was, and would remain, preoccupied with reorganising the industry, there were some changes that it could make meanwhile. For instance, more careful planning of small-scale investment expenditure in individual works on a standard method could have immediate effect. None of the plants or divisions visited had a plan or target for cost saving. The BSC's own "target" for cost reduction was merely the difference between their proposed selling prices and the required rate of return. Programmes for cost saving could quickly be set. The two main impediments to improving efficiency were the absence of a uniform standard costing system, and of "soundly engineered" work standards. Both of these hindered plant bargaining for productivity agreements. The White Paper required that every effort to absorb cost increases should be made before prices were increased. As this condition seemed not to have been met, the full price increase could not be recommended. But by how much should it be reduced? There was no convincing answer. The PIB wanted to relate its recommend-ation to a "firm estimate" of potential cost savings; but none had been found. Price increases should therefore be approved only to the extent of an increase of £40 million a year of extra revenue, instead of the £50–55 million proposed by BSC.

The distribution of the increase over separate products should also, in the PIB's view, be done in a different way from the BSC's proposal. The Government had pledged that competition between the BSC and the remaining private sector should be fair, though it was far from clear what this would mean in practice—especially as the target rate of return had not been set. The PIB interpreted it to mean that it should not abuse its market power. Reductions should therefore be made where the Corporation had a predominant share of the market, and where its proposed price exceeded what could be justified in relation to costs. The PIB then went on to specify a list of carbon steel product groups where all the reductions (against the proposed prices) were to be made—the most bitterly opposed of all its recommendations. The BSC was to decide how the reductions should fall between products within the group, given that the whole reduction was to be made within it.

This recommendation was met with an outcry from BSC, on the grounds that it had the commercial responsibility, it had duly exercised its commercial judgment in devising the price structure, and it was not therefore for any other body to impose anything different on it. The Government had to offend either the BSC or the PIB. The Iron and Steel Consumers' Council was consulted, and took the side of the BSC. The Government then allowed across-the-board increases, as the BSC had demanded.

Shortly after this, in August 1969, the PIB was again asked to examine a request for increased coal prices, at very short notice. The urgency was so great that the PIB was specifically told to suspend its function of reviewing efficiency, though the Government at the same time recognised the need to consider the scope for cost savings. Consequently the PIB's second review of the industry was very similar to the first, in merely reviewing management practices having a direct bearing on costs and prices (No. 124). Increases in price had been sanctioned by the Government on the lines set out in the PIB's report No. 12 of 1966. These had yielded only enough extra revenue to cover extra costs. Since then, a deficit had once more appeared, and the NCB wanted to raise enough extra revenue to cover a forecast loss of £14.6 million in 1970–71. Again the forecast increase in deficit was due more to declining revenue per ton, in spite of increased prices, than to increasing costs.

Productivity was still rising and was expected to rise substantially more. The PIB "gained a generally favourable impression" of standards of management, and there did not seem to be much scope for cost reductions beyond the NCB's forecast. But a review of the statistics showed that the NCB was vulnerable to a charge of over optimistic forecasting. Performance was worse than previous estimates, and on the trends shown in the figures, the prospective deficit could be twice as high as the forecast. If the proposed price increases were approved, they might soon be followed by another round, which might spoil the market for coal in the long run. The PIB's preferred remedy therefore was to do the estimates again, and make revised (higher) price increases from 1 January 1970. If this could not be done, there was no alternative but to approve the NCB's proposals.

Barely three months later the NCB was proposing further price increases; and these were referred back to PIB (No. 138). This time NCB wanted an average increase of 10 per cent, to yield extra revenue of £65 million. The increases approved by PIB in No. 124 had actually been in operation only one month. Meantime, the NCB had recalculated its forecast of productivity, costs and revenue (as PIB had recommended), and had found (as PIB had forecast) that their prospects were much worse than they had presumed three months before.

One factor accounting for the change of forecast was a major strike, and the subsequent wage settlement. This would increase costs by £9 million. But the expected deficit had increased by £38 million. The largest single item (more than twice as large as the combined strike loss and extra wage bill) was the reduction in expected productivity increases, largely attributable to production difficulties and "some decline in morale among workers" before, during and after the strike. The consequences of the new wage settlement had to be accepted as a datum, since the PIB had not been asked to examine the pay settlement. It noted, however, that "the pay increase exceeds the estimated increase in productivity".

There was "a wide range of uncertainty" in the estimates of revenue. It was certain, however, that even on optimistic assumptions, the proposed price increases would not be enough for the NCB to cover its costs in the two years up to March 1971. The PIB had no alternative to allowing the proposed immediate general increase of 10 per cent.

The structure of prices in the NCB's proposals had not been reviewed since 1951. The PIB therefore set about reviewing this matter, as well as looking further into the background of the productivity estimate, in a follow-up report. But meantime the NCB had applied for yet another price increase, for coking and "general purpose" coals, the third in a year. Once more, productivity was rising less fast than forecast, costs were consequently higher, and prices needed to be raised to restore revenue. The PIB had to hurry on its report (No. 153), so that the price increase should not be too long delayed. Nevertheless, the bulk of the report was concerned with the principles of price determination, and the general scope for raising efficiency. It is the only one of the four on coal that constitutes an efficiency study of the industry.

The most important part of the report concerned pricing in relation to resource costs. The NCB aimed to charge average costs for all collieries together, and for separate markets (coking coal, smokeless fuel for domestic use, and industrial coal). But marginal costs were much higher than this, because they related to the costs of mining in the least productive pit remaining in production. Marginal cost pricing would involve a steep increase in price and this would reduce demand, precipitating a faster contraction of the industry. Apart from the social reasons for not doing this, costs might well rise in consequence, due to the effects of demoralising present miners and deterring potential recruits. However, the coincidence of possible excess demand for coal in the winter of 1970–71, and the expiration of the industry's current financial target (to cover its costs) in March 1971, gave it an opportunity to modify its pricing policy. The PIB suggested that resource cost, rather than accounting cost, was the relevant concept to which price ought to be matched. In principle, resources ought to be valued in relation to their alternative uses were they to be released from mining, instead of in relation to present cash rewards. Miners in "high-cost" areas might remain unemployed for long periods, or be prematurely retired, if coal mining ceased. The value of the extra coal to the consumers might well be greater than its real cost in terms of the resources used, even though the price would not cover the cash expenses. The Government should take such calculations into account in setting the industry's financial target. Data were already available as a result of the NCB's planning work to make such estimates a practical possibility. All that was needed was for the Ministry of Technology to have access to relevant data in the possession of the NCB and the electricity industry, and for the two nationalised industries to exchange information.

Such changes could not yield any savings to meet the NCB's

immediate need. But the PIB did not agree to the size, nor to the form of the price increase proposed. The NCB had made some allowance for a pay claim shortly to be presented. This should be disallowed, on the usual grounds that pay increases of indeterminate size should not be anticipated in price increases. To the extent that wages did increase, the only alternatives would be a price increase, or increased Government borrowing, or increased taxes, a dilemma for the Government to resolve. The NCB was also aiming to cover colliery costs by revenue from coal in 1970–71, though the industry's financial objective and statutory obligation both required only breaking even over all activities (including opencast-mined coal and other activities). Though the PIB approved the more rigorous aim in general terms, it disapproved implementing it at once, since the steep rise in coal prices necessary to achieve it would inhibit demand and perhaps therefore damage its finances even more. Given the more modest aim of breaking even over all activities, a major price increase was still necessary however. This should take the form of a rise of 15 to 16 per cent on coking coal (compared with the 12½ per cent proposed), a rise which would still leave British prices lower than those in other countries, at a time of world shortage. But there should be no general increase in industrial coal prices. The justification for the increase in coking coal prices was that the scarcity responsible for driving up world prices was likely to continue, a market justification rather than a change in structure to bring prices more in line with marginal costs.

Two technical supplements to No. 153 were published in the last days of the PIB's life, completing the two efficiency studies begun in 1970, in connection with the second report on coal prices. The first contained two papers: one, a study of a price policy based on marginal resource costs (that is the real costs incurred in keeping extra men and other resources in coal mining, rather than releasing them to whatever alternative employment was available); and second an up-to-date statement of the NCB's revised prices. The other supplement also contained two papers: one on hours of work, overtime and shiftwork-ing; the second the results of the PIB's earnings surveys of two colliery areas.

The National Freight Corporation (NFC), whose costs, charges and productivity were referred in the last days of the Labour Government, was the last public-sector case reported on (No. 162). At the time of the reference, the NFC had only existed for a year and a half. It was a public holding company, consisting of a large number of disparate haulage companies formerly in various other parts of the nationalised industries. However, the important companies determining the results of NFC as a whole were the British Road Services companies and the two former rail divisions, Freightliners and National Carriers Ltd. BRS

Ltd operated mainly in general haulage, mostly in full lorry loads between large firms. This was a very competitive market, where a national network gave no particular advantage. BRS Parcels and NCL were both parcel carriers, enjoying a distinct advantage in having a national network, but competing mainly with one another, and with the Post Office for the lighter, less awkward items. Freightliners were in competition in a general way with other long-distance hauliers. A Freight Integration Council, set up at the same time as NFC, had reported—not surprisingly—that there was overlapping between public-sector carriers for parcel traffic, so that capacity might be ill-used.

NFC had only one year's trading accounts. Though it could distinguish between the activities of its various subsidiaries, the exercise was of little value, since there were no separate accounts for NCL and Freightliners for previous years. Both were making considerable losses, balanced by small profits elsewhere. All charges were related to published tariffs, but much modified in practice to meet competition for particular traffic over particular routes. How actual charges were related to costs on each route or traffic was impossible to discover. The PIB recommended that avoidable costs on each type of traffic should be the basis of all charges.

Tariff rates for BRS Parcels had increased five times in two and a half years, in all by nearly 50 per cent. Revenue had risen, but not as much as costs. Both labour costs and vehicle costs had risen, the latter mainly due to the Transport Act 1968, and increased oil duty. BRS Ltd had increased its revenue by increasing its business. The PIB could only conclude that the increases in charges, "though very considerable", were justified—given existing levels of efficiency.

All the companies were labour-intensive, the relationship between pay and labour productivity was the main determinant of cost. This depended most on the quality of management, and the techniques of control used. The PIB found that quality of management good in having "experience and expertise in managing men and getting things done"; but more modern techniques needed to be applied and depot managers should be trained in their use. However, any improvement at the depot level would be trivial compared to the effects of the strategy adopted by the NFC to match its market for parcels carriage. A shrink-ing market, rising labour productivity and increasing vehicle produc-tivity (by larger size, better roads, better handling) all tended to reduce the vehicles and depots required for a given service. NCL and BRS Parcels together might have to face a reduction to half their size in three or four years (partly due to low levels of productivity in NCL). Major changes in the functions of the two would clearly be needed. The PIB could not itself choose among the alternatives: it merely urged evalua-tion of them, as "failure to adapt now will lead to far more drastic and painful adjustment later". Such drastic changes would clearly need drastic changes in manpower. "Frank discussions" should begin with the unions on a manpower plan. The more transfers between depots were made, the less redundancy there need be. Transfer would be greatly eased by common grading and pay structures, for clerical and supervisory as well as manual workers. Negotiating procedures were still based on the constituent companies, and resulted in substantially different pay levels and conditions.

BRS Ltd (general haulage) operated in a different market, and had to adapt to its market by meeting frequent new demands quickly and cheaply. Management needed scope for quick decisions, and the NFC should content itself with requiring appropriate financial results. The Government also should restrict itself to approving the criteria and techniques used for appraising new investment, leaving the NFC and BRS free to buy and sell within the rules, and within market limits, as they saw fit. The past succession of price increases that gave rise to the reference were inevitable within the existing circumstances. But the circumstances clearly needed some drastic reform for costs to be contained, charges to remain competitive, or profitability to be restored. Meanwhile, the PIB could only conclude that the increase in charges "though very considerable", were justified—given existing levels of efficiency.

The reference was more fruitful than some, in that it invited the PIB's suggestions in an interval between particular pay negotiations or tariff changes, when changes in the determinants are more likely to be considered. But in this particular case, it could only be regretted that some such investigations, involving industrial relations and pay negotiations, as well as management questions at the policy planning and operational levels, could not have been made earlier in NFC's life, preferably before its birth.

BRS companies gave their employees another general pay increase in May 1970, on the old lines. But by early 1971 a new structure applying to 23,000 workers had been prepared. The existing basic rates (more than 100 of them), would be grouped into a few broad standard grades. The immediate result for the workers was a substantial pay increase for many of them; the ultimate result for the managements was the ability to make better use of their labour-forces, within the between depots.

The PIB's only case involving local authorities was rents of local-authority housing (No. 62). During the standstill, no local authority had wanted to incur the odium of putting up rent in spite of rising costs, since many faced new elections in the spring of 1967, and many were fighting a losing battle after the high tide of Labour gains in 1964. But by the summer of 1967, the local elections were over. The problem of unbalanced housing accounts remained, and something had to be done, severe restraint or no. But, as the rumours of rent increases grew, public protest grew; and, more important to the Government, many trades unions supported the tenants' protests. The question was referred to the PIB in December 1967.

The principles of rent determination had previously been distinguished by their absence. Actual rent levels varied between 16s 2d a week to 86s 9d (for a similar house). Varying costs of construction, land and repairs accounted for some of the difference, more of it by whether the housing accounts were subsidised from the rates, or different methods of relating rents for different types or ages of houses. The proposed increases varied also, but rents would be somewhat nearer in line after them. All costs were increasing, especially interest charges.

The circumstances of the tenants proved to be as varied as the policies of their landlords. About one in four were found to have insufficient means to pay standard rents. Another one in four had incomes well over the national average. Moreover, tenants in privately-owned houses were significantly less well off than the tenants of the local authorities. Local authority rent-rebate schemes had gone some way to meeting the needs of the poorest, but this was only part of a proper solution.

The PIB attached importance to the uniformity of standard rents and a uniform increase, on the grounds that "an increase in rents in one place may give rise to a claim for increased earnings which is then copied elsewhere without any prompting rent increases". Rents could also be too low, in that they induced an "unrealistic" demand, the outcome of which was long waiting-lists. Low rents would also inflate the demand for other goods and services.

Some rents were far below replacement cost, some about equal to them. Local authorities should all make "strenuous attempts" to contain costs, since management costs showed the same wide discrepancies as other costs. When costs had been reduced to a reasonable level, rents could be related to them, either to historic cost (as some authorities did) or to replacement cost (as few of them did). The PIB chose to recommend replacement cost in spite of the steep increases in rents in many places as a result. As standards were continually rising, as well as cost, historic-cost rents would not take into account the increasing expensiveness of replacement. But the increases should be mitigated by moving in steps of not more than 7s 6d a week. Within the limits of the reference the PIB's passion for the efficient allocation of resources was well to the fore.

The PIB succeeded in modifying price increases in nationalised industries to only a minor degree. In capital-intensive, expanding industries (gas, electricity, telecommunications) this was due to the inflexibility of the financial obligations. In others (coal, road and rail transport), it was due to the inevitable swelling of costs in labour-intensive, contracting industries. Standards of management were reviewed more thoroughly than in the private sector; but most of the reviews revealed no weaknesses peculiar to the public sector, nor evidence of slackness. Perhaps the most outstanding (and surely culpable) general weakness was a failure to apply what are supposed to be accepted principles of pricing and price structure. But this was at least as much the fault of Government Departments' policies as of nationalised industries' management.

Reports

No. 7   Electricity and gas tariffs (Cmnd 2862)

No. 12   Coal prices (Cmnd 2919)

No. 59   Bulk supply tariff of the CEGB (Cmnd 3575)

No. 57   Gas prices (Cmnd 3567)

No. 56   Proposals by London Transport Board for fare increases in the London area (Cmnd 3561)

No. 112   Proposals by London Transport Board for fare increases in the London area (Cmnd 4036)

No. 159   LTB fares (Cmnd 4540)

No. 72   Proposed increases by BR in certain country-wide fares and charges (Cmnd 3656)

No. 137   Proposed increases by BR in certain country-wide fares and charges in the London commuter area (Cmnd 4250)

No. 102   Gas prices (Cmnd 3924)

No. 155   Costs and efficiency in the gas industry (Cmnd 4458)

No. 58   Post Office charges (Cmnd 3574)

No. 121   Post Office charges, inland parcel post and remittance services (Cmnd 4115)

No. 111   Steel prices (Cmnd 4033)

No. 124   Coal prices (Cmnd 4149)

No. 138   Coal prices (Cmnd 4255)

No. 153   Coal prices (Cmnd 4455)

No. 162   Costs, charges and productivity in the National Freight Corporation (Cmnd 4569)

No. 62   Increases in rents of local authority housing (Cmnd 3604)

Part 3

Incomes

9

First principles: A norm for pay

The first incomes case referred to the PIB was a wage agreement recently made in the printing industry (No. 2). All incomes cases were to some extent *sui generis*, especially in the eyes of the parties. But printing was well chosen to establish some of the ground-rules of incomes policy. Though the referred agreement left out workers in national newspapers, the highest-paid in the industry, it still covered workers known to be among the highest-paid in the country. Printing was also notorious for enduring restrictive practices; an industry where technological development made traditional distinctions between craft and non-craft workers and between one craft and another increasingly anachronistic. Moreover, it was sufficiently distinct from other industries for the connection between wages and prices to be direct and obvious.

The agreement had been negotiated by the federation of printing unions (the Printing and Kindred Trades Federation) and two employers' associations (the British Federation of Master Printers and the Newspaper Society). The unions' claim was decided in January 1965, communicated to the employers late in February, and the settlement reached on 17 May 1965. All the negotiations therefore took place after the general lines of the prices and incomes policy had been agreed, and after the first prices and incomes policy White Paper was published. Both the unions and the employers considered that the settlement conformed to the policy. A previous agreement had secured four increases in pay from September 1962 to January 1965. A third week's holiday with pay also came into effect in 1965, though the extra cost was supposed to be offset by changes of working practice. The 1965 agreement came into effect immediately. If the last payment under the 1962 agreement, and the first under the new one were added together, there was no doubt that the increase would be in excess of the norm. However, the unions and the employers claimed that settlements made prior to the policy, whenever they were effective, should not be taken into account and the PIB accepted their argument. In justice it felt it could do no other. But it was obvious that, in consequence, the totality of decisions made in respect of individual cases would come to something more than the $3\frac{1}{2}$ per cent which prudent economic management required, even if all parties to future settlements adhered to the policy.

The next point to emerge was that the norm was an annual rate of increase, as it obviously must be for economic management purposes. But negotiated wage increases did not occur regularly each year. Nevertheless the percentage increases were expressed as increases above the previous level, regardless of how long the new one was intended to last. In the printers' case, a $3\frac{1}{2}$ per cent increase in basic rates had been made in May 1965, and another $3\frac{1}{2}$ per cent would follow in January 1966. This gave an *annual* rate of $3\frac{1}{2}$ per cent only if each calendar year was regarded as a separate period, ignoring the date from which new settlements applied. This was obviously an interpretation that would make nonsense of economic management if it were generalised.

There was a wide gap between wage rates, the subject of the settlement referred, and wage earnings, the subject of the incomes policy. There were no figures of actual earnings, and the PIB was not yet in a position to collect its own. But earnings were clearly well in excess of basic rates, and increasing faster. Pay increases could only be within the norm on the assumption that house (company) bargains about merit rates, house rates, and incentive bonuses (so-called), would not follow after the national negotiations, as they had done for so long before, and ignoring increased overtime rates automatically following from increased basic rates. The White Paper referred clearly to earnings: the PIB must judge the settlement in terms of its probable effect on earnings, taking history into account, as well as the narrow content of the agreement.

There had never been any real doubt of the intent of the policy. It could refer to nothing but take-home pay. But it had not been clearly understood by some, if not all, trade-union leaders. A $3-3\frac{1}{2}$ per cent annual increase in basic rates, with take-home pay remaining in the same relation to basic rates as in the recent past, would be no great change. It was a prospect that most could cheerfully accept, especially when there were the various exceptions to add, notably for the low-paid and scarce workers (most at all levels being both in their own eyes). But an overall annual increase of $3-3\frac{1}{2}$ per cent after taking into account everything but equivalent extra work, implied a much more drastic change. On the face of it, the PIB's judgment of the printers was surprisingly mild. To the unions, including some of the printing unions, it was something of a shock.

A more serious complication was the cost-of-living bonuses. For 15 years there had been a flat-rate addition to wages as a separate payment, not counted in the basic wage rate used for the purpose of calculating overtime, shift or other extra rates, which increased automatically with increases in the Index of Retail Prices, the bonus being revised annually since 1962. From time to time part of the bonus was consolidated, by adding it on to the basic rate, so that extra rates were calculated as a proportion of a higher base. The bonus was to increase twice yearly in larger steps from January 1966, when there would be a further consolidation. Even if any further increase in the Retail Price Index was left out of account, the new basic rate plus cost-of-living bonus would rise by four per cent for the craftsmen and $4\frac{1}{2}$ per cent for the lower-paid workers. But the index was obviously going to rise, and a modest rise would yield five or six per cent instead.

That there should continue to be cost-of-living bonuses at all was considered to be inconsistent with a policy whose purpose was to stabilise the cost-of-living. The PIB observed that the cost-of-living had been rising for 20 years because earnings increased faster than productivity. Some further rise was to be expected; but if earnings were related to the rising cost-of-living, no stabilisation of prices could be achieved. Cost-of-living bonuses should be eliminated, by consolidating them with basic rates. After the printers, there were no further cases involving cost-of-living supplements until the pottery workers in 1970 (No. 149). But by then the PIB was recommending not just consolidation but moving to a new pay structure, based on job evaluation, in which cost-of-living bonuses would have no relevance.

The PIB did not conclude, however, that the printers' settlement was entirely beyond the terms of the policy. This was its first pay report, a settlement had already been reached by the two sides, and the first payments under the new agreement had already been made. The increases could manifestly not be justified on the grounds that printing workers were exceptionally low-paid, or exceptionally scarce. But the extra payments could be justified retrospectively by "a major change in working practices making a direct contribution towards increasing productivity".

The PIB's own enquiries suggested that improvements in output per man-hour might reach 10 to 25 per cent, without more capital. What the PIB in effect recommended was that, having negotiated the agreement, the parties should see to it that it turned out to be within the terms of the policy, by increasing productivity.

Another conclusion, having wide general implication, was that conditions of work should be taken into account, as well as rates of pay, as the incomes policy clearly intended. In particular, the effect of extra holidays or changes in minimum or notional hours of work during a standard week, as well as any changes in actual hours worked, must be included in the calculations. A reduction of one hour in the standard working week from 41 hours to 40 hours (when 41 hours or more were actually being worked) with no change in hours worked, was equivalent to an increase of nearly $1\frac{1}{4}$ per cent, with overtime rates at time-and-a-half. An increase in paid holidays from 17 working days to 19 working days was an increase of nearly one per cent. Neither of these changes looked anything but minor matters, and both were common constituents of wage settlements whose major provisions were increases in rates or earnings. But these two "minor" improvements together amounted to more than half the norm, even in the comparatively lush days of a 3½ per cent norm.

Finally, the PIB concerned itself, as it continued to do, with changes in institutional arrangements to allow and encourage the changes in working practices to take place. The outstanding characteristic of union organisation in printing was the degree of central control exercised by the unions. The industry had recently formed a Joint Manpower Committee to consider relaxation of the rules about apprentices. The PIB recommended that this Committee should take on a much wider function. It should first provide both sides (especially the unions) with "full and objective" information about the industry, earnings, labour and capital productivity, and profits. Secondly, it should concern itself with manning and pay on new machines. An independent Chairman, with the necessary staff, would give it more authority and more impetus. New house arrangements, following on and in addition to the national settlement, should be registered with this body, so that there could be a clear relationship between national and local settlements.

Apart from its impact on printing, the general result of the PIB's first wages case was to establish that incomes policy was going to relate to pay, in its normal sense, and not to some heavily-qualified national or basic rate. It had also given an explanation to a wider public of what the norm was to mean.

The point soon receded in importance. With either a standstill or a norm of nil at least the arithmetic was less confusing. But by the time journalists' pay was investigated in 1969 (No. 115), there was a ceiling of 3½ per cent. It was still no more straightforward to establish the right figure of actual increases to compare with the rules. The referred settlement established minimum rates for the first time. About one in three journalists were directly affected by it; and the salary bill would increase by just over three per cent, clearly within the ceiling. But newspapers intended to pay other journalists varying sums to maintain differentials. Taking these into account, the salary bill would rise by nine per cent. Moreover, a second stage would increase salaries by another 1½ per cent in a year's time, consequential increases bringing the salary bill up another five per cent. This later case showed that the relevant standard to the PIB was the total pay bill, the measure having the closest relationship to national economic policy, though the percentage increases in either negotiated rates or individual pay could be something quite different. The journalists' agreement, unlike the printers, was found to be unacceptable.

All the early pay cases concerned wages; and it was rare for wage-structures to include regular increments, pay reviews or other built-in "career prospects". Many salary structures did include increments, often by annual progression up a scale, sometimes depending on merit. But there was nothing in the first White Paper about increments. The only general principle was that incomes should be confined to the norm, and that the policy was supposed to have regard to social need and justice. Annual increments could absorb all or more than the norm for individual salary-earners. If increments were to be included (like holiday pay and shorter standard hours) increases in salary scales would have to be justified in relation to the exceptions and nothing else.

The issue did not arise until late in 1965, when the pay of the armed forces (No. 10) and of higher civil servants (No. 11) were both referred. Armed forces pay was decided at triennial reviews, and certain of the referred civil-service grades (mainly assistant secretaries) were on incremental scales. The PIB decided in relation to pay of the armed forces that the pay reviews were a commitment and part of the remuneration bargain. Until a new bargain were made, the old one should stand—norm or no.

In relation to civil servants, no mention of increments was made at all. The norm was applied to the scale. The PIB rule was that the salary bill (or, later, the wage bill) should be confined to the norm, the bill to which the rule was applied depending on the limits of the case referred. Hence the actual rate of pay increases accruing to individuals was no particular concern of incomes policy, so long as their pay was determined according to the rules. This was an interpretation made explicit by the Government in July 1966, when annual increments were specifically excluded from the standstill. This was quite consistent with economic management requirements: it was applying the norm to the income flow. It was less clearly consistent with "social need and justice". Increments were after all increases of cash paid out, whereas increased holidays involved no increase of cash, but usually less work for the same pay. Also in spite of increasing overlap, those on incremental salary scales were better-off than those on uniform wages. To have included increments as part of the norm would have involved a far more radical restructuring of incomes, and would no doubt have met great opposition. But the essential injustice between one individual and another contributed to the later breakdown of popular support for the policy.

The relation of pay to basic rates and standard hours was the crucial issue in another early case, that of plant bakery workers (Nos. 9 and 17). The basic working week had already been reduced from 42 to 40 hours in May 1965; but hours actually worked were over 50 on average, and one-tenth of the workers put in 60 hours or more. Weekly earnings had, in consequence, increased by about seven per cent. There had been no reduction in the labour-force, and no increase in output, which was limited by steadily falling demand. In August 1965 (immediately before the publication of the PIB's report on bread prices, No. 3, see p. 55, the Bakers' Union put in a claim for an increase in basic rates to give a minimum wage of £15 a week for a five-day week of 40 hours. The May increase in pay had been well in excess of the norm, without compensating increases in productivity, as the PIB had pointed out in connection with bread prices. Having refused the full increase in price the industry wanted, it now had to review an additional claim, pressing more strongly on costs. The union's claim was for an increase from 5s 9d an hour to 7s 6d an hour. Assuming that 50 hours a week continued to be worked, this was equivalent to an increase of about 18 per cent, with a wide range depending on hours worked, and the pattern of work over the week. Before the case was referred to the PIB, after one strike and with the threat of a second, the union had offered to settle for an "interim" increase of £1 a week, equivalent to $5\frac{1}{4}$ per cent on earnings.

Bakery workers' basic hourly rates were low (though not remarkably so; basic hourly rates in engineering were still only £9 7s 4d. The rail-waymen's case was being investigated by the PIB at the same time; their lowest basic rate was barely £10. On the other hand actual earnings, at about £19 10s a week average, were not low. The PIB's view was that low pay was low pay per week, and not per hour. The whole case thus turned on whether an increase could be justified in compensation for reduced hours of work to produce the same output.

The room for manoeuvre was very small, given the industry's structure. Four national groups fought to maintain or increase their share of the shrinking market. Low returns on capital and competition among the few had squeezed out many inefficent plants and made excess capacity too expensive a luxury to be very widespread, and there was not much flexibility in working the plant. Numbers and grades of workers were more or less fixed in relation to each production line; many plants had only one production line and few then had more than two. With a perishable product, the industry was effectively locked in to a 100-hour week (against 168 hours in three shifts, seven-days a week) by the pattern of demand: a quarter of the weekly total had to be produced on Friday (for sale on Friday or Saturday), with the other three-quarters spread over Sunday to Thursday.

The market restriction naturally increased the industry's unit costs. But agreement on wages and hours between union and employers increased them further by imposing other limits on daily hours of work. The standard basic five-day week could be worked in only four ways: in five days of eight hours; or in four days of $8\frac{1}{2}$ hours and one of six hours; or in four days of nine hours and one of four hours; or in two days of nine hours, two days of eight hours and one of six hours. Overtime became payable each *day* after basic hours had been worked, regardless of whether basic hours were worked on any other day or not. Managers could not reduce costs by matching output to agreed basic hours because of market requirements, nor could they match basic hours to the pattern of demand, because none of the four weekly cycles matched it.

An agreement of this kind was of the utmost importance to the union, since it kept take-home pay well in excess of basic pay, in spite of the pressures on the managements to cut unit costs to improve their returns. With low basic rates (and even lower fall-back pay) in a declining industry in the process of further concentration, such a defensive policy was neither surprising nor reprehensible. But equally, the interests of employers and employees could be advanced together by a new bargain, allowing better matching of hours and output, with consequent reduction in overtime. Some overtime pay would then be available to raise basic pay a bit nearer take-home pay, at the same time reducing the long hours needed to earn it. The solution was the more viable, in that union leaders firmly and repeatedly expressed the view that their members were really interested in cutting long hours, rather than finding another pretext for raising take-home pay.

Hence the PIB recommended an interim settlement to provide for more flexible shift working, this being a "substantial change in working practice" on the part of bakery workers. Plant managers should aim at an average cut of two hours a week. Pay could be increased by 15s a week the earnings for two hours, without increasing labour costs or prices. The extra 15s a week should be a special supplement, not part of basic rates, so that it was not part of the base for calculating overtime, and did not increase the incentive to preserve it.

This would allow a reasonable pay increase without prices increasing further; but the old parallel climb of wages and prices would be resumed unless the labour-force could be better used. Thus the final report (No.17) was largely a management consultancy exercise to demonstrate the possibilities. The problem was to find ways of improving labour use even in the best, and of improving matters in the mediocre, without new investment, and without supposing that all managements could overnight reach some uniform standard of best performance. A more detailed survey still was done into production, hours and patterns of work, partly by questionnaire and partly by a number of case studies on the spot. All of this together amounted to a more comprehensive and far more thorough account of the industry than had been done before.

As might be expected, the results of detailed surveys of production methods showed that there were no obvious or universal remedies. But there was an accumulation of small changes, to give more effective labour use, which together could improve matters radically. The PIB's summary of its detailed recommendations was that changes should be made, and these changes would justify allowances being paid to cover: greater variation in lengths of shifts, the adjustment of starting times, rotating rest days on different days of the week (including Sundays), and amalgamation of grades to make transfer between jobs easier. A five-day, 40-hour week had little real relevance to actual working in the industry; yet the unions based their demands on this as it seemed the only way of getting a reasonable income. Agreements needed to be based on what actually went on. Production workers should be paid a guaranteed minimum wage "bearing a closer relationship to the minimum hours they are likely to be called up on to work". The minimum working week should therefore be 46 hours instead of 40 (still well short of average hours actually worked in the industry, but closer to a six-day working week). Basic pay could then be raised by nearly £3 a week (with the important consequence that fall-back pay would be considerably increased).

The effect would be to give an immediate pay increase to all workers working less than 46 hours. Those working more than 46 hours would get little more immediately, though all would get greater stability in earnings from week to week, and shorter actual hours of work. Wage bargaining on new lines would open further possiblities of improvement in pay and productivity.

The most important general conclusion drawn by the PIB in the bakery wages reports was that a 40-hour, five-day week was not necessarily an object in the best interests of workers, In the case of the bakers it had worked out to be restrictive and depressing to the bakery workers' conditions. Realistic standards of working would more easily lead to realistic standards of pay and greater security—and to the prospect of better pay, consistent with the national interest.

The PIB investigated plant baking four years later, and found that its early view of the industry was still largely justified (No. 151). Hours worked had gone up to 54 a week, still spread over six days for most workers. The pay agreement after report No. 9 had incorporated the amendments suggested by the PIB, and both workers and employers seemed to have profited by the change. But developments in the industry only emphasised the problem of overtime. Long hours were necessary because labour turnover was high and labour scarce, but turnover was high also partly because of the long hours. The industry was locked in to a new inflexibility. But recruitment and training were expensive, probably much more so than managements imagined. Cutting them down might finance better pay, and hence a more stable labour-force, working fewer hours.

The general attitude to take to overtime working was a question which continued to nag the PIB until almost the end of its life. In its first case (road haulage, see p. 53), it dealt with an industry where overtime hours were not even always worked, but often paper hours for making pay up to an acceptable level (a practice not unknown in printing). Overtime in such circumstances could clearly be condemned as inconsistent with the policy, since it prevented any control by management or labour over the relation between pay and performance, and hence over unit labour costs. Neither productivity nor price stability could be promoted this way. But there were equally clearly cases where universal disapproval of overtime working would undermine productivity, or service to the customer. Railways were a case in point and hospitals another. Plant bakeries were similar, in that some overtime working was a more efficient way of meeting uneven demand between different days of the week, than employing a larger labour-force. It could even be more efficient to go on working overtime in a large brick-works, at a time when demand had fallen well below capacity, to avoid the costs incurred in disrupting work schedules and losing experienced workers who would not stay in an arduous job for basic rates only.

Yet, difficult though it might be to formulate any general principles on the subject, the PIB's accumulated experience of pay problems only emphasised its importance. Opportunities to work overtime were the main means by which time-workers' pay could be kept up with piece-workers, in engineering, civil engineering and many smaller industries. They were the most important protection against inordinately low pay for some workers in the public sector on very low standard rates. They could be a way of making up the pay of workers in small firms to that of workers in large firms better able to organise incentive schemes, as in building. Nevertheless, overtime working could obviously involve wasteful use of capital and inefficient management control, and most productivity agreements had had reduction of overtime as one of their major aims. Eventually (but not until the spring of 1969) the "length and pattern of the working week" was referred to the PIB, in particular overtime and shiftwork and their effects in earnings, costs and productivity. There resulted, in the last months of the PIB's existence, the fattest, most close-packed of its reports (No. 161).

There were no conclusions, in the sense of specific recommendations, nor of universal principles. Rather there were a number of propositions of general relevance to pay, costs and productivity. One of the most outstanding factual results was that male manual workers mostly worked regular overtime, women workers seldom; and this was a major reason for the wideness of the gap between men's and women's pay. Shiftwork, sometimes involving overtime, was increasing rapidly (up to about one-fifth of manual workers in 1970), and was an important means of raising incomes. Where overtime did not exist, "moonlighting" (a second paid job) was widely used to raise pay.

Though overtime and shiftwork could be to the advantage of employers, the PIB's view was still that high overtime working was usually a warning that inefficient working existed. The level of management at which overtime working was decided varied very widely, and the adequacy of the data available to make rational decisions was as varied, as well as its use where it was available. Management decisions about hours or patterns of work were "largely based on intuition" rather than proper calculations, in spite of the major effects of those decisions on costs and profits. Trying to remedy low standard pay by a sharp increase in basic rates without changing methods of work, would merely increase the incentive to work overtime, without reducing the need to work it. Costs would rise even faster than before and prices with them.

Useful action to control the increasing overtime worked would depend on the way in which pay was negotiated. In industries where negotiations were highly centralised, and supplements to nationally agreed rates small or infrequent, hours might be controlled and reduced through national agreements. Where company supplements and production bonuses were important, hours would have to be determined by company (or plant) arrangements. In any case, there was room for more experiments in patterns of work.

The PIB also surveyed the workers' preferences, and found that most would prefer longer holidays to shorter weekly hours. Within weekly patterns of work, four days of ten hours might be preferable to five eight-hour days for both workers and managements; but a simple re-peating cycle of shifts was not necessarily the most preferred pattern for workers, nor the best for management. Where changes were contem-plated, there should be early discussion with workers before changes were made. The lack of statutory control on hours in the UK (in contrast to other countries) meant an absence of external pressure on manage-ments to use their labour effectively. It allowed much greater freedom of choice to workers and employers; but it also left much greater re-sponsibility on management to see that the result was something other than the joint endurance of long hours and low performance. But there were few conclusions, few principles and fewer prescriptions for reform that would fit most situations in most industries. The PIB's case-by-case approach turned out to be a peculiarly apt one, to investigate the diversity of needs, circumstances and institutions by which pay, as well as prices, was determined.

Reports

No.   2   Wages, costs and prices in the printing industry (Cmnd 2750)

No. 115   Journalists' pay (Cmnd 4077)

No. 10   Armed forces pay (Cmnd 2881)

No. 11   Pay of the higher civil service (Cmnd 2882)

No.   9   Wages in the bakery industry (1st report) (Cmnd 2878)

No. 17   Wages in the bakery industry (Final report) (Cmnd 3019)

No. 151   Bread prices and pay in the baking industry (Cmnd 4428)

No. 161   Hours of work, overtime and shiftworking (Cmnd 4554)

10

Pay and Productivity

Pay and productivity was the central theme of the PIB's first report—even though it was prices, and not incomes that had been referred. Having investigated road-haulage rates, one of the main conclusions was that obstacles to increased productivity needed removing, by means of pay agreements which would finance increased wages out of higher productivity. This was the kernel of the PIB's pronouncements on prices and incomes policy. All the early wage cases were building up background and general principles that changed and developed little in its six years. The first case to show emphasis on productivity, almost to the exclusion of other considerations, was one that was politically crucial as well, the railwaymen.

The PIB had railwaymen's pay (No. 8) referred to it while it was considering bakers' wages. The railwaymen's problems were in many ways similar to those of the bakers. Basic pay was low, hours of work long, and the industry declining. But the problems were the more acute since it was a public service, and there were restrictions of long standing on labour use. All the issues then important in incomes policy, notably the principle of comparability, and the indentification of the low-paid were raised. Comparability had to be considered because it was the explicit principle on which pay was then decided, and low pay because in union eyes—and probably many more—the railwaymen were notoriously low-paid (see also p. 173).

The PIB then turned to the central issue, what "in the light of the financial plight of the railways" could be done to improve efficiency and enlarge the scope for increased earnings?

The history of pay negotiations for the railwaymen had been unhappy. A generation before, they had been among the most privileged of workers, not so much for their pay, as for the security with which they enjoyed it. Now the railwaymen's security had disappeared with the inexorable running down of railway transport, while many workers were vastly improving theirs. The unions' bargaining strength was also further weakened by the weakness of the railways' finances, at a time when railway deficits had become a political issue. This uneasy situation had been materially changed in 1958, and from the unions' point of view somewhat improved. An independent committee of enquiry produced the so-called Guillebaud Report, which promulgated a more objective formula for deciding pay in relation to pay elsewhere (see also p. 191 below). As a result strikes and threats of strike had disappeared until late 1965. But industrial relations nevertheless were far from good. As the PIB found it: "the management felt that the unions were endeavouring to obtain rates which they held to be comparable with those elsewhere without sufficient regard to the railways' inability to pay."

Railwaymen had kept pace with industrial earnings generally for the five years to 1965. The latest negotiations over increased rates and shorter hours had broken down, after the unions had rejected an offer from the management which would have given increases of $6\frac{1}{2}$ to $7\frac{1}{2}$ per cent. The claim, and the employers' offer was, on the face of it, in excess of the norm. It, and any improvement, would have to be justified by exceptional circumstances. The PIB turned again to productivity, which could clearly be improved by the removal of a variety of restrictions. A new approach was needed, based on the joint interest of management and unions in the efficiency of the railways and thence higher pay for the railwaymen. The onus must be on management to negotiate the change. But it also required an "appropriate structure for negotiation and consultation" and the application of broad principles governing the sharing of gains from improvements in productivity. Productivity objectives were specified in the report; but they were not intended to be a list of restrictive practices to be removed. They were generally directed towards the more flexible use of manpower and reduced overtime working. In some cases the number of men required for particular jobs could be reduced; in others, men could do a wider range of jobs.

A new approach to bargaining should be on the same lines as in road haulage and printing, namely that pay and productivity must be discussed, negotiated and settled together. Pay and Productivity Councils ought to be set up, at which management and unions could discuss and negotiate pay and productivity, not only at national level, but at every lower level also. The Councils should begin immediately on a programme for negotiating productivity-linked pay increases for the following year, the size of the increases depending on the savings made. But the savings were neither to be pre-empted entirely by the workers, nor to be the subject of a battle between management and the workers directly involved. The interests of workers not directly involved, and of taxpayers and consumers must also be considered. The taxpayers' share was the reduction in cost, and hence in the deficit that had to be financed. The consumers' share was an improvement in the service offered, or a relatively lower price.

The extra payments should take the form of separate productivity increments for the same reason as in the bakers' case, so that overtime working should not become more attractive, as a consequence of increased basic rates. The increments would not be uniform, any more than the scope for reducing the working week was uniform. There would consequently be new problems of the relationship in pay between one grade and another, problems for the Councils to solve at a later stage. By this means railway pay could be increased; but meanwhile, nothing more than the rejected offer was due.

Railway workshops had been added to the case soon after the reference, when they too failed to reach agreement with the British Railways Board (BRB). Most pay there consisted of piece rates, on similar lines to the engineering industry. However, increases in the rates followed increases in the rates paid to other railwaymen, rather than to engineering workers. They had no special claim to an exceptional increase as they had kept up with both the railwaymen and engineering workers. Work study, and incentive schemes based on them had been introduced into some shops, as the unions had agreed nationally, but some local committees had not accepted it. There was scope for increasing earnings in the workshops if the workers accepted work measurement as a basis for reforming pay.

The railway clerks, in contrast to their colleagues, had a case for some immediate general pay increase, as their pay had fallen out of line with clerks elsewhere. But neither clerical nor supervisory work should be excluded from the efforts to make better use of labour. Productivity payments to the manual workers might leave the clerks with a sense of grievance. Yet organisation and method studies did not seem to have been applied, to see whether similar increases could be negotiated for them. Further mechanisation or greater flexibility of work might help management to contain costs and at the same time provide clerical earnings comparable with the manual workers' pay.

Finally, a firm date (October 1966, only eight months away) was set by the PIB for the preparation of a comprehensive programme, including the new negotiating procedure for manual workers, the introduction of work study schemes in railway workshops, and an examination of the possibilities for improved clerical work.

The railways' case was the most important of the early ones, in establishing the primary importance of linking pay increases to productivity. It opened the way to a radical change in pay negotiations, especially in the public sector, putting an end to wage increases on the old pattern. Increases of pay were to be related neither to pay increases in comparable occupations, nor to increases in retail prices.

The railwaymen were bitterly disappointed with the PIB's conclusions, mainly because so little in the way of immediate pay increases was forthcoming, and this little consisted of the management's already rejected offer. A national strike was called, as had widely been expected. Eventually, the Government had to negotiate directly with the unions, and finally the Prime Minister himself became the chief conciliator. As a result of meetings at 10 Downing Street, the recommended pay increases were paid and the standard week was reduced to 40 hours one month earlier than recommended. The strike was called off at the last minute. The concessions raised an outcry that the incomes policy had been fatally weakened, because the PIB's interpretation of the railwaymen's case had not been entirely defended by the Government. But this was to overlook a change of direction, while worrying about the precise speed at which the matter was to develop. What was to be paid out in the coming year 1966 was somewhat increased in total. But the principle of linking pay and productivity on the railways, instead of pay on the railways to pay elsewhere regardless of productivity on the railways, was established and defended without modification. The PIB had put into the Government's hands, and through it into the BRB's hands, the arguments for the change of direction towards pay and productivity, and specific proposals showing how it ought to be done. To keep the principle intact, at the temporary expense of what was after all a minor concession, was the more important issue. It opened the way for the railways' management to start a series of notably successful pay and productivity deals in the following two to three years. Without these it is difficult to see how railway workers could have achieved fair pay for the work (and hours) they did, especially as the railway network was still being run down. As other workers were pushing up their earnings by productivity deals, the railwaymen would have been left to chase increasingly volatile pacemakers and the management would probably have faced increasing unrest.

The situation of the busmen was very like that of the railwaymen. A seven-day service, with long hours, had to be provided in a declining industry with very low basic rates. The workers were disgruntled, and well organised for channelling their discontent. The *Pay and conditions of busmen* (No. 16) was another case which turned on major changes of working practice as a means and justification for pay increases, in spite of other criteria being obviously relevant to some degree.

Pay was mostly settled by two collective agreements and a series of local ones. Municipal bus undertakings negotiated with the two unions in the National Joint Industrial Council; and bus companies (dominated by two large employers, the Transport Holding Company and British Electric Traction) negotiated with six unions in the National Council for the Omnibus Industry. But though these two agreements covered a large majority of bus workers, both negotiations followed settlements in London between the London Transport Board (LTB) and the TGWU. The immediate cause of the reference was a proposal by the LTB to increase pay by six per cent. A committee of enquiry in 1963 into the pay and conditions of busmen in London (the Phelps Brown Committee), had recommended increased basic rates, and further increases in earnings associated with productivity improvements in specified ways. There had subsequently been three further pay negotiations, based on the Phelps Brown recommendations, of which the PIB's case was the third. But the repeated negotiations had turned the Phelps Brown suggestions into a rigid formula, even though the Phelps Brown report itself deprecated any system involving an automatic link with what happened elsewhere.

The LTB defended its offer solely on the grounds of shortage of labour. But the PIB rejected this argument out of hand. There was no evidence that the relatively large increases paid as a result of the Phelps Brown report had mitigated the shortage of labour; and the White Paper required that any such increase should be "necessary and effective" to redistribute manpower. The remedy for a shortage of labour was to make better use of the existing labour-force. The PIB therefore considered the claims in the light of the scope for improving productivity, an approach in any case in the best interest of the employers, since exceptional pay increases justified by better labour use would also protect them against losses of manpower.

Better use could be made of busmen's time with existing methods and equipment by altering union-imposed rules on breaks between journeys, limits on spreadover duties, speed of vehicles and demarcation between drivers and conductors. Further services could be manned more economically by one-man operation, which showed cost reductions of 15 to 20 per cent below the usual two-man crew. Since staff costs were 70 per cent of the total, agreement on one-man operation was vital to the prosperity of the industry, and the potential savings high enough to provide rising earnings and more stable fares.

A start had already been made in linking pay and productivity; and the workers considered they had secured annual pay reviews, according to the Phelps Brown formula, in return for agreeing to productivity improvements. The PIB concluded therefore that to prevent the employers settling on this occasion "would be to go back on a tacit understanding", and therefore bring into question the improvements already agreed to. The existing agreement did not meet the PIB's requirements; but there was a link, and a moral commitment to it. Hence, in spite of its excess over the norm, the settlement should be allowed.

But this conclusion did not in itself offer anything to the municipal or company busmen outside London. As the previous negotiating arrangements were clearly undesirable, whereby the pay of 190,000 workers in the provinces automatically followed negotiations for only 44,000 in London (where bus operation was uniquely difficult), the PIB had to consider whether all the negotiating bodies should be merged into one. However, it recommended against this on the grounds that pay and working practices ought to be negotiated together; and since operating conditions and existing practices differed radically between one sector and another, each should continue to negotiate separately.

These conclusions settled the matter only temporarily. A year later, further claims were put in by the TGWU to both municipal and company employers. The Government urged employers to respect the incomes-policy rules for standstill and severe restraint. Many undertakings were in any case manifestly unable to finance extra costs. In face of increasing union militancy, collective bargaining broke down altogether in the municipal sector, and a few large undertakings then reached separate productivity agreements. Some of these were referred to the PIB in July 1967 (No. 50).

The TGWU had meanwhile produced a Busmen's Charter, comprising four main principles: a larger share in cost savings for the staff; longer holidays; compulsory trade-union membership for all employees; and a minimum basic rate of £15 a week. The Charter was clearly in conflict with the PIB's recommendations. In justification, unions and employers referred to the difference in pay between the provinces and London, and comparison with earnings in other occupations.

The general policy context was still less helpful than before, as sterling had been devalued before the report was ready. The policy White Paper covering the period after severe restraint gave no general norm. Developments in the industry were also the reverse of helpful. More municipal undertakings were going into deficit; and the LTB was being subsidised. Companies were better off, but returns on capital were "modest".

The PIB again reviewed the benefits that might be expected from one-man operation. This time, it appeared that the prospects of profitable one-man operation varied widely from place to place. Little difficulty faced companies operating rural routes: but for inter-urban and urban services the problems were still formidable.

The busmen's claim was to raise the provincial basic rates to the London level. Basic rates were considerably higher in London than in the provinces, but there was scarcely any difference in earnings, because of longer hours of work in the provinces. London busmen's pay compared well with industry in London; but in the provinces, hourly pay was considerably lower, though weekly earnings compared well with other workers.

The claim, in the form in which it was made, could not possibly be reconciled with the rules of incomes policy. But increases commensurate with the claim could be justified by productivity negotiations to change limits on methods or hours of work.

The PIB stressed more strongly than before that the most effective remedy for an undertaking suffering from labour shortage was to make better use of the labour it already had. The London case was the most straightforward, as negotiations had already started. Once more, it recommended that productivity payments should take the form of special bonuses, not forming part of the basic rate. In the provinces, productivity bargaining had still to be started; and employers were advised to work out a suitable national framework, within which local productivity agreements could be negotiated. The PIB recommended a bonus of 10s a week for all platform staff agreeing to one-man operation as it represented a major change of working practice affecting the whole industry.

But before the PIB had reported, the municipal sector had begun national negotiations again, and had agreed an extra £1 a week without conditions, a rise of $7\frac{1}{2}$ per cent. The Government invoked the Prices and Incomes Act to prevent payment for the statutory three months, while the case was referred once more to the PIB as required by the Act (No. 63).

The case now made was that the municipal busmen were low-paid, that there were "crucial staff shortages" operating against the national interest, and that the differential between London and the provinces was too large, in spite of the PIB having twice by now refused to regard this difference as significant. The agreement clearly did not involve productivity conditions; so the $7\frac{1}{2}$ per cent increase would not be offset by more effective use of manpower. There was no provision for talks on productivity, though the unions said that local productivity discussions would follow it. At best, it constituted a promise to talk productivity, which did not satisfy the criteria for an increase.

A PIB survey showed that there was indeed a shortage of labour, and that the shortage had grown worse between 1967 and 1968. But this covered a period of industrial unrest which both discouraged recruitment and lost established staff. Relative peace after January 1968 soon resulted in better recruitment. If one-man operation increased significantly, and other productivity improvements were negotiated, extra pay could be offered to reduce wastage and attract recruits. No more evidence was found of low pay or that busmen were seriously out of line. The £1 could only be justified by changes in working practices, half of which had already been recommended in return for agreement in principle to one-man operation. Considerably more could come from further local productivity bargaining. The DEP should now set up a working party to draft the code and get on with the job.

The busmen's case was still not over. A number of local authorities had made agreements in November and December 1967 while national negotiations were in abeyance. These were notified to the DEP under the early-warning procedure, and referred to the PIB. There followed five more reports (Nos. 69, 78, 85, 95, 96) dealing with seven such agreements. For the first two, Liverpool and Glasgow, the PIB gave a qualified approval, as pay was "seriously out of line" with that of other provincial cities of similar size. But it regretted that a framework of nationally agreed tiers of rates relating to the "effort and strain" involved in city conditions did not exist. For all the rest, the PIB could only report that the agreements were not in accordance with the terms of the prices and incomes policy, though there was scope in all cases for agreements that did.

The £1 a week increase in the basic rates agreed by municipal employers had applied to garage workers as well, and had been subjected to the twelve-month standstill order. Craftsmen had also had an increase of £1 a week in the summer of 1967 under a separate agreement, but this was not stopped. In June 1968, maintenance workers in company garages had reached agreement on an increase of 25s 1d for skilled workers and 15s a week for semi-skilled and unskilled, increases of 8½ and six per cent respectively—well over the ceiling increase of 3½ per cent. In September 1968, the workers in municipal garages lodged a new claim, and pay and productivity among maintenance workers in garages was therefore referred to the PIB (No. 99).

Enquiries into maintenance operations also showed ample scope for proper productivity agreements. A national framework agreement was needed, accepting work study, shorter apprenticeship, employing experienced workers who had not been apprenticed, training for more versatility, bus operation by maintenance workers, and a commitment to work out a code to control piece-rate systems. Company agreements could follow, applying the principles as appropriate in the circumstances. Increased earnings would occur through incentive bonuses, but no further addition to basic rates should be added to the national increase. Thereafter relations in the whole industry improved as one-man operation spread, and the PIB was not again involved.

A few industries are so large that changes in their pay rates have national repercussions, even if they cause no imitation whatever in other industries. The consistency of engineering agreements with incomes policy determined to a material degree whether incomes policy could be effective or not. Moreover, engineering agreements had important consequences elsewhere, partly for institutional reasons and partly through market pressure. If incomes policy was to be taken seriously at all, it would have to apply to engineering pay, and to pay in building and construction. Engineering was referred to the PIB in the summer of 1967, and building and construction in 1968, both concerning payments by results systems and productivity bargaining.

Pay and conditions of manual workers in the engineering industry was referred (No. 49) as a new pay claim was being prepared. Staff

F

workers (represented by six unions) were in various stages of negotiation with the employers, and their pay and conditions were referred simultaneously with the manual workers. As the manual workers and staff workers were operating one industry (and the PIB had previously urged employers to develop comprehensive manpower policies), the two references were dealt with in one report (No. 49).

National agreements for manual workers were the result of *ad hoc* negotiations between the Engineering Employers' Federation and the Confederation of Ship Building and Engineering Unions, leading to general increases in minimum time rates and piece rates. A three-year "package deal" in 1964 had also established "minimum earnings levels", superimposed on time rates and piece rates. One million workers were directly covered by the agreement; but there were another million workers in engineering or other firms whose pay in fact followed engineering settlements, though they were not party to them. One million more had pay affected to some degree by the engineering agreements. Some 60 per cent of all manual employees in manufacturing were affected in one way or another by the engineering settlement. As this agreement covered pay increases up to January 1968, the actual changes could not be investigated at the time of the reference. The PIB had to base its report on a general investigation.

Wage drift (a continually increasing gap between basic rates and earnings), was notoriously a characteristic of engineering and it had been abnormally high (between $3\frac{1}{2}$ and 5 per cent a year), only some of which would be due to increases in productivity. Piece rates continually crept upwards, either through frequent changes in the job, or through a continual re-assessment of a job. They had to be settled at shop-floor level, where there was most pressure to keep production going. Time-workers either worked overtime to keep their earnings up with the piece-workers, or received "lieu bonuses" to keep them up; time-workers' hourly pay was generally less than that of piece-workers. But more serious anomalies than this were probably widespread: semi-skilled and even unskilled earned more than skilled, usually because of the disproportionate effects of piece rates. The structure of earnings within plants was distorted so as to cause "as much concern on grounds of equity or justice as does the position of the low-paid workers", by inadequate or reverse differentials for skilled workers. Relative pay of manual workers showed similar anomalies, such as supervisors earning less than skilled piece-workers. Equity required that skill and responsibility were both suitably rewarded.

The package deal was intended to begin reforming the structure of earnings, particularly by raising the minimum earnings of the low-paid without corresponding increases for the better-paid. It was also intended that plant bargaining should relate to productivity increases, all ostensibly very much in the spirit of the prices and incomes policy. But the PIB found that few plants had implemented the package deal as intended. Minimum earnings levels had been paid earlier than the agreement provided, or to workers not entitled to them; they had also been consolidated into new minimum basic rates, thus raising the base from which overtime or shift rates were calculated. Some firms had even paid across-the-board increases on the old lines, with no relation to productivity. The gap between minimum earnings levels and average earnings had actually widened, the opposite of the intention of the agreement. The only structural effect had been to narrow the gap between the pay of women and unskilled men, and to compress the range of women's earnings. Total earnings had increased by nine per cent annually, while productivity increased by five per cent, the same relation as before the agreement; and there was no evidence that control of wage determination at plant level was generally better.

The package deal had not conformed to the prices and incomes policy, and the PIB saw no virtue in national wage increases in such a heterogeneous industry, where they could be related neither to productivity, nor to the needs of individual firms. Nor were they needed to protect the workers, the vast majority of whom were mainly dependent on plant bargaining. Moreover, national increases made it increasingly difficult to remedy anomalies and inequities by pre-empting some of the money available to do it.

A future national agreement should make the good intentions of 1964 effective. It should consist of guidelines on productivity and pay and minimum earnings levels for each group. For a start, a one-year agreement should be made giving a uniform cash increase only to those on minimum levels. The new minimum earnings levels should then be used to calculate overtime and other premia instead of the minimum time rates. But raising minimum earnings levels would compress internal differentials further, some of which would need restoring. The new agreement would give firms opportunity to begin revising their whole wage structures, the only solution to wage drift. It was clearly the responsibility of managements to effect such reforms.

Bargaining with staff workers was at an altogether more primitive stage, with salaries fixed by firms according to their own systems. Some larger firms had made a start on job evaluation, but it was unusual for the unions to be directly involved, or even fully informed of the system used. The clerks' unions had recently reached a settlement with the employers. But the pay of young workers, and the relation between clerical and manual pay, and clerical and managerial pay were important outstanding issues. Draughtsmen were in dispute over pay, and their union wanted a national scale of minimum rates, a particular grievance being that young qualified draughtsmen earned less than manual workers. The EEF had produced a so-called charter of standard conditions, to apply to all staff, the first time any such national standard had been offered. But this had been rejected by the unions because conditions might become generally worse if all were restricted to the standards that backward firms agreed to nationally. The PIB considered that staff workers and their employers both suffered by the lack of a national structure properly rewarding skill and responsibility, and recommended that they should negotiate a charter of minimum conditions.

National negotiations for staff and manual workers could effectively influence only minima, and would have to be supplemented by local agreements. The problems in engineering were largely due to the failure to look at pay in plants as a whole. Fragmented bargaining meant fragmented and inequitable settlements. Efforts to remove anomalies and inequities were mostly in vain, though inflationary in effect. The normal Joint National Council machinery of employers and unions might not be enough, as strong leadership by the appropriate experts in job evaluation and pay systems would be necessary. The PIB suggested the appointment of an independent Chairman, who could also have regard to national needs expressed in the prices and incomes policy. He might publish a report every six months on developments in the industry, and in the last resort report on firms or unions frustrating his efforts.

A second report on engineering (No. 104) was published when the results of the final stages of the 1964 deal had been reviewed; but little of substance could be added to the argument. Earnings of the lower-paid had still changed very little. Management and unions would both need to change their attitude, and to introduce more written company or plant agreements to make much improvement. Particular sectors might need collective agreements designed to suit their own special needs. Large multi-plant firms might well need different agreements from small ones. Larger firms in the EEF as well as outside it, should consider establishing their own negotiations with the unions, in consultation with the EEF. The EEF would then negotiate national pay agreements on behalf of smaller firms, and a national framework agreement covering all firms, setting only minimum conditions and rates. Staff workers would also benefit from bargaining within a national framework agreement, which could include general guidance on categories of staff, and factors to be taken into account in grading systems (using job evaluation). The PIB's recommendations might have made a major improvement in control of labour costs and the rate of pay increases eventually. But there was little it could do to alter the immediate prospects.

The PIB had recommended payments-by-results schemes in earlier reports, where pay systems were still primitive. The first was the industrial civil service (No. 18), where only 15 per cent of the workers had incentive pay. More direct incentive schemes were recommended, in the interests of better management, cost restraint, and better pay. Existing schemes needed improvement through work measurement and systematic review of the systems used. This would probably show the scope for more schemes. By early 1970, a second report on industrial civil servants (No. 146), still recommended the managements of regrouped establishments to introduce incentive schemes to "realise the potential" of the work-force, as well as maintaining earnings comparable with private-sector workers

An even larger public-sector work-force, the manual workers in local authorities and National Health Service, were recommended to look to incentive schemes for better pay and better management (No. 29). A few local authorities had introduced schemes by 1966, with some major improvements in both output per head and earnings; but only half the schemes had been accompanied by work study. Both pay and savings could be considerably increased by properly planned schemes, as the unions had been urging onto reluctant authorities. The greatest problem was long preparation time. Work-study staff were scarce and major improvements in supervision and management were needed.

A certain amount of method study had been done in the National Health Service, but it had usually not led to incentive schemes. The unions had become so exasperated at the slow progress and limited objectives that they had ceased to co-operate in method study, even though it was originally they who had pressed for incentive schemes to be introduced. Both industries were advised to press on to properly controlled incentive schemes. A national advisory service for managements in each sector would make economical use of scarce experts, and spread best practices to backward authorities.

Water supply was another industry where labour use could be vastly improved by similar means (No. 29). Work and method study were little used in 1966, and there were hardly any incentive schemes. As it had a smaller work-force, occupied on a single activity, the industry could introduce incentive schemes much more quickly than either local authorities or the NHS. The only real obstacle was persuading management and workers in some undertakings that such schemes were in their interests. The PIB suggested that technical advice might be given by the national advisory service proposed for the local authorities. For all three activities, payment-by-results was one recommended technique for achieving a closer relationship between pay and performance.

The water-supply industry took the PIB's advice to heart, if not very quickly. When its pay structure was again referred in 1970 (No. 152), work-studied incentive schemes were much more common. As a result, labour productivity in distribution had shown spectacular improvements, and unit labour costs had been reduced by 20 to 35 per cent. By 1971, more than one in three manual workers would be able to earn productivity bonuses. However this was bound to lead to more pressure for across-the-board increases unrelated to productivity from others. To prevent costs rising and water rates increasing, work-studied schemes must be accelerated. As incentive bonuses spread further, consequential payments to men whose work could not be included would be made, to complete pay structures with proper rewards for effort, skills and responsibility.

In contrast to water supply, gas-supply manual workers (also covered in No. 29) already had work-studied payments by results schemes. Here, the PIB, though "having no wish to upset this line of development", urged the industry to consider moving on to new systems, by trying area agreements, rather than local ones, an opposite movement from that recommended to engineering.

As the incomes policy became more restrictive, it became more necessary to clarify the PIB's general attitude to incentive schemes. Payments-by-results was by far the oldest and most widespread form of incentive bonus, and as it was recommended in some cases and deprecated in others the PIB itself asked for a general reference on PBR which it duly received (No. 65).

Some four million workers, something like a sixth of the work-force, were covered by PBR schemes in 1967, though more than twice this number were affected by them, through schemes in other parts of their employers' enterprise. The primary purpose of PBR was one which at first sight was entirely in the spirit of incomes policy: the relation of pay to effort, and hence to output. But many things could and did go wrong. For PBR to be consistent with incomes policy, pay had to increase in step with productivity so that the level of unit costs did not creep upwards. But a properly designed scheme would not achieve good results indefinitely nor automatically. PBR represented a constant administrative weakness to incomes policy since changes in earnings or changes in piece rates under PBR schemes did not constitute an agreement or settlement which need be notified. The best of PBR could also undermine the policy by using up the proceeds of extra productivity, leaving nothing to provide non-inflationary increases for the low-paid, or for workers in activities where productivity rose less fast.

The PIB's survey of different systems confirmed that PBR schemes were an important root of wage drift. Pay rose generally above minimum or national rates because of "the work-place margin", due to bonuses of one kind and another, over and above extra payments due to extra hours of work. Moreover, when drift occurred among PBR workers, it tended to be compounded by "secondary drift", as time rates were raised to preserve acceptable differentials for time-workers. The result was that national drift had occurred at about twice the rate that official estimates suggested. Average hourly earnings had increased by eight per cent between 1963 and 1966. Nationally agreed increases had contributed four per cent, the other four per cent being drift.

PBR systems were subject to a kind of decay. A good PBR system seemed to produce drift amounting to one or two per cent a year. But as control relaxed, annual increases up to eight per cent were found. Earnings rose with increasing productivity due to technical progress as well as to effort; workers became more deft with experience of a given procedure (the so-called "learning curve" phenomenon); increases in hourly rates were secured where jobs changed ("piece-workers' creep", suggested the PIB); and there was a universal assumption that new rates must be better than the previous ones (the "ratchet effect"). Friction over differentials was often a consequence of PBR; and where time-workers also enjoyed increased earnings even though their own efforts were not increased, drift approached the higher figures.

Wage drift was often called a symptom of inflation rather than its cause, on the grounds that excessive demand for labour drove up its price, whether it took the form of PBR or not. But the PIB considered that the mechanism of wage drift itself contributed to the degree of drift, a conclusion in line with its repeated view that institutions contributed materially to inflation. Bargaining conventions on piece rates and time rates were mainly responsible. But the outcome was neither inevitable, nor to be blamed on market pressures: firms in similar market situations did not show similar rates of drift, so it could not be "altogether unamenable to managerial or joint control". Persisting with incomes policy might lead to something better.

If PBR was to minimise costs, it should meet four requirements: the work should be measurable and directly attributable to particular workers; the pace of work should be within the workers' control; management should be able to maintain a steady flow of work, in spite of fluctuations of demand or output; and the jobs should not be subject to frequent changes. Method study and work measurement to establish standard times for jobs were the keys to effective control. A viable PBR scheme should also be relatively new, namely something under three years old. A scheme five years or more old, was probably in decay, as management control first improved during the design and introduction of fresh schemes, but soon petered out when the effort was relaxed. Regaining control required redesigning the scheme. Management at the highest level would have to take a much greater interest in the matter than many of them did. Above all, the PIB's case studies showed that no payment scheme was a substitute for effective management, or management and union control over the system.

The content of a non-inflationary and fair agreement was easier to describe than how it was to be negotiated. Though PBR rates were negotiated at the work place, with the closest possible connection between pay and output or effort, the system was clearly anything but encouraging to either productivity or harmony. National agreements were not particularly conducive to efficiency either, since they had sometimes become merely a first stage in a bargaining ritual imposed on all firms regardless of their different circumstances. Indeed, it was in engineering, dependent to a relatively high degree on PBR, that the PIB had found national agreements were nullified most completely by work-place arrangements.

The PIB's solution was to change the nature of the national agreement, and the level of work-place agreements. National agreements were a main cause of cost inflation, since national increases were added to work-place PBR rates, which had already taken increases in productivity fully into account. But in spite of their weaknesses, the PIB concluded that they could still serve as a framework for work-place bargaining. A proper framework agreement would contain five provisions: standard conditions such as hours and holidays; standard procedure for plant or company bargaining; guidelines for payment systems; methods of correcting faults appearing in the systems; and selective wage increases for special groups, such as the low-paid. Given framework agreements, the details of pay rates and jobs would have to be negotiated. at whatever level managements could keep control of the system. This might be plant or company level, depending on the size of the company, and its organisational structure.

But given new-type framework agreements, there would not be much effect on pay systems or take-home pay very quickly. However, about two hundred corporations, including the nationalised industries, between them employing five million workers, could largely determine whether or not wage drift was contained and pay systems reformed. They could ensure that plants operated pay systems approved or negotiated by joint agreement. "They have the power," observed the PIB, "and can have the expertise, to bring and keep their units in line with the requirements of national incomes policy."

The PIB was then asked to investigate pay, and particularly wage drift, in a major employer of PBR labour, the building and construction industry. There were three main references, preceded by two supplementary ones, following the divisions of national negotiations. The main ones were on pay and conditions in the building industry (No. 92), civil engineering (No. 91), and other construction (No. 93) published simultaneously; preceded by the two smaller ones on an agreement relating to the pay of sawyers and wood-cutting machinists in the saw-milling industry (No. 82), and on a settlement relating to the pay of certain workers employed in the insulation-contracting industry (No. 84).

At the time of the references (May 1968), the National Joint Council for the building industry was considering a claim for an increase of 12 per cent in hourly rates, with, as the reference pointed out, no evidence that productivity was increasing at such a rate. The Civil Engineering Construction Conciliation Board had received a broadly parallel claim, and other sections of the industry would be influenced by settlements reached by the building Council.

Though the construction industry was notorious for reliance on PBR, the PIB's investigations revealed that PBR was not so important as commonly assumed, nor was wage drift as acute as in engineering. Large firms used PBR widely; small firms did not. As a result two-thirds of the craftsmen had no bonus, though the bonus was an important part of their take-home pay for the rest.

Even civil engineering which the employers' association described as "a traditionally PBR industry" turned out to be much less dependent on output bonuses than had been thought. Less than half the firms operated PBR schemes for half the labour-force, and the bonuses were a relatively small part of the pay packet. However, wage drift had been of about the same order as in industry generally, the main reason being overtime pay. Drift had been worst in the large firms, some of which used long overtime as a means of increasing pay. But productivity was low because of wasted time, due to inadequate management and slack supervision, itself the result of insufficient differentials and lack of training. The PIB thought the remedy partly a matter for the larger companies, and partly for the national bodies. As the large companies endured the worse abuses of the pay system, it was for them to negotiate company agreements and improve their management. At the national level, there was need for a framework agreement, which would lay down the principles of good PBR schemes, and a set of job-evaluated national rates.

Some of the peripheral industries (such as exhibition contracting, felt-roofing and mastic asphalting, fencing, furnace building, glazing, heating and ventilating engineering, and monumental masonry, No. 93), could also develop incentive schemes with profit to themselves and their employees. All ought to review whether they should continue to be parties to the main building agreement in future, or whether separate negotiating machinery and separate agreements would not serve their interests better. Separate machinery should not exist, merely to reproduce building settlements more widely.

Similarly, building workers in local authorities, Government Departments or elsewhere should have their pay settled in relation to their performance and the requirements of their own employers, and not to building workers in the construction industries. The more increases in pay were related to increases in productivity, the less reason to pass them on automatically to others without the productivity.

The two construction industries referred separately (sawyers and wood-cutting machinists [No. 82] and employees of the thermal-insulation industry [No. 84]) were also sufficiently different to need separate machinery and a new pay structure.

However, the PIB increasingly took the view that productivity agreements provided a better link between pay and productivity. It is to these company-type productivity agreements that we now turn in the following chapter.

Reports

No.   8   Pay and conditions of service of British Railways staff (Cmnd 2873)

No. 16   Pay and conditions of busmen (Cmnd 3012)

No. 50   Productivity agreements in the bus industry (Cmnd 3498)

No. 63   Pay of municipal busmen (Cmnd 3605)

No. 69   Pay and conditions of busmen in Belfast, Glasgow and Liverpool (Cmnd 3646)

No. 78   Terms and conditions of employment of busmen in Rochdale (Cmnd 3723)

No. 85   Pay and conditions of busmen in Dundee (Cmnd 3791)

No. 95   Pay and conditions of busmen in Wigan (Cmnd 3845)

No. 96   Pay and conditions of busmen in Great Yarmouth (Cmnd 3844)

No. 99   Pay of maintenance workers employed by bus companies (Cmnd 3868)

No. 49   Pay and conditions of workers in the engineering industry (1st report) (Cmnd 3495)

No. 104   Pay and conditions of workers in the engineering industry (2nd report) (Cmnd 3931)

No. 18   Pay of industrial civil servants (Cmnd 3034)

No. 146   Pay and conditions of industrial civil servants (Cmnd 4351)

No. 29   Pay and conditions of manual workers in local authorities, National Health Service, gas and water supply (Cmnd 3230)

No. 152   Pay and productivity in the water-supply industry (Cmnd 4434)

No. 65   Payments-by-results systems (Cmnd 3627)

No. 91   Pay and conditions in the civil-engineering industry (Cmnd 3836)

No. 92   Pay and conditions in the building industry (Cmnd 3837)

No. 93   Pay and conditions in the construction industry other than building and civil engineering (Cmnd 3838)

No. 82   Pay of sawyers and woodcutting-machinists in sawmilling (Cmnd 3768)

No. 84   Pay of workers in thermal-insulation contracting (Cmnd 3784)

11

Productivity Agreements

The PIB had approached productivity agreements in general with great caution throughout its first year. Though prepared to recommend company agreements to the road haulage industry, and something analogous to plant agreements to the railways and industrial civil service, it was not yet backing productivity agreements as generally more desirable than other methods of negotiation. In its first general report, prepared in the early summer of 1966, it asked for a reference to investigate the results of a number of productivity agreements already in operation for long enough to show the effects. Seven agreements reached by five enterprises were included in the reference: Esso (two agreements, covering two refineries, and distribution activities); electricity supply (the "status agreement" with manual workers); ICI (the Manpower Utilisation and Payments agreement for manual workers on four trial sites); British Oxygen (Gases Division, covering process and distribution workers); and Alcan (covering manual workers employed at the Rogerstone works).

Meantime the standstill had started, and extra productivity was virtually the only way for most workers to get increases in pay at all. The PIB was therefore asked to report generally on pay and productivity for the severe restraint period (No. 23). It reported (on the basis of provisional results of its investigations of the seven agreements) that higher pay in return for increased productivity would be justified during the period of severe restraint—and at any other period while the incomes policy lasted—if the productivity agreements were on recommended lines. Almost overnight, the idea of productivity agreements developed from a fairly advanced fashion practised by the sophisticated few, into a workaday tool that everyone was willing to lay hand to.

All the seven agreements exchanged improvements in pay and conditions for changes in performance and practice throughout the plant or plants to which they referred. But the PIB thought that to restrict admissable agreements to plant or company agreements might be too narrow a definition. Similar agreements relating to one department, or even one group of workers might have similar purposes, and similar beneficial results, a view not borne out by its own later experience of many difficult cases where partial agreements had disturbed pay structures, so that costly consequential settlements followed. On the other hand, productivity agreements "ought to be more than a means of 'buying out restrictive practices', a label commonly used". Rather they should be "designed to secure changes in working practice in general with a view primarily to make more effective use of available resources". The objection to item-by-item negotiation over a "shopping list" of restrictive practices was its lack of effectiveness. The PIB had found agreements of this kind where a considerable "price" had been paid for some restrictions, leaving others to be bought out later on.

The aim of a proper agreement should be a closer correspondence between basic pay and total earnings, so that take-home pay need not be dependent to an important extent on overtime or bonuses. It would not be one in which increases in pay were "accompanied by a vague promise to increase output"; it would introduce "new standards of work measurement and new methods of control" to ensure that agreed standards were met. The advantage to employers of seeking productivity agreements was the better use of their resources. The advantage to the workers was higher pay, better conditions (especially shorter hours) and greater security of earnings.

New agreements of an acceptable sort could not become widespread immediately; preparing, negotiating and installing sound agreements would be a lengthy process. Experience might shorten the process somewhat, but most managements were "far from ready" to undertake the preparation, negotiation and control required for success.

The first step was to calculate all gains and losses which such an agreement would bring to the whole company or plant. The agreement could only be judged in terms of forecast effects on the use of all resources. Proper work and cost standards should be constructed before the forecast was made. This might be difficult, but nowhere impossible. Standard techniques and costings already worked out in some difficult environments could be more widely applied. A general revision of the whole pay structure throughout companies might have to be considered, to give adequate control of costs as well as proper pay relativities. Only when managements were well informed enough to do all this were they ready for productivity negotiations. But demanding though the preparations might be, managements unable to work out the standards, estimates and costings would be "ill-advised to embark on a productivity agreement".

There might be gains and losses to others besides the firm itself. Some of the benefit of productivity agreements should accrue to the community in the form of lower prices or improvements in quality. It was widely thought to be a weakness of productivity agreements that they inevitably led to higher pay elsewhere (without the productivity) because of the pressure for comparability in settling pay. But the PIB could find no evidence that this had generally happened. Nevertheless it thought such a danger remained, and could appear with the further spread of productivity agreements.

Another danger was that a bad management might buy out restrictive practices not endured by its better-managed competitors; and the increases in pay to get rid of the slack practices of a few would apply to all alike. Alternatively, an enthusiastic management might offer pay increases justified in terms of its own productivity, but far beyond pay in comparable occupations. The PIB could only urge managements to use their judgment about what might be "too high", in the sense that a general increase in costs and prices would follow. Other rewards such as lump-sum payments or personal rates might be used to avoid spreading increases over an industry by the conventions of wage bargaining.

The PIB's advice was summed up in seven guidelines to be used by the Government for vetting agreements notified during severe restraint. The workers must be shown to be making a direct contribution to increasing productivity by accepting more exacting work, or major changes in practice. Forecasts must be derived from proper work-standards. Calculation of gains and costs must show that unit cost would be reduced, taking into account any extra capital cost. There should be controls to see that the extra pay was only made as the extra output or changes of practice were forthcoming. Clear benefit to the consumer, in lower prices or improved quality must be shown. Agreements covering only part of a plant must bear the cost of consequential increases in cost elsewhere. In all cases, "negotiators must beware of setting extravagant levels of pay which would provoke resentment outside".

The seven guidelines appeared once more in report No. 36, the fuller report on productivity agreements. But some amendent was made, as difficulties had already appeared. There were some cases where units of output could not be distinguished clearly enough to make a calculation of gains and costs. There were others where the units and unit costs were clear, but changes could not be forecast because the effect was too indirect. In both types of cases it was nevertheless common sense to approve the agreements and this was recommended.

However, productivity bargaining was no panacea for industrial peace. Even when it had been established well before the incomes policy itself, and espoused with some enthusiasm, disputes could arise as well as settlements inconsistent with the policy. One such case that came to the PIB concerned the industrial workers in the Atomic Energy Authority (No. 51). The National Joint Industrial Council was in the course of negotiating a new pay agreement when the policy was introduced. Both sides thought that some improvement in productivity would have to be negotiated to justify the pay increases being discussed. But a dispute resulted. An arbitrator recommended unions and employers to investigate the scope for further increases in productivity, and consequently the pay claim was still not settled before the standstill. The Authority eventually made several offers, all of them rejected by the unions. By this time the TUC had set up its wage vetting committee, and the unions submitted their claim to this. The TUC committee suggested amendments, and the Government referred the revised claim to the PIB.

Scope for increasing productivity was found by the PIB to consist of reducing overtime working; using craft and general workers on a much wider range of tasks; and using method study to cut down wasted time. The possible savings were considerable, and there was justification therefore for increasing pay by the £3 to £4 a week the unions claimed, in two stages. The PIB recommended higher standards, and higher pay for the disputed agreements than the employers offered; and so smoothed the way to a settlement.

Another public authority, the Electricity Council, had also started far-reaching productivity agreements, well before the incomes policy. The Productivity and Status agreements of 1964–65 had been among those studied in the general reference on productivity agreements. Overtime working had been reduced, a certain amount of overtime was worked without extra pay, and extensive changes were made in the pattern of work (by earlier starting, later finishing, and spreading five days' work over seven days in various shift patterns). Pay related mainly to time worked, and the time worked had been adapted to the industry's needs. But difficulties arose over what sort of agreement should follow. By the summer of 1967, the National Joint Industrial Council found it impossible to agree on a further pay increase for manual workers. Work study had been agreed, and the unions wanted a five per cent pay increase "in recognition of the high level of co-operation". The Electricity Council offered a lower increase, in return for accepting work study and allowing management "to deploy workers in the manner they required", as a result of it. At this point the question was referred to the PIB (No. 42). The main point at issue was what improvement the introduction of work study was likely to bring.

At the PIB's request, Area Boards estimated the likely increase in labour productivity, and the PIB recommended pay increases inside these estimates. It urged the Electricity Council to press on with work study, by taking more responsibility for co-ordinating and improving information available to Area Boards. The Council had a statutory duty to ensure "proper arrangements" for pay; and in the PIB's view, this meant it ought to assume responsibility for improving performance, in order that pay could be improved with it. It should therefore compile a register of the best labour practices of the industry, and press for their adoption. It should set up detailed yardsticks for measuring labour practices of the industry, and press for their adoption. It should set up detailed yardsticks for measuring labour productivity, to stimulate the improvements as well as measure performance. Where the Electricity Council had been given a duty to manage, it should manage, and firmly. A settlement with the manual workers was reached immediately afterwards on the lines suggested by the PIB, and soon after that connected agreements for technical, administrative, clerical and managerial workers. Yardsticks for measuring manual work were adopted by all the Area Boards, and the Electricity Council set up a register of best practices.

The following year (1968) a new agreement was signed, introducing so-called productivity bonuses again. A code laid down in "national guidelines covering productivity payments", was referred to the PIB (No. 79). The form of the new agreement was tantamount to admitting that putting manual workers on salaries did not achieve the full increase in performance open to the industry. The question therefore was whether new arrangements would elicit the improved performance, and whether the improvements would cover the full cost of the scheme.

A standard level of performance for each job had been set, with a bonus for above-standard performance. This was an old-style incentive scheme, and not a productivity agreement in the PIB's sense (or according to the incomes policy). The remaining scope to improve performance was obvious. With standard performance at 100, incentive bonuses were to begin at performance rated only 65. This was a low enough standard to set; current performance, however, was even lower. Progress on the different Area Boards had varied greatly. Some had taken advantage of the previous agreement to introduce work study; some had begun by measuring capital costs and only later turned to measuring labour performance. The PIB thought there was a case for incentive schemes; but varying rates of progress by different Boards would inevitably mean that wide variations of pay appeared between areas, though the workers were all doing the same job in the same industry, and this would only lead to resentment.

Costing the schemes was impossible, since performance when the incentives were introduced could not be forecast. The PIB's calculations showed that it was possible to cover the extra cost. It therefore recommended that the new agreement be applied, if the Electricity Council assumed responsibility for the consistency of schemes, for seeing that benefits matched the costs and for maintaining work standards. The Government should reserve the right to investigate progress in reducing unit labour costs, but no further PIB report was requested.

Soon after this, the PIB began to get cases of productivity agreements made in response to the incomes policy rules. The first of these, relating to road haulage (No. 94) was partly due to recommendations of the

PIB itself (in Nos. 1, 14 and 48). After national productivity negotiations broke down, the PIB had urged large firms to take the initiative
themselves; but eventually the TGWU had initiated successful agreements with a number of firms, the subject of the PIB's case.

The main effect of all the agreements was to raise the maximum
speed used for scheduling journeys from 30 to 40 mph, in return for an
increase in minimum basic rates. In some cases (other than those
specifically referred to the PIB) major cost savings had been achieved,
notably by firms using work study to establish standard times. But
many others had conceded pay increases without being in a position to
take advantage of high scheduling speeds, or even, in one or two cases,
without drivers being aware of what was expected of them.

The public sector of road haulage, British Road Services, had also
negotiated a productivity agreement with its garage maintenance workers
giving pay increases of 12 per cent in return for increase in productivity.
The increase in pay could clearly only be justified by major improvements, and the occasion was taken to refer the agreement, and the
general scope for the improvement of productivity to the PIB (No. 90).

The labour-force was relatively poorly paid in terms of basic rates,
compared with the engineering industry (the alternative source of employment for many workers). The result was familiar: long hours of overtime
to make up pay, and an ageing labour-force through failure to attract
young recruits. Increases in productivity would accrue from extending
shift working and increasing flexibility of work between grades. The
question was whether this would enable costs to be reduced sufficiently
to finance the 12 per cent increase negotiated. The PIB found that these
and other possible changes would not save more than 10 per cent a year,
unless work study and work measurement were added. Once more, the
main burden would fall on management. But given changes in management techniques, the pay claim could be earned and the cost absorbed.

Another more specialised, but private enterprise section of the road
haulage industry, the car-delivery industry, was referred in October 1968
(No. 103). The industry covered collecting cars from manufacturers,
sorting them at the delivery firms' depots, and delivering them to dealers
(for home sales) or to the docks (for export). A large number of firms
competed keenly on price. But they all negotiated wages with one
strong trade union, the TGWU. The PIB found that the firms had "clearly
incurred increases in costs which outweigh any advantage to the consumer
deriving from competition in price".

Firms seemed to be neither sensitive to their costs nor responsive
to public policy. The DEP's attention was drawn to the fact that
"notification to it of agreements in the industry has been minimal"
(in spite of the legal requirement to do so). Moreover, not a single firm
had costed the result of extensive increases in wages negotiated the

previous year; nor did their prices relate to costs in a reasonable way.

To make a start on improving an indifferent situation, the PIB thought larger employers should try to form an employers' federation, which could eventually advise on pay and productivity bargaining, for which there was plenty of scope. Although labour costs were relatively high, costs and prices could be better stabilised by proper agreements on productivity with the union.

At the same time, the PIB had under review a series of productivity agreements from the opposite end of the range of industrial management: the agreements made by ICI Ltd with its manual workers (No. 105). The firm had itself pioneered modern pay structures, and had been using work study and job evaluation for many years. Job evaluation was used to add a differential on to basic rates for general craft workers according to the jobs actually done. Work measurement was used to add an incentive bonus on to this. The whole structure was negotiated centrally. ICI claimed, and demonstrated to the PIB's satisfaction, that it had firm control of its wages bill and had not allowed drift.

Productivity had undoubtedly increased and would continue to do so. Increases in pay due to the bonuses for job appraisal or by work measurement were related to actual improvements under management's control. Overtime was not being worked unnecessarily. But though the productivity increments could not have been made without the co-operation of the workers, it was found impossible to quantify the direct contribution of labour, as distinct from the effects of technical improvements in the use of other resources (mainly capital or management).

The latest agreement gave increased earnings amounting to 6.8 per cent of the wage bill of the workers covered by it. The settlement was made possible by "continuing co-operation" in changes in work; and the parties had declared their intention to adopt a new pay and productivity structure, which would give staff status and annual salaries to all payroll employees from top to bottom (the Manpower Utilisation and Payments agreement [MUPS], which the PIB had reviewed two years before). Only $3\frac{1}{2}$ per cent under the new settlement had been paid on the due date, by agreement with the DEP while the PIB investigated. Anything beyond $3\frac{1}{2}$ per cent had to be justified either because it was a major reorganisation of structure in the interests of productivity and efficiency, or because there was extra productivity and efficiency enough to pay for more than $3\frac{1}{2}$ per cent, and leave something over for the consumer. Though the settlement had "a clear relationship to increased productivity", the PIB was suspicious of a suggestion (by ICI) that an increase of 6.8 per cent was needed "to match increases elsewhere". The PIB had the impression that this "played at least as significant a part in the conclusion of the settlements as the argument based on productivity". An agreement which sought a figure for increased pay to be arrived at by reference to increases elsewhere, and afterwards found "productivity" reasons to justify it was not in the spirit of the policy, or its guidelines. Perhaps it was too easy for firms like ICI to make productivity improvements. The policy would be defeated if such companies, able to increase productivity faster than most, "appropriated an undue share of the gains for themselves and their employees", instead of spreading the benefits through lower prices.

On the other hand, though the MUPS was then only being tried out in a few places, the full scheme would justify a bigger general pay increase. Therefore, anything over $3\frac{1}{2}$ per cent could be justified only if the company and the unions signed a revised agreement to introduce MUPS on a permanent basis. Some part of the extra increase could then be paid in all plants to bridge the gap in those where MUPS was not immediately introduced. This was regarded as one of the PIB's harsher judgements, on the grounds that it withheld increases in a well-managed firm, where productivity was increasing and industrial relations relatively advanced. If it was harsh, the main reason was to guard against creating new privilege for workers or management, fortunate enough to work in rapidly progressing, technology-based industries. Nevertheless, an agreement to improve productivity further was reached soon afterwards; and this settlement was approved by the Government.

The PIB was soon back with an industry where labour costs largely determined charges, and where good industrial relations were much more difficult to establish. A productivity agreement had been made by the exhibition-contracting industry in February 1969, consisting of increases in basic rates of $3\frac{1}{2}$ per cent, plus a bonus of 10s a day, in return for measures to increase productivity (No. 117). A standstill was imposed on the settlement while it was reviewed. A $3\frac{1}{2}$ per cent increase could only be justified on grounds of productivity improvement (leaving something over for the customer).

The main productivity provision was that men should work regularly on weekdays, as well as at the weekend (at double time rates). But the PIB's enquiries showed that absenteeism was not as serious as the employers believed; even if it was eliminated, the savings would not be great. In any case, improvements were not likely as the workers had not accepted the agreement supposedly made on their behalf. It could not therefore be approved.

In spite of the PIB's opposition to an increase, the Standstill Order was not effective for the full 12 months. After more strikes, leading to some exhibitions being cancelled, a general pay increase was negotiated, and accepted by the DEP. The Standstill Order was lifted in August 1969, after seven months.

The PIB had an opportunity of checking up on its own general principles, when productivity agreements were again referred (No. 123).

This time the PIB surveyed agreements in 40 companies. Two detailed studies of the effect of productivity agreements on local labour-markets were also made. There was a wide range of agreements from detailed and cost-controlled comprehensive agreements, to the essentially spurious kind, invented to get past the incomes policy requirement. Nevertheless, whatever the gloss put on the facts, an unprecedented extension of productivity bargaining had taken place in a short time. This was the more impressive since the average length of negotiations leading to the agreements was about eleven months (ranging from six weeks to two-and-a-half years or more).

The impact of productivity bargaining on cost, prices and profits was found to be generally anti-inflationary. In three-quarters of the cases the net effect was lower costs per unit of output, or "worthwhile reductions" in wage or salary bills. But the PIB was wary of claiming more than the evidence would stand, and its conclusions were that "our studies do not suggest that productivity bargining has so far inflated earnings in relation to increases of productivity and has therefore been on balance disadvantageous from a national point of view; rather the reverse". To which was added a further precautionary note: "whether the balance could become unfavourable in longer term, time alone can show".

This was a much more sceptical tone than the first report on productivity agreements. But the PIB had gone to considerable lengths to discover firms which had increased pay rates to match a competitor's productivity-based increases without the productivity, and no such case was discovered. In the local labour-market studies, "very wide ranges of pay" for similar work in a restricted area appeared. No doubt the differences were to some degree compensated by different conditions and non-monetary benefits. But in one of the PIB's areas, a hierarchy of local pay rates had been "completely disrupted" by a productivity agreement, and still no consequential increases in rates had been discovered elsewhere. What also appeared was that "comparability" was an acceptable argument in favour of opening wage claims, and in managements being prepared to negotiate. But settlements were eventually reached on other grounds. It could even have been that managements forced to concede "comparable" pay increases were forced also to find comparable productivity.

Companies had made more progress than national negotiators with framework agreements which they had found necessary to control the main lines of productivity agreements in separate plants. Conventional industrial agreements were still an obstacle to company agreements where uniform pay increases were negotiated. Obstacles from the past had to be removed, rather than pronouncing general prescriptions for the future. It would be desirable if national institutions would lay down general guidance on this backed by effective and influential advisory service. But whether this was possible depended particularly on the strength of the employers' associations, and these were too often lamentably weak, as the PIB was constantly discovering.

Non-manual workers might require different treatment from manual workers. In principle non-manual workers could contribute as effectively as manual workers to productivity. Work measurement could be applied to many jobs, clerical or otherwise, but agreements for future changes in working practice were often unnecessary, because of their "generally co-operative attitude". The habit (where it existed) of continuously changing working practices to adapt them to whatever technical changes were introduced by their employers, without compensating pay increases, was often feared to be an unfair burden on non-manual workers imposed by the incomes policy. Many public-sector workers suffered this handicap, especially where Organisation and Methods units were used. When pay increases were restricted to current norms some resentment was caused among these workers by their lack of approved bargaining power, the lack of something to sell. Had no modification of the rules of the standstill, severe restraint and post-devaluation periods been made, this weakness would have penalised some non-manual workers increasingly. It was in recognition of this problem that the PIB finally decided to extend its interpretation of productivity agreements in a major way, by inventing the concept of "efficiency agreements".

An efficiency agreement was one which provided for "appropriate and effective means of raising productivity and efficiency" without specifying changes in working practices, and where the extent of the increase in productivity could not be measured. The objective was "to make possible the constant raising of efficiency", and required "close and continuing co-operation between management and workers so as to achieve and maintain the highest standard in the use of both equipment and manpower", and only "where appropriate" should changes in working practice or method be specified.

Second-generation productivity agreements existed by then, and demonstrated that because a company has negotiated a productivity agreement, this did not imply there was no scope for further agreements. Technology continued to change and continuing adaptation to it was needed. Where the adaption of working practices had reached such a height of achievement that further changes no longer needed to be formulated in the agreement or directly paid for, a wider efficiency agreement might be the desirable form. In general, the scope for increasing productivity was found to be so great among relatively efficient companies as well as inefficient, that there was little grounds for fear that opportunities for productivity and efficiency bargaining would dry up.

As a result of all this, the seven guidelines for proper productivity agreements needed further amendment. In essence they were very much the same as before, apart from the extension of productivity bargaining to "efficiency bargaining" in general. It was now required that the major changes justifying the pay increase should be specified in the agreement. The more likely disputes over the interpretation of the agreement, the more detail it ought to contain. Work measurement, or indices of performance must be applied to all activities covered by efficiency agreements. A reduction in the total cost of output or service was still required "normally" to be shown as a result of calculating gains and losses. Managements should be in a position to confirm that the increases in efficiency were effected before the extra payment was made. "Clear benefits" to the consumer must be shown. Partial agreements should include the cost of any consequential increases elsewhere (especially of extra supervisors' pay to maintain differentials). Finally, "negotiators should avoid setting levels of pay or conditions which might have undesirable repercussions elsewhere."

A case where the concept of an efficiency agreement was relevant, rather than a productivity agreement, was that of the pay of employees in film processing (No. 131). The employers and the union had decided that they could not negotiate a productivity agreement on the lines of report No. 36. The output of the industry consisted not only in feet of film processed, but the speed with which the process was done, and the quality of the work. Labour costs had been held down in the past by rapid changes of method, and improvement of work flow, within the limits of fluctuating demand. No restrictions on labour use prevented the fullest use of machines or laboratories. An agreement had consequently been reached to include increases in minimum rates, an extra hour of overtime pay on afternoon and late shifts, a reduction in the working week for all clerical grades, and an increase in holidays. In return, meal and tea breaks would be staggered to avoid interruption to production, afternoon tea-breaks would cease for clerical staff, and the union gave an assurance that members would support better mobility of labour. The net effect was to bring annual increases in earnings well above the $3\frac{1}{2}$ per cent ceiling.

The PIB could find no case for exceptional treatment. Extra costs would evidently not be met by the changes of practice, since some firms proposed to raise prices. The industry needed to negotiate an efficiency agreement. The workers would then secure a fair reward for their continuing contribution to the raising of the industry's productivity. Companies should develop techniques by which productivity improvements could be attributed properly to their source (labour, new equipment or management). Better training could increase the versatility, as well as the skill of labour. A sanction against a new pay agreement going beyond the White Paper criteria would be to prevent the industry raising its prices. The customers should not agree to pay higher prices caused by higher labour costs (if they were in a position to know).

Further than this, the Government should keep itself informed of price lists, and enquire into the justification for them, in spite of the industry not being subject to early warning on prices.

The bulk of the PIB's reports on wage cases concerned efficiency rather than equity or welfare. Pay increases successfully linked to productivity increases, either by relatively crude methods such as PBR, or more advanced ones such as productivity and efficiency agreements, would secure more stability in unit costs of product or service. Incidentally to this, welfare would be served by allowing pay to increase faster than it otherwise might. But conditions of work would only be improved where efficiency required it, as in cases where overtime working was inefficient, or where improvements, such as extra holidays, were accepted as an alternative to pay increases. Equity between workers of one kind and another would also incidentally be improved, where they were working within the same enterprise or collective bargaining sector. Between groups of workers in different enterprises or sectors, however, equity might well be reduced, as the opportunities for improved productivity depended often on past circumstances, such as the competence of management and current technical advances in production, management or marketing. Furthermore, the social problems arising from pay problems, particularly the poverty of the low-paid, would not necessarily be improved, and might be relatively worsened in sectors where productivity increases were not to be had. The pay of the low-paid therefore had to be exceptionally considered under the policy rules, and interpreted as such by the PIB.

Reports

No. 23 Productivity and pay during the period of severe restraint (Cmnd 3167)

No. 36 Productivity agreements (Cmnd 3311)

No. 51 Pay and productivity of industrial employees in the Atomic Energy Authority (Cmnd 3499)

No. 42 Pay of electricity-supply workers (Cmnd 3405)

No. 79 National guidelines covering productivity payments in the electricity-supply industry (Cmnd 3723)

No. 94 Productivity agreements in the road haulage industry (Cmnd 3847)

No. 90 Pay of vehicle-maintenance workers in British Road Services (Cmnd 3848)

No. 103 Pay and productivity in the car-delivery industry (Cmnd 3929)

No. 105 Pay of general workers and craftsmen in ICI Ltd (Cmnd 3941)

No. 117 Pay and conditions in the exhibition-contracting industry (Cmnd 4088)

No. 123 Productivity agreements (Cmnd 4136)

No. 131 Pay in the film-processing industry (Cmnd 4185)

12

The Low-paid

The question when workers were to be considered low-paid was first raised by the case concerning railwaymen (No. 8) though the report in the end never mentioned it. The railwaymen were notoriously badly-paid; the reference was made in the knowledge that a strike was a possible—and disastrous—outcome of a failure to reach an acceptable conclusion. There was a good deal of sympathy for the railway workers from other unions. Moreover, the special exception in the incomes policy rules for the low-paid worker was the only real answer to left-wing (including union) opponents of incomes policy, who objected on the grounds that restraint and uniformity of treatment made prospects more difficult for the relatively poor. All this was just as obvious to members of the PIB (and some of its staff) as it was to anyone else; there was no lack of zeal in setting out to discover and document the low-paid. But the report did not reveal the balance of arguments that had been considered and rejected. The PIB appeared at the time more naïve, more superficial, altogether more reactionary than its behaviour justified.

There was no doubt that wage rates and drift were relatively low for all the workers covered by the reference, including clerical and supervisory grades, and workshop staffs. But earnings were universally above basic rates, the highest earnings to a considerable extent. However, it was only extensive overtime that made railwaymen's incomes comparable with others: railwaymen worked two hours a week longer on average than industrial workers generally. Average weekly earnings of the conciliation (operating) grades ranged from £16 to £23 a week (at a time when average weekly earnings in industry were £19 11s 9d). Railwaymen had become no worse-off relatively to others in the five years previously, and probably a little better-off. But the PIB did not discuss hourly earnings in its report.

The problem, somewhat ill-concealed, was a thorny one. Some overtime was only maintained by a rigid framework of working practice. Both were preserved together to maintain earnings. As in the bakers' case (under investigation at the same time), if an increase in basic rates were recommended on the grounds that hourly earnings were too low, overtime was not likely to be reduced and the railways' labour costs would inevitably increase. Had the PIB accepted overtime working as entirely necessary to maintain the railway service, it would have been faced more starkly with hourly pay as worked. Though acknowledging that some work outside normal hours was inevitable, it nevertheless found scope for reducing them. Increases in productivity were not only possible, but immediately attainable; and they would be more easily achieved if pay increases were directly related to them.

The provincial busmen were another group with low hourly pay made up by long hours of work. The PIB's general attitude to them was precisely similar. When new claims for provincial busmen and an agreement for London busmen were first reviewed (No. 16), the PIB established that most busmen had improved their position relative to other workers in terms of percentage increase in weekly earnings. Again, low pay was not mentioned in the PIB's report. Busmen too could justify exceptional increases of pay by productivity (see p. 145 above). When the PIB reviewed busmen's pay again in terms of hourly pay (No. 50), it admitted that though weekly earnings compared reasonably well with similar work elsewhere, hourly earnings were "considerably lower" than others. But even if busmen were "seriously out of line" with others, so far as hourly rates were concerned, the only general route to exceptional increases in pay was productivity.

By the time the PIB needed to be explicit about low pay, the standstill was nearly over and the era of restraint begun. In the autumn of 1966, the statutory Agricultural Wages Board proposed increased minimum rates for agricultural workers. The case was referred to the PIB (No. 25) specifically having regard to "the complex aspects" of the criterion about the lowest paid workers.

The White Paper sanctioned exceptional pay increases where pay was too low "to maintain a reasonable standard of living". A reasonable standard of living had been defined in various studies of poverty, and it was often assumed that the standard set by supplementary benefits was a convenient communally decided minimum. The PIB first looked for some such yardstick. But all the calculations involved highly arbitrary assumptions, as all were based on the needs of a household or family of some given structure, and no one of them could usefully be treated as representative. Hence, a "reasonable standard of living" could not be expressed as any particular cash figure to be paid as wages. Since there was no absolute standard of need to be found, the only alternative was to sort out the lowest paid workers in relation to others. Those who came at the bottom at any one time (taking due account of conditions and fringe benefits) were *ipso facto* low-paid and therefore deserving of exceptional increases within the terms of the policy.

Weekly earnings among agricultural workers were shown to be lower than in any other industry, and hourly earnings even more so. The PIB had no misgivings about recommending that the proposed increases were paid, even during severe restraint.

This report was an advance since railway pay and busmen's pay. The Government had made changes in the White Paper, as a result of trade-union leaders' disappointment over the report on railway pay, so that hourly pay had to be taken into account, as well as weekly earnings. But the PIB's attitude to overtime had not changed. It looked for evidence that some of the long hours worked on farms were merely a means of supplementing poor incomes, but this time found none.

A second report on agricultural wages (No. 101), was published late in 1968. Agricultural workers were still as low-paid as two years previously. Average weekly earnings were still lower than in any other industry, and the gap between agriculture and other industries was greater in hourly earnings than in weekly earnings. There was a higher concentration of low-paid workers in agriculture than elsewhere, and agricultural workers were demonstrably "the lowest paid body of workers of significant size in the country".

By this time, the policy rules were much harsher in effect to the low-paid; and had they been strictly applied, it would have been impossible to remedy the situation. The incomes policy for 1969 had imposed a ceiling of $3\frac{1}{2}$ per cent applying to all exceptional cases, excepting only productivity bargains and reformed pay structures. As neither of these latter considerations applied, the policy allowed the agricultural workers an increase of no more than $3\frac{1}{2}$ per cent, 8s a week on basic rates, instead of the 17s agreed on by the Agricultural Wages Board. Merely preventing further deterioration would be frustrated by the White Paper itself. The PIB therefore recommended that the policy be broken, the first (and last) time it did such a thing. The Government would be justified in considering "whether a special exception to the requirements of the White Paper ought to be made in this case".

The narrowing of differentials, the most sensitive point in determining acceptable incomes, was an important consequence of exceptional increases for the lowest paid. The PIB was more explicit about its general principles in the first agriculture report than it had been before. Though improving the lot of the low-paid necessarily implied narrowing differentials, not all differentials ought to be narrowed. The White Papers already allowed exceptional increases to correct serious anomalies, as well as low pay. There should, in principle, therefore, be adequate differentials for genuine differences of function. Where a labourer worked with a skilled man earning little more than he, it might be "economically unwise and socially unjust" to leave the skilled rate of pay untouched. But the PIB proposed no general rule about what the differences should be; there was no presumption either that they should be preserved, nor that they should never be widened.

The difficulties of helping the low-paid where differentials were critical, were illustrated in the case of the engineering industry (Nos. 49 and 104). The national negotiators had attempted their own incomes policy for the low-paid in the package deal of 1964. Minimum earnings were to be set, and minimum earnings levels raised in stages. For the time being low earnings were to be raised to the minimum agreed levels by means of special supplements. At the end of the three-year agreement (on 1 January 1968), minimum earnings levels would be consolidated into basic rates.

Engineering was a high-paying industry on the whole, heterogeneous though it was. Yet its previous procedures for pay agreements had created a formidable low pay problem. It was the PIB's work on this case that conclusively demonstrated that low pay was one problem of most wage structures, regardless of averages, rather than a problem confined to a few industries. Basic time rates in engineering were still spectacularly low. The reason lay in the procedures for settling pay. Minimum basic rates relating to a few key grades of workers only were settled nationally. But not all employers belonged to the Engineering Employers' Federation; and though it had been established that non-federated firms must pay no less than the agreed minima, they could, and some did, pay more. Some federated firms also paid more, in spite of the collective agreement. Company or plant minima were usually renegotiated every time a new national agreement was made, together with overtime rates and PBR. The bigger the difference between the national minimum rates and take-home pay, the more difficult it became to increase the national rates substantially. But some workers were trapped on or near the minimum rates, in firms or jobs where overtime or PBR was not worked.

Before the package deal, the labourers' minimum national time rate was just under £9 a week, and the fitters' (a skilled grade) under £11 a week, the women's, skilled or unskilled, under £8 a week. The PIB could not discover (for all its accumulated skill and facilities) how many workers were actually on these minima, or below the new minimum earnings levels. But there were enough of them for the new minima to create even worse structural problems than already existed. Workers with pay near the national minimum rates were clearly low-paid, and had a good case under the incomes policy rules for an exceptional increase. But the consequences for other workers illustrated the difficulties of improving their lot without tight controls. Up to January 1967, before the new minimum earnings levels were to be consolidated into basic rates, minimum earnings were supposed to be raised by 12.8 per cent for skilled (male) workers, and 12.3 per cent for unskilled. But earnings for the standard week (excluding overtime payments) went up more than this for all workers, except for the lowest paid, the unskilled time-workers. There could have been good reasons for this, such as greater productivity, or higher payments for increasing skill and responsibility. The fact remained that the low-paid ended up relatively worse off. The only exception was that poorly-paid women probably finished relatively better-off in relation to other women, and to the worst-paid men. In the last year of the package deal, from January 1967 to January 1968, a little of the lost ground was made up relatively. But the cash gap between minimum and average earnings continued to grow.

The PIB's solution was further agreements with similar intent, but in a different form. National minima should be set, on the understanding that no general increase of rates was to follow them. Criteria for plant or company bargaining on pay and productivity, and machinery for maintaining proper differentials should be the other subjects of national negotiations. The lowest-paid would benefit relatively from this, to the extent that exceptional increases in the minima were negotiated.

Some industries were found to be poor payers, because they were poor earners, or in the public sector, or both. The total number of low-paid workers in relatively small groups in high-paying industries might be higher than the large groups in low-paying industries. But the PIB had most work to do on the relatively poor-paying industries.

Three such low-paying sectors were manual workers in water supply, local authorities and ancillary (manual) workers in the National Health Service (No. 29). (The pay of manual workers in gas supply was also referred, because of historical links in the negotiations; but gas-supply workers were not particularly low-paid, and had adequate opportunity to increase their earnings by productivity bargaining.)

Water supply manual workers included considerable numbers of the low-paid, about one in six earning less than £15 a week, though not nearly so many as in local authorities or the NHS. They suffered from the low level of labour use in the industry. The real difficulty was persuading managements and workers alike of the advantages in work-studied incentive schemes (see p. 153). The few large undertakings should give a lead to the rest. There would be no need for further unconditional general pay increases unless managements made "unduly slow" progress in productivity bargaining.

Pay in water supply was referred again four years later (January 1970), after yet another general pay increase on the old lines (No. 152). The unions defended the settlement on the grounds that progress had indeed been unduly slow. The PIB found something in their contention, but the workers had meantime ceased to be specially low-paid. A part of the low-pay problem had evaporated under the pressure of technology.

There was no doubt about the local authority manual workers being entitled to exceptional treatment on the grounds of low pay. They included large concentrations of workers, among the lowest paid in the country at that time (1966). But the case was not nearly as straight-forward as the agricultural workers, who already had a high and rising output per head, as a result of a combination of more capital, better management and more skill. Steadily rising productivity meant that the wage increases recommended need not cause prices to rise. Here productivity was low and recruitment difficult. A straight pay increase inevitably meant that rates or taxes must rise in consequence. Much the same circumstances applied to the NHS workers, though they were not so unequivocally low-paid.

The central proposition in the PIB's report on both local authority and NHS workers was that low earnings were the result of limited opportunities. Basic rates were not unduly low, and pay negotiations related to these alone. The primary reason for the differences between their pay and comparable earnings elsewhere (£3 to £4 a week for local authorities and £1 to £2 a week for the NHS), was lack of opportunity for working overtime. Like industrial civil servants (see p. 152), though they had been statutorily protected by national bargaining machinery, this did not pre-vent them actually falling down relatively to the private sector. The reason was not incomes policy, but outdated institutions and principles.

It was not easy to decide an immediate recommendation. By the time the report was ready, there had been two cases where exceptional increases on grounds of low pay were recommended: agriculture and retail drapers (see p. 180), in both of which hourly pay as well as weekly pay was undeniably low. In this case hourly pay was not so low. Also, it was still the period of severe restraint, and the rules to apply after June 1967 had not yet been published. The case for an all-round increase, resting merely on low pay, was not overwhelming. It might also be a risky course to recommend, from the national point of view, since the workers covered by the reference made up a considerable sector of the national labour-force. Over one million workers were covered by the whole case, at that time the largest number in a single case. More-over, there was undoubted need, and undoubted scope, for more effective labour use of labour, which could lead to higher earnings with-out additional cost or reduced service. On the other hand, if workers were paid substantially more for the same work without a change in methods, an unreasonable burden would be imposed on ratepayers or taxpayers, and the result would be incompatible with the aims of incomes policy. Therefore any solution among these lines was ruled out. The cause of the low pay was low productivity; and so the proper remedy was not in doubt: to introduce schemes relating pay and productivity.

But desirable though such an outcome might be, immediately and conscientiously applied though particular schemes might be, they would take time to produce any results. Some authorities had already got far enough with incentive bonus or other productivity agreements for their workers to reap some of the benefit. What of the rest? Recommending an immediate unconditional wage increase would not contribute to spreading or speeding up better standards of work; but relying only on future performance to bring future rewards would not meet the case in justice. "It would be a harsh message for local authority and health service workers to tell them that they are relatively low-paid, that the remedy lies in a better use of their labour by their employers, but that many of them will have to wait for several years for the remedy to begin to work." Therefore, apart from granting, with modifications, the particular settlement and related claims for 10s to 11s 8d a week which were the origin of the reference, there must be some immediate step towards the longer-term object. Some means of relating pay and productivity were required, that did not need "exhaustive expert study", reorganisation, much training, or make "heavy demands upon standards of management". It therefore had to be a relatively simple and crude device. The device was to be a productivity increment parallel to a saving in manpower; 10 per cent more pay all round should be offered for 10 per cent saving in manpower all round (to apply to NHS workers also).

It was only too easy to find fault with such ideas. It would be unfair between one authority and another, and therefore between their employees. Even a crude scheme required some change in management. It might be particularly hard on progressive and efficient authorities and their employees. The 10 per cent was not securely enough established as immediately feasible, and so on. But in the last resort, too great a regard for the reasons why not, leads to acceptance of the *status quo* indefinitely—a consequence which is the opposite of a policy for productivity.

The immediate pay increases recommended by the PIB were implemented. Some response was made to the exhortation to greater productivity. Both sides of the NJC for the local authorities were invited by the Government to discuss the possibility of a national advisory service on productivity and incentive bonus schemes. The NJC itself began discussing an appeals procedure for incentive schemes and approached the PIB to discuss further the possibilities and technical details of job evaluation, and the PIB's interim scheme. It then decided to commission consultants to look further into the technicalities.

But as it turned out the PIB was too optimistic about the capacity of some local authorities to alter the situation. The dustmen's strikes of 1969 and 1970 arose directly out of the failure of some authorities to provide workers with proper opportunities for more or better work. The Court of Enquiry after the dustmen's strike drew attention to the lack of any advance in three years in some of the most troubled areas.

When the PIB itself had the NHS workers again referred in 1970, it found much to criticise in the way its recommendations had been adopted (No. 166). Both the Department of Health and the Regional Hospital Boards had failed to adopt a coherent strategy, and methods and results varied widely from Board to Board. Organisation and Methods and work-study staff were unevenly divided between regions and their work of varying effect. Some incentive schemes were over-detailed, and consequently wasteful; some were insufficiently supervised, and also wasteful. Schemes had been prevented by lack of standard equipment, such as floor-cleaners, or agreed standards of work, such as how often wards were to be cleaned. Above all progress had been slow. At the rate of progress of 1967–70, it would have taken 13 years to cover the whole work-force with work-studied incentives. Not unnaturally, the PIB urged more rapid improvement, "given the waste represented by the continuance of current low levels of efficiency". Renewed effort based on the experience of the best hospitals was necessary. Pilot studies could lead to model schemes in all the main activities, with target dates "not much more than three years hence". An Ancillary Work Efficiency Scheme should be negotiated by the Ancillary Staffs Council. In the NHS, as well as local authorities, slow progress and persistent low pay was clearly due to deficiencies of management and the structure of management.

The statutory wage-fixing bodies, especially the Wages Councils, were supposed to protect the weakest and lowest-paid workers, so it was not long before the PIB was considering their functions. The first report to raise the question was on the pay of workers in the retail drapery, out-fitting and footwear trades (No. 27).

The immediate occasion of the reference was a proposal to increase wages during the period of severe restraint, and the reference again specifically mentioned low pay. The majority of the employees here were women. As many more women were low-paid than men in industry generally, the PIB decided to compare earnings in retail drapery and in other trades separately for men and women. It then easily con-cluded that men on the statutory minimum remuneration (of £9 15s to £10 11s a week for sales assistants) were among the lowest paid. Similarly, women on the statutory minimum (of £7 5s to £8 1s a week for sales assistants) were low-paid, within the meaning of the policy. But (unlike agriculture) only a minority of workers were on or near the minima. The majority of workers therefore had no case for exceptional treatment as low-paid, and the PIB thought the differential between the minimum pay of assistants and the minimum pay of managers was such that it should not be further compressed. Hence, only workers at or near the minimum should receive the pay increase proposed by the Wages Council. A tapering proportion of it should be paid in the case of those just above the minimum, except for increases necessary to preserve the differential for managers on minimum pay. The same principle applied to women, though the band over the minimum within which tapered increases were to be allowed was only £1 a week compared with £3 a week for men.

The Wages Council had not been entirely effective in protecting low-paid workers, and its role was in other ways undesirable. The Retail Drapery Council was only one of twelve in retail distribution, each covering only a limited section of trade, though all employed the same kind of labour. All usually settled for similar increases in wages at similar times. The same unions represented the workers on all the Councils, and the same employers' organisations represented employers on several. Some employers had voluntary agreements with the unions, where minima were higher than the Council, but followed the statutory Wage Council increases. There was even a recognised sequence of settlements: an agreement between USDAW and the Co-operative Union (negotiating for retail Co-operative Societies); followed by negotiations for an increase in the Drapery Wages Council rates; followed by voluntary agreements; followed by similar increases in statutory minima set by other retailing Wages Councils. Although the Wages Councils overtly negotiated only statutory minimum rates, in fact they were the means of transmitting most pay increase to the whole of retail distribution, employing some $2\frac{1}{2}$ million workers.

The two worst features were that the process began with a settlement in the lowest-paid sector (the Co-operative shops), but then rapidly spread to all others, so that the lowest-paid sector was prevented from getting any relative benefit. Secondly, this went on in the total absence of information about either earnings or costs, in drapery or other retailing. It was impossible therefore to relate changes in pay, costs and prices. Both of these practices were obstacles to the aims of incomes policy.

The Wages Councils themselves were disinclined to take any account of the policy. All the members, including the independent members, seemed to think that their powers under the Wages Councils Act of 1959 actually debarred them from considering anything other than the statutory minimum. But a "reasonable" minimum level of pay was discussed in relation only to increases in pay elsewhere (selected impressionistically), increases in retail prices (often equally impressionistic) and various unsubstantiated arguments about possible effects on costs, output and prices. This caused the PIB to question whether the Wages Council system served its original purpose at all. The system required radical reform in any circumstances. But the prices and incomes policy in particular would be "under a grave handicap" so long as Wages Councils regarded themselves as debarred from taking it into account.

The Drapery Wages Council rejected the PIB's recommendations, and repeated its original proposals, urging that a Wages Regulation Order be made immediately. As the Minister of Labour had no power to amend a Wages Council proposal, and as outright rejection was not an

G

appropriate response, the Order was made. But the Minister also directed that a notice was sent at the same time to all employers setting out the Government's (and the PIB's) view of the settlement. Though this notice had no statutory force (unlike the Wages Regulation Order) a considerable number of large employers, perhaps a majority, conformed to the Government's suggestion and paid the increases only to workers near minimum rates.

Not all Wages Councils guarded their traditions so jealously. When the PIB reviewed road haulage wages and charges for the second time (No. 48), the unions were claiming a £1 a week increase across-the-board. After the report, showing that average earnings were not low though basic rates were, the Council awarded the £1 increase only to those earning less than £14, and to those earning £14 to £15 the amount necessary to bring them up to £15.

The effects of Wages Councils was reviewed again in a later report (No. 110) on the clothing manufacturing industries. Again the PIB found that the Councils were not fulfilling their intended purpose, and in some ways actually impeding it. The lowest paid were not protected, and voluntary collective bargaining could well have developed more strongly without them.

This time the whole industry was referred, where pay was covered by a chain of Wages Councils, which in turn had links with voluntary collective agreements. No less than ten separate Councils (two of them being separate Councils for Scotland) covered the various sections of 11,000 firms and 440,000 workers (whereas the Retail Drapery Wages Council negotiated for 340,000 workers). The sections had distinct methods of work, different sizes of firm and, to some extent, different products; but they competed in the same labour-market.

The only really effective voluntary agreement in the industry was between the National Union of Tailors and Garment Workers and the Clothing Manufacturers Federation (the large ready-made clothing firms). A percentage increase in minimum basic time rates and piece rates was negotiated annually. The Federation then recommended its members to apply the same increase to all workers. The Wages Councils then met in turn, and concluded agreements following broadly on the Council rates in ready-made clothing (though details like holiday entitlements might differ). Though the only active union and employers' association controlled a minority of the industry, they were able to use the Wages Councils to make their agreement effective throughout the market.

In an industry fragmented, ill-organised and relatively badly paid, an effective agreement about minimum rates was obviously desirable. But the Wages Councils appeared to have done nothing to alleviate the problems in their 50 years' existence. The clothing workers had been made no better-off, relatively to others. As usual, a major cause of the low pay was low productivity (mainly through excessive handling of materials and waiting for work), and the remedy must be to raise productivity. Pay structures relating pay to skill and giving adequate rewards for contributions to higher productivity would offer a better prospect of dealing with low pay, and company agreements should be made to this end.

Collective bargaining was hampered by employers' indifference, and the unions' weakness. The Wages Councils had much to do with both, since they furnished a ready-made means by which negotiated settlements were given statutory force. The fact that minimum wage rates and wage movements were determined by the decisions of statutory bodies remote from the shop floor made it harder for the union to persuade workers that it was of real benefit to them. The Wages Councils had at once reduced the unions' powers of recruiting greater numbers, and robbed them of the need to take an initiative in protecting their members from the erosion of their real income by relatively greater progress elsewhere. It could not be said that matters were any more satisfactory from the national point of view. The Wages Councils worked in a way contrary to the incomes policy, and in a way which failed to promote the efficient use of resources.

With such a conclusion, the PIB could hardly do less than recommend that the Councils should cease operation. But if the weak were badly protected by Wage Councils, it did not follow that they would be better-off without them. There would be no guarantee that other effective arrangements would take their place. However, the new powers proposed in the White Paper *In Place of Strife*, then recently published, for supporting unions and enforcing agreements were intended for just such cases. If the DEP was to advance at all in strengthening collective bargaining, and by it, to improve working performance, here was a case in point. The DEP should draw up a "programme of action" with the unions, the employers and independent members of Wages Councils to promote voluntary bargaining machinery, so that the Wages Councils could be replaced as rapidly as possible. The Commission on Industrial Relations might also give help or advice, or might be given powers to recommend the abolition of the Wages Councils, and institutions to replace them.

Protecting the interests of the lowest paid during the transition period after the abolition of Wage Councils would then have to be done in a more continuous and comprehensive way than occasional intervention by the PIB could ever do. The Wages Inspectorate could still be used for this purpose (as the Donovan Commission had recommended), and they could conduct their own earnings surveys to monitor progress.

Meantime the incomes policy rules would not allow further across-the-board increases in the clothing industry on the grounds of low pay. Minimum rates should be increased, the increases going only to those on or near the minimum. For the rest, increases would have to be justified, either by removing serious anomalies that would otherwise arise, or as part of a productivity bargain at plant level, or by a reorganisation of wages structure in the interests of greater efficiency.

One subject conspicuously not discussed in the clothing report was the question of women's pay. The PIB had by now investigated all the main groups of women employees: local authority manual workers, health-service manual workers and nurses, engineering, retail drapers and clothing. (It had also reported on laundries, though charges—and not wages—were the subject of the case.) In all of them, the evidence was quoted of low pay for women, and the even worse pay of women supervisors relatively to men. In all of them, general consideration of women's pay was studiously avoided. In each activity, women's earnings were compared only with other women's earnings. As these varied within a much narrower range than men's, as well as being at a lower level, no female labour-force was found to deserve exceptional pay increases, except some clothing workers, who were clearly at the bottom even of the women's heap.

In the first engineering report, some minimal comment was necessary, since one objective of the industry's own incomes policy was to begin closing the gap between men's and women's pay, at any rate at the lowest levels. This part of the agreement had rather more effect than others. In both reports on engineering, the first based on changes up to 1967, the second including the last stage of the package after 1 January 1968, evidence was given of some success in this. But the PIB was not to be disturbed so easily from its masterly neutrality. Once more, by comparing women's earnings here with other women's earnings it finds that "the resultant minimum earnings cannot be said to be unduly low ... It would be difficult therefore to justify, on the low paid criterion, a further increase of any significant amount ... It follows that yet another step towards equal pay cannot be taken at the present time. It would, however, be wholly unjustifiable in our view to widen the differential between male and female workers against the movement in the industry towards equal pay."

In the clothing report, the "right" rate for women was taken to be about two-thirds of men's rates—a rather lower proportion than the Wages Councils took them to be. The lowest paid were to be protected by a percentage increase in minimum rates, which would, of course, close the gap somewhat between the lowest-paid women and the rest. But the absolute gap between women and men was automatically made bigger. On the face of it, the more successful the PIB's recommendations the larger the earnings gap between the poorest-paid women and men workers would be, were it not for the legislation on equal pay. This was a theme appearing again before the PIB, in the last phase of its existence, after the Equal Pay Act, 1970, was law.

Another case where minimum rates of pay were decided by Wages Councils was milk distribution (No. 140). Again, in spite of their intended function they had not paid any special attention to the problems of lowest-paid workers, and did not negotiate pay and productivity together. Consequently pay rates remained low and productivity low. Overtime and rest-day working made it more difficult to attract and retain labour. But the general shortage of labour perpetuated the need for long hours of work.

The PIB's enquiries confirmed that there was a good deal of scope for improving productivity, through better management, and less waiting about. The PIB had "no hesitation" in recommending that it was time for better negotiations in place of the Wages Councils.

In its general study of overtime, the PIB concluded that overtime working was a regrettable way, and often a costly way, of providing tolerable or acceptable incomes for poorly-paid time-workers; but it could still find no general remedy. The only lasting solution lay in improving the value of the output of labour, by some form of productivity scheme.

One of the reasons for accumulating hostility to the incomes policy in 1969 was a growing awareness that low pay had not been alleviated by it. The final White Paper admitted as much, and promised special investigations. In furtherance of this, three low-paid industries were referred to the PIB three weeks before the general election of 1970: ancillary workers in the NHS (No. 166); the laundry and dry-cleaning industry (No. 167) and contract cleaning (No. 168). The PIB's posthumous survey of these three was supplemented by a general report on low pay (No. 169).

Workers in laundries and dry-cleaners were found to be undoubtedly low-paid. Efficiency was low, mostly because plant was under-used as demand declined. The work was suitable for, and even attractive to the weakest members of the labour-force, namely women with family commitments, the elderly, and the disabled. There was a Wages Council, whose rates were even lower than earnings (still £11 a week for men and under £9 for women in 1970). The PIB could find no great scope for increasing efficiency generally, except as the consequence of greater concentration in the industry, as the market continued to shrink. It wished to see the Wages Council rates raised, if only because they served no purpose as low as they were. Many employers paid rates well above the statutory minima, though the statutory increases set the standard for increases in basic rates. But the PIB put the onus of deciding a suitable increase back on the Wages Council. The faster it pushed up its minimum rates, the faster the industry might contract. It would have to choose between more jobs at relatively low pay, and fewer jobs at more adequate pay (a choice doubtfully appropriate to such a body).

No negotiations had begun about implementing equal pay for women, as required by the Equal Pay Act. Women workers already had equal pay for doing men's jobs; but few of them did men's jobs. As men's rates were in any case "not particularly high", the PIB foresaw that the Act might not have much effect, and might not do much to eliminate low pay. There could be little comfort here for the low-paid, men or women.

The contract-cleaning trade (specialist firms contracting to clean office or other buildings) was found to be not particularly low-paid. This conclusion was due to the great predominance of women workers, and of women part-time workers. "Low pay among women in the trade is no greater in extent than that elsewhere," observed the PIB. But the real weakness of women's position in contract cleaning was shown in the low pay of full-time night workers. Night workers actually earned less than day workers, and an average of 39 hours a week at night yielded an income of only £13. On the other hand, the relatively few male workers (often doing external window or other cleaning not normally done by women) were found to be definitely low-paid (in relation to other men). Average weekly pay for full-time men was almost £21, including considerable overtime.

Productivity-linked pay schemes were not thought to be very promising. Better organisation of work was the main means of increasing output, and this was a management function. Improvements in training junior managers and supervisors, the PIB thought, might be required. The large employers and the unions should "begin to develop some continuing relationship with each other", perhaps eventually leading to a joint Council. Meantime the DEP might begin discussions on pay for night workers. In spite of its special review in depth of more low-paid industries, the PIB's view was basically the same as it had been in 1965: if the low-paid could not earn better pay through higher productivity, so much the worse for the low-paid. The primary consideration was whether increases would be inflationary or not, that is whether costs would be increased or not. Of course, any increase of pay not related directly to increased productivity would be inflationary in this sense.

After reviewing the three separate low-paid industries in this equivocal light, especially concerning women's pay, it was not to be expected that the general report on low pay would draw any very definite conclusions (No. 169). As a research study in some of the circumstances surrounding low pay, it was another advance, and another contribution in the PIB's own style. But perhaps the nature of the references, and the lateness of their occurrence prevented the PIB from ending on a crest, with a policy for low pay.

Low pay has been something to be deplored for a long time. But the nature of the problem has not been much explored before. The PIB took as its starting point the principle that all normal workers ought to be able to earn a higher real income than the socially-provided and socially-decided standard available to non-workers. But the socially-provided minima (available through pensions and supplementary benefits) take family circumstances into account, and even some commitments such as housing costs. The PIB was consequently led into a survey of the "net resources" of its low-paid, a rough measure of the way of life open to them, given the size of their families. In the three industries referred, over one in ten of the men full-time workers, one in seven women full-time workers, and one in eight of the women part-time workers earned within £4 a week of supplementary benefit levels. As might be expected, the PIB also found that many other factors besides low earnings determined whether a family came inside or outside its measure of poverty. Nevertheless, it had clearly established that low pay (on its definition) did not provide a significantly higher standard than the social minimum. Moreover low pay was a persistent, even growing problem. Distributions of earnings showed remarkable stability, even during the post-war years of full employment. The lot of the low-paid had at least not deteriorated during the first phases of the incomes policy, up to about 1968. From 1969 onwards, a relative slide had begun again. The PIB concluded that taxes and social security, together with full employment and economic growth, had secured what improvement there had been in the standard of living of low-paid workers relative to the rest.

The problem of the low pay remained. But the PIB could not in fact protect the low paid. A national minimum wage was once again rejected, in report No. 169, on much the same grounds as in the agricultural wages report five years before. Any improvement would only be temporary, and would result in reduced employment. Differentials would reassert themselves, and raising the level of the minimum could be a "dangerous source of cost inflation"—the same old bogey. But it was not conceded that it could form part of an "overall strategy" to promote growth in conditions of full employment, by raising the lowest pay, forcing the inefficient out of business and releasing workers for the more productive. Informing and training the squeezed-out workers of the new opportunities would also have to be part of the strategy. The disabled and the elderly, prominent among the low-paid, would need "special help" to find suitable jobs.

But there seemed to the PIB to be no common cause of low pay among the three reference industries, and so no general solutions. Differentials were difficult to change, and "there are sound economic reasons why they exist". Not all of them could be so justified, but no responsibility for changing them was suggested for anyone, except the unions. Their role was "of crucial importance". They must, however, beware of the cost inflation which would follow from "raising general levels of pay substantially". They must "recognise that a relative improvement of the position of some must mean a relative worsening of the position of others". Otherwise, the Government should promote studies into particular industries including low-paid workers to establish causes.

The three PIB studies leading to this conclusion had been based on a limited view of the low-pay problem, as they all concerned low-paid industries. But the PIB itself had pointed out some years before that many very low-paid workers existed in industries where the general level was high, engineering being the obvious example, and there was no reason to suppose the total of such workers to be smaller than the total in low-paid industries. As these reports turned out to be the PIB's last chance of throwing more light on the circumstances of low-paid workers, if not on the remedies, it was even more regrettable that the DEP did not refer a reasonable selection of the whole problem at once.

In sum, the PIB's view of low pay, having studied the matter in general terms, was no different from the accumulated conclusions from earlier reports. The low-paid who qualified for exceptional treatment were the absolutely lowest paid, men in relation to other men, women in relation to other women, weekly as well as hourly earnings being considered. Where earnings were low because few opportunities existed for shift-working, overtime or piece work, immediate improvements were difficult, and general increases in basic rates or minimum earnings might be made, providing in most cases, it was confirmed to about £3 a week from the bottom for men, and about £1 a week for women, so that differentials were very little disturbed. Any consequential adjustments to differentials could be dealt with if "serious anomalies" arose, on the lines discussed in chapter 13. The only important difference in the late reports was that no recommendation for increases in rates at the bottom were made; but neither policy nor powers existed any longer to give practical effect to it.

Reports

No.   8 Pay and conditions of British Railways staff (Cmnd 2873)

No. 16 Pay and conditions of busmen (Cmnd 3012)

No. 25 Pay of workers in agriculture (Cmnd 3199)

No. 101 Pay of workers in agriculture (Cmnd 3911)

No. 49 Pay and conditions of service of engineering workers (1st report (Cmnd 3495)

No. 104 Pay and conditions of service of engineering workers (2nd report) (Cmnd 3931)

No. 29 Pay and conditions of manual workers in local authorities, NHS, gas and water supply (Cmnd 3230)

No. 152 Pay and conditions of manual workers in local authorities, NHS, gas and water supply (Cmnd 4434)

No. 27 Pay of workers in the retail drapery, outfitting and footwear trades (Cmnd 3224)

No. 110 Pay and conditions in clothing manufacturing industry (Cmnd 4267)

No. 166 Pay and conditions of ancillary workers in NHS hospitals (Cmnd 4644)

No. 167 Pay and conditions in laundry and dry-cleaning industry (Cmnd 4647)

No. 168 Pay and conditions in the contract-cleaning trade (Cmnd 4637)

No. 169 General problems of low pay (Cmnd 4648)

13

Comparability and the Market

W e have to deal here with one general principle of incomes
policy, and two of the criteria for exceptional increases.
"Less weight than hitherto" would have to be given to comparisons with incomes elsewhere in settling pay. However, exceptional pay
increases might be justified where it was essential "in the national interest
to secure a change in the distribution of manpower", or where there was
"widespread recognition that the pay of a certain group of workers has
fallen seriously out of line with the level of remuneration for similar
work". These together concerned the way labour-markets worked, how
far the conventions modified market rates, and how far they could or
should be modified by incomes policy.

A summary of the views behind these rules might run as follows:
demand for certain skilled or specialised kinds of labour might pull up
its rewards; where supply was limited by restrictions on training, a
closed shop or lack of mobility for social reasons pay might be even
higher. All pay might be pulled up in time on the tail of market forces,
because comparisons with others was accepted as good grounds for
claiming—and getting —increases in pay. The process became continuous
and cumulative since comparisons were done group by group, according
to the traditional boundaries of negotiations; and there was always some
group at the end of the line with a "good" case on comparability grounds.
However, comparability could not be overthrown entirely because there
were large groups of workers whose pay was determined by little else,
especially in the public sector; and it was not at all clear whether there
was any other acceptable way of doing it.

But the market could not be overthrown altogether. Demand for
workers increased when demand for their product increased. A policy
that prohibited demand-induced increases in pay would inhibit movements of labour into expanding and more efficient employment: it would
be an anti-productivity policy, so far as structural changes between
industries or between firms was concerned. The only solution was to cast
general doubt on comparability and market forces and then allow both

of them as possible reasons for exceptional treatment. The market should only work where it was essential in the national interest, and where "a pay increase would be both necessary and effective". Comparability required not only "widespread recognition", but pay needed to be "seriously out of line" as well as in the national interest for (relative) improvement to take place.

Railwaymen's pay (No. 8 also discussed on p. 142) first raised the issue of comparability explicitly and unavoidably. The Guillebaud Committee had been set up to settle "a fair and adequate wage", so that the railwayman "should be in no worse case than his colleagues in a comparable industry". It accordingly set about establishing comparability to indicate appropriate rates of pay. But exact comparisons were seldom to be found, and analogies were no help, since the range of wage rates was so wide that no particular rate for railwaymen suggested itself. The Committee made up a list, only one item of which was published, a comparison between the lowest scale for railwaymen and twelve outside labourers' rates. No comparisons at all were found for any higher grade. For the salaried grades the result was the same: a workable comparison for the lowest grade and nothing for any higher grade. Nevertheless, the railway unions had seized on comparability as an officially-blessed formula for getting relatively better increases than they had succeeded in getting before, and constructed their own list of analogues to support their claims. The management had, in fact, joined the argument on these lines, though they had "not held themselves to be bound by any particular comparisons".

The PIB found good reason for disapproving of the principle and its application. "Basic rates" meant different things in different cases; bonuses had been consolidated into basic rates in some industries. Moreover, even if earnings were compared with earnings (rather than rates with rates), whatever relationship happened to exist between railways' pay and the analogues' pay in the base year would be perpetuated, regardless of changes in technology, responsibilities, or the employers' management methods. All this made comparability unjustified in relation to the needs of the railways, and unlikely to be in railwaymen's interests.

There was a further consideration of the national interest. Comparability linked the pay of one group with another, not only in a long chain, but actually in a circle. A large number of Government industrial workers (already then being investigated by PIB, see also p. 152) received pay linked to the "M" (for miscellaneous) rate. The M rate was also determined by reference to pay increases to a list of comparable workers; and the basic rates of the railway conciliation grades were among those on the list for the M rate. The M rate had been increased in late 1964, partly as a result of an increase in railway rates; then the increase in the M rate became one of the grounds on which the railway unions based their 1965 claim.

Comparability had been deliberately introduced piecemeal into many parts of the public sector because it seemed to offer fair treatment for public servants; and a sense of fairness was one of the most important elements in both pay claims and acceptable settlements. But equally, the public sector could not continue to pursue a principle directly counter to incomes policy. It was too big a sector, and it had an overriding duty to be a good employer by setting a good example, as well as in protecting its employees. The PIB therefore rejected comparability as emphatically as it could as an acceptable method of determining fair wages.

Further implications of this rejection for public-sector employees were worked out in relation to industrial civil servants (No. 18). The most important result of the PIB's investigations was to show that the principle of comparability, to which both employers and employees were so attached did not in fact give comparability. The whole elaborate exercise had become a shadow play. The reason was familiar enough in other public-sector incomes cases: restricted opportunities for earning, compared with the private sector. The most meticulous comparison of rates of pay could not bring earnings into line, once a major (and growing) part of outside earnings consisted of overtime pay and bonuses. Firm Treasury control of Government establishments had prevented both overtime working and incentive schemes on anything like the scale outside. This, in itself, was not necessarily a fault of Government; it might be a sign of weak management outside. But the result had been to make Government employment an increasingly unattractive alternative to private-sector employment. Meanwhile, many establishments were left with a relatively aged labour-force and high labour turnover, as well as an unusual shortage of skilled labour. Comparability had failed to work; in its place, market pressures were repelling new recruits and a stable, skilled work-force.

There was a case for an exceptional increase on market grounds (where a change in the distribution of manpower was desirable), and on the associated comparability grounds (where pay was recognised to be seriously out of line). But there were objections to any such easy solution. The first was the issue already raised in the railways' case, that it made the Government follow everybody else at the very time it was urging on others the need to attach less weight to comparisons. Secondly, it ignored the different conditions of work outside Government service. Finally, the formula used was based on rates not earnings. As other industries reformed their pay structures, the comparisons were even less valid.

The decisive argument was the demonstrable ineffectiveness of the whole system, not only in actually achieving comparability (and therefore fair wages), but also in maintaining an adequate labour-force. But what was to determine increases in pay, if not comparability? One set of negotiations covered a heterogeneous collection of establishments, performing different functions, with different workers, with different interests. There was little to be said for the practice, except that it made tight control by the Treasury more effective. However, the PIB considered the industrial civil service to be a number of industries with one employer, most of them having reasonably close analogues outside, in spite of the absense of commercial objects. The larger establishments (employing the great majority) ought to be grouped according to their industry, each with its own pay structure, related to conditions and performance in the industry. Once a new structure was established, the pay of particular grades could be related to their counterparts in private employment. There would still have to be some central negotiations covering small, scattered groups. But this would be on a very much smaller scale than before, and so would not give rise to the same difficulties as the existing system.

Such changes were not to be made overnight. Meanwhile many of the workers had a case for an exceptional increase on the grounds that pay had fallen "seriously out of line", and manifestly needed improvement. Therefore, as the PIB had not been asked to comment on a particular settlement or level of pay, it suggested a demanding target date, April 1967, nine months ahead, for the new pay structures to be introduced, combined with some immediate increases to put right the worst anomalies.

Some time later, after the PIB had resolutely continued its campaign against comparability through many salary cases, the pay and conditions of industrial civil servants was again referred (No. 116). The structure of pay had by then been changed, and new rates based on it were paid on 1 July 1967. Twelve groups had been formed, to correspond with recognisable groups of private-sector workers, with whose basic rates Government pay was to be aligned. The re-grouping and re-aligning had involved rises averaging $7\frac{1}{2}$ per cent. In 1968, a $3\frac{1}{2}$ per cent increase (up to the ceiling) had been allowed, on grounds of again being seriously out of line. In 1969 the twelve groups had been consolidated into four, and the number of pay grades reduced. Increases averaging $8\frac{1}{2}$ per cent had been allowed, partly to prevent pay falling out of line, partly as a payment for more efficient working.

But the groups, whether twelve or four, cut across departmental boundaries and did not seem to the PIB to be "natural entities" for management purposes. The new structure was therefore "unable to withstand the strong tendency for the method of pay determination to revert to its previous form". Comparability had flowed back. The PIB's enquiries showed that not much had changed. Men still earned less than workers outside, women rather more. The twelve groups had had to be abandoned because workers doing similar work got different rates of pay by being aligned with different industries outside. Some, but not all anomalies had been removed by reducing the groups to four.

The structure originally suggested had gone wrong because pay negotiations did not correspond to the structure of management; and no good purpose had been served by reforming pay structure in advance of reforms of management.

The PIB reported that the new structure had neither reduced workers' dependence on comparability, nor much increased the link between pay and performance. Reforms of management were then still in train, generally in the direction of giving managers more responsibility. Where there were establishments suitable to become "autonomous organisations under public control", the PIB thought it desirable to put pay and conditions under the control of the management. But it might be unwise to abandon central negotiations altogether, as few managements were in control of their costs adequately, and to allow them to decide wage rates without being clearly responsible for total costs would lead to weaker constraints on managers.

Nevertheless, it was impossible to negotiate pay increases in return for contributions to productivity centrally. Progress must therefore be made with both central and local negotiations. Central negotiations ought to aim at establishing a framework of pay and conditions. There should be no return to the old M rate negotiations; but rather "guidance on the basic pay which workers in comparable circumstances in outside industry are actually receiving". Existing anomalies should be eliminated by abandoning the four groups and negotiating a single basic rate for craftsmen and unskilled workers throughout the civil service. This would also help to eliminate low pay among men workers. Local negotiations on productivity should give priority to method study and work measurement, as a basis for soundly based incentive schemes.

A smaller group of public-sector employees, showing some of the same problems as the industrial civil servants, was the maintenance workers of British Road Services (No. 90). The engineering industry and maintenance shops in road transport were both relevant standards of comparison for pay. Pay had fallen out of line with both, and industrial relations had worsened as a result. The management maintained that this had caused a serious shortage of labour. The PIB doubted this, since the alleged shortages were based on estimates of requirements assuming only current productivity. If productivity increased, the labour shortage would disappear. But public-sector niggardliness to its industrial employees was also having its usual side effects: the average age of the workers was high, and losses of skilled staff heavy. Earnings had been kept up by working overtime.

The PIB looked to productivity improvements for a solution. A productivity agreement had been made as a result of incomes policy; but taking all the improvements into account, the pay increase that could be justified was less than the settlement (7½ per cent as against 12 per cent). Future pay increases would have to be reviewed in relation to cost savings actually realised, rather than to outside rates. The workers would depend heavily on management for pay increases comparable with others.

Most of the railwaymen, industrial civil servants, and BRS employees were in jobs where output or performance was readily measurable and often also related to individual effort. The strongest case for comparability—and hence the most difficult problems for the incomes policy —occurred where performance was difficult to measure, and where the relation between the pay and performance of individuals was more tenuous. The most outstanding groups here were non-industrial civil servants and teachers. But the PIB was never asked to investigate a major claim or settlement for either. The only case involving non-industrial civil servants came very early on (late 1965) and related to the smallest group, at the top of the administrative class, and this was dealt with without much reference to comparability at all.

The only cases involving teachers also related to relatively peripheral cases. The pay of Scottish teachers was referred in the early period (January 1965), and university teachers were made the subject of a standing reference in the summer of 1968. In addition one boundary of the teaching profession was relevant to part of the case of nurses' pay, where the pay of nurse-tutors had to be considered separately.

The reference on Scottish teachers' salaries (No. 15) asked the PIB what salary increase would put them into "a fair relationship with teachers in England and Wales", on an "overall comparison". The PIB's view was that as there was little movement of teachers between Scotland and England, and as movement did not occur where the difference in salaries was greatest, the practice of matching pay increases served no "useful economic or social purpose". Two independent education systems required two independent salary structures (as both employers' and teachers' representatives agreed). Increases in pay should therefore also be independent.

Determining university teachers' pay involved comparisons with others, but not with other teachers, as the PIB saw it. A particular point of comparability was with consultants and other clinical workers in the NHS, since some of them were also university teachers, graded in the same way as others. But doctors were another important group whose pay was never reported on by the PIB. (An investigation was begun in May 1970 of the case for half an increase of 30 per cent recommended by the doctors' independent review body, the Kindersley Committee. But the case was withdrawn by the new Conservative Government of June 1970 before a report could be published, though rumour had it that the PIB had found good technical grounds for objecting to the way the Kindersley Committee had reached its conclusions, quite apart from

the obvious questions of principle and consistency.) Comparability perforce had to be accepted, at least in the sense of comparability of
increases for university teachers, though the PIB's reluctance to admit the
obnoxious principle showed plainly enough (and accounted for its
difficulties in reaching a conclusion on its first report, see p. 228 below).

In all these cases, the PIB established mainly a negative principle—
that general comparability was to be rejected; and a pertinent observation—that markets, insofar as they worked, were far more fragmented
than occupational groupings would suggest. But if comparisons of all
kinds were to be rejected, extra pay for extra performance would be
virtually the only way to exceptional increases in pay (or any increase at
all after July 1966); and this would inevitably mean that many public-
sector employees, and others performing skilled services would fall
increasingly behind. There must, therefore, be some kind of comparisons
to prevent this happening. The White Papers allowed comparisons in
making a case for an exceptional increase under criterion (iv), where
pay had become "seriously out of line" with pay for similar work. Having
thrown out general comparability, the PIB allowed a limited function
for it at particular points where market pressures were felt. For instance,
in the case of nurses' pay (No. 60) there were two such points relating to
tutorial staff, and to local authority nursing staff, were pay was said to
be out of line with going rates for alternative employment, the one in
Colleges of Further Education, the other in social welfare jobs. But
relating the pay of either of these small groups of nurses to outside groups
would cause great resentment among other nurses. The solution was to
give both groups better opportunities for promotion to more highly-paid
jobs in their own hierarchy. The structure should be improved to open
the way for more qualified and experienced tutors to do more responsible
teaching jobs in nurse training, justifying the higher pay they would
get on promotion. Hence the PIB's recommendation that nursing schools
should be grouped and enlarged (in the interests of students as well as the
teachers). Market pressure should be met where it was actually felt: by
seeing that the mobile individuals—the relatively well-qualified—were
rewarded in terms of pay and of the size of the job enough to retain them
where they were most needed.

The local authority nursing staff worked with other social welfare
staff of local authorities, though their pay was linked with hospital
nurses. It had been claimed that they should be paid according to local
authority scales, which were higher than hospital nursing scales. The
PIB did not accept their case, on the grounds that the change would
have created even greater problems of inequity with other nurses than
those between local authority nursing staff and other social welfare
staff. There was more mobility between hospital and local authority
nurses than between local authority nurses and other social workers.

Pay negotiations for the industrial civil service had excluded Her Majesty's Stationery Office (HMSO) because the printing workers were largely "trade-rated", that is, their pay rates were whatever was decided at national negotiations for the printing industry. Pay structure within HMSO, however, was referred to the PIB in 1969 (No. 135). Comparability with printing workers elsewhere was maintained by means of the industry rates, and overtime earnings were considerable. But accurate comparison of earnings with other London printers was difficult because of the wide range of pay found among the other printers. It appeared that earnings in HMSO might be rather less than elsewhere, but fringe benefits were considerably better.

HMSO could not isolate itself from the rest of its industry, but equally it should not merely follow after. It was a major employer, facing the same general problems as others. Like other major employers it should negotiate house agreement with the unions. There was no alternative to trade rates, but improvements could nevertheless be made. House extras could be consolidated into an "HMSO rate", which could be the basis for productivity discussions. Disputed relativities between maintenance and production workers could be settled by job evaluation. HMSO would eventually pay more attention rather than less to comparability, but with the rest of the industry in the private sector. It must continue to have regard to market rates; but it should also make suitable arrangements to get as good a bargain as other major employers could get.

All public-sector employees should be protected in the last resort by comparisons. But first their pay, or supplements to pay, should be decided in relation to the requirements of the unit of management. Pay should be related to performance; and internal relativities adjusted to make a structure both fair to workers, and effective for management purposes in securing their due share of the labour available, and an adequate supply of supervisors or higher staff. Then when the result came to be compared externally, earnings levels for exactly equivalent grades should be compared, making due allowance for differences in conditions.

Pay which was "in line" and allowed a nationally justifiable distribution of manpower was, generally speaking, the pay which allowed employers power to retain a labour-force. This conclusion emerged from a string of cases, beginning in the early days with the first report on busmen's pay (No. 16, see also p. 145), when some evidence of labour shortage was found. But it did not follow that an exceptional pay increase would alter the situation. Exceptional pay increases in 1964 had not been matched by other employers of similar labour in London; but no addition had been made to the labour-force on the buses. Pay had manifestly not solved the problem once; there was no reason to suppose it would on other occasions. Even if one major employer succeeded in remedying his shortage of labour by increasing pay relatively to the rest he would be only too likely to be followed by the others. If all were suffering from the effects of a general shortage, the only result was to increase pay all round for a given amount of work. The only useful remedy for individual employers or the country was better use of existing labour-forces. This conclusion implied that no claims on supply and demand grounds that arose basically from general shortages of labour in one area, or one competing group were consistent with the incomes policy. Thereafter the only cases where distribution of man-power arguments were accepted as justification for exceptional increases were all cases of demonstrable failure to retain certain small groups or at certain levels.

Mobility at a particular point in an occupation was found to be a key to the case of the General Accident Assurance Group (No. 41). There was a failure to retain experienced staff. Therefore, though the PIB recommended that a proposed general increase be implemented, it also recommended that the pay of experienced and more senior staff should be radically altered, by a system of annual reviews, with increments according to individual merits.

The market for office staffs in London was also investigated by the PIB in connection with the pay of staff employed by the office staff agencies (No. 89). It was widely believed (including within the Government service) that the temporary staff employed by the agencies and supplied by them to London employers set inflated levels of pay and attracted recruits away from permanent employment. The reference itself stated that: "the levels of salary paid to staff whose services are provided to other employers on a temporary basis has become a significant factor influencing the general level of pay for office staff." But "the market" was failing to work, as there was too little response from the demand (employers) side to scarcity and increasing prices. Case studies showed that "immediate steps" could be taken to improve the effectiveness of the staffs' efforts, and to reduce turnover. The demand on agencies for temporary staff was thus stronger than it need be.

There was no evidence that the pay of temporary staff set an inflated level to which the pay of other office staff adjusted. A survey showed that the labour-force consisted very largely of women who would not seek permanent jobs if no market for "temps" existed. The gap between the pay of the "temps" and of permanent staff was not "significantly greater" than could be accounted for by the value of fringe benefits such as sick pay and holiday pay, received by the permanent staff. The market appeared to be reasonably effective in equating net advantages.

In spite of its general rejection of comparability as a principle, plenty of comparisons can be found in the PIB's report in wages and salaries alike. Leaving aside the two largest sectors, engineering and building (where comparisons are hardly helpful since they cover so large a part of the average or general level themselves), all reports on pay levels (as opposed to systems of pay) contain comparisons with average levels of earnings, or movements of earnings in a related sector. Whatever the policy rules, pay had to be judged partly in relation to the pay of some other group. Comparisons of pay and pay increases helped to establish whether or not there was a problem that ought to be solved by means involving an increase in pay. In case after case, having made its comparisons to establish the facts, the PIB found that pay was relatively low where productivity was low—as might be expected if pay was market-determined. But what the PIB also found was that in many low-productivity areas, productivity could be improved relatively quickly and relatively significantly (as would not be expected in a model market economy). The prescription was demonstrated by the PIB to apply even in cases where comparisons seem to be the only standard, and in cases where previous official committees on pay had resorted to such comparisons to settle disputes.

Markets only worked in the direction of equalising the prices of labour where knowledge of what was offered and required was good. This knowledge was found to be often seriously lacking, even in very local markets, both among buyers and sellers of labour. But given better information, comparing like with like was a formidable task, as conditions of work, or the exact nature of the job itself varied widely, behind the same job descriptions. The PIB rarely found market pressures creating difficulties that were likely to be remedied by general pay increases. Pay structures could and did become unbalanced (especially in the public sector), by failure to recognise and pay for responsibility or skill at certain points. The market must in a general way influence the flow of labour available to a particular enterprise. But within the severe limits of markets divided by educational and other qualifications, many employers matched conditions, prospects and jobs to the work-forces at given levels of pay, rather than the other way round. How well or ill the matching was done was a matter of management rather than market economies.

Reports

No.   8   Pay and conditions of British Railways staff (Cmnd 2873)

No. 18   Pay of industrial civil servants (Cmnd 3034)

No. 116   Pay of the armed forces (Cmnd 4079)

No. 90   Pay of vehicle maintenance workers in British Road Services
          (Cmnd 3848)

No. 15   Scottish teachers' salaries (Cmnd 3005)

No. 60   Pay of nurses and midwives in the National Health Service
          (Cmnd 3585)

No. 135   Pay structure within HM Stationery Office (Cmnd 421)

No. 16   Pay and conditions of busmen (Cmnd 3012)

No. 41   Salaries of staff of General Accident Assurance Co. Ltd (Cmnd
          3398)

No. 89   Office staff employment agencies charges and salaries (Cmnd
          3828)

14

Reform of Pay Structures

From the first, the PIB made its recommendations on the pay claims referred to it with longer-term reforms in mind as well as the rules of incomes policy. Differentials between working groups or levels of responsibility in one enterprise often needed radical change, even when they were not in dispute. To make them correspond better to real differences in work content meant working out internal pay relativities systematically, and hence introducing new pay structures. Differentials between manual and clerical work, between production workers and their supervisors, between craftsmen and process workers, as well as between one skill and another all became outdated as technology and management progressed; and the need for reform was accentuated as productivity agreements brought more rapid and varied changes in working methods. The need was soon found to be widespread and important enough to make it desirable to add reform of pay structures to the list of special cases justifying exceptional pay increases, the only major addition made (in 1968).

Where labour productivity could be raised by workers carrying out wider ranges of work, re-grading into wider and more appropriate categories of function, skill or responsibility was usually necessary. Regrading into fewer groups with appropriate changes in pay, was one of the reforms urged on the railways (see p. 142), and on plant bakeries (see p. 135). The pay of industrial civil servants (see p. 152), local authority workers and NHS workers (see p. 177) had become confined within narrow bands, with far too many ineffective differentials. Some distinctions between jobs in Government industrial establishments had lost their purpose altogether, while grossly inadequate rewards for responsibility "militated against the efficient running", and probably was one reason for the leisurely pace of work found in some places. Manual workers in local authorities, public utilities and the NHS needed to have their pay related more to their own sector and less to one another. Indeed the PIB's report was designed to "enable each industry to develop pay systems" determined by their specific needs. Work measurement and job evaluation were the accepted techniques, whose adoption or extension was urged on all these public authorities.

The electrical-contracting industry (No. 24) had negotiated a new pay structure before the PIB's report, based on a radical new grading, embodied in a three-year agreement (1966 to 1969). Rates and conditions throughout the industry had previously been effectively controlled by the National Joint Industrial Council and incentive bonuses were not allowed, on pain of expulsion from the employers' association. As a result, the only important difference between national rates and earnings was overtime pay. The new agreement made provision for getting rid of "mates", and reclassifying other workers according to their technical qualifications, the objects being to improve management–labour relations, as well as the skill of a reduced and more adaptable labour-force. The restructuring was to be supervised by a newly-formed Joint Industrial Board (JIB), consisting of employers and unions with an independent Chairman.

The first wage increase under the new agreement was prevented by the standstill. But as it was believed that the agreed increases would be spread to other industries, by the "trade-rating" of electricians employed elsewhere (including Government establishments, local authorities, and the NHS), the whole agreement was referred to the PIB. Specific provision for an exceptional increase to allow a major restructuring of pay had not yet been added to the White Paper. The PIB therefore had to approach the case by reference to productivity rather than the restructuring. The employers claimed that the increase was justified because electricians in the contracting industry had got "seriously out of line" with other electricians, or craftsmen working on building sites alongside electricans. But it was found that the electricians had merely done a little less well than similar workers, in contrast to a relative improvement intended by a previous agreement of 1963.

The PIB was highly critical of the new agreement. Although the prospect of co-operation between management and union to promote productivity was warmly welcomed, the proposals relating to productivity had not been worked out in detail, and only provided a framework for proper measures. The final size of the pay increase was uncertain. The first instalment would add 13 per cent to standard rates; but the increase in the wage bill in the second and third years depended on the number transferred to each of the new grades. The increase for the three years would probably be between 20 and 33 per cent, a formidable increase to have to cover by increased productivity, and some firms had already declared their intention of raising charges. The PIB decided that the reform should go ahead; but the second and third stages should be re-negotiated in the light of progress to ensure increases in productivity, and of economic conditions at the time. Meanwhile, a standard method of measuring output should be developed, unnecessary overtime should be reduced, and "pair working" reduced. Employers of electricians in other industries should no longer copy the contracting industry's rates.

The first stage increase was duly paid, at the end of the standstill, and the Government decided to give electricians in the NHS the 13 per cent increase at the same time. Many private-sector employers also gave the 13 per cent, but a number did not follow (for the first time). The second stage was discussed by employers and unions with the Ministry of Labour, and it was agreed that a second pay increase should not be made for another year. The definition of grades, and the procedure for regrading was also agreed.

A further reference to the PIB was made two years later, after the implementation of the second stage (No. 120). Pay increases had been made to depend on possessing a JIB card (which meant that they depended on regarding), as had been agreed with Government as a result of the first PIB recommendations. Moreover, the PIB now found the JIB to be an admirable institution—even one to be recommended for the consideration of other industries. It had adopted enlightened employment and training policies, and the regrading had been handled with "notable success". A data bank of standard times would soon provide guidance to firms on measuring productivity and on costing. In short, it was the right sort of national body to supervise a framework agreement, by now being recommended generally by the PIB.

However, when pay in engineering and then in construction were referred to the PIB, far more chaotic pay structures were documented, with effects arguably far worse than the primeval rigidity of public-sector pay structures. "Gross anomalies" affected staff as well as manual workers. Supervisors were sometimes regularly paid less than those they supervised, skilled men paid less than unskilled, and qualified people less than unqualified—in the same plant. The PIB's remedy as we have seen (p. 152), was negotiating comprehensive company agreements, eventually within a national framework agreement, a primary purpose of which was to establish orderly pay-structures earnings, with differentials generally defensible in terms of the job to be done.

Building and civil engineering also suffered from inequitable and inefficient pay structures, with a multiplicity of rates within a narrow range. Grades in building still related to traditional crafts, whereas new techniques required different skills, and less demarcation between them. A fresh analysis of grades was necessary; and large companies might undertake job evaluation schemes, or adopt model schemes worked out nationally.

The civil-engineering industry was even more in need of job evaluation, at either company or industry level. New jobs had been introduced with new equipment and techniques; but they had been fitted into the old grading, rather than the grading adapted to the jobs. As a result, there were over 100 different "plus rates", ranging from only 2d to 2s 3d an hour. The plus-rating system had virtue in making it easy for ambitious or industrious workers prevented from entering a craft to increase their earnings. Nevertheless so large a number of rates was bound to cause friction. The PIB had sympathy with the unions's aim to reduce the plus rate to a series of grades, and recommended job evaluation with this aim for industry or company agreements.

When dealing with salaries, the PIB advised all major employers to consider their structure as a whole. For instance, the banking salary structure (No. 6 see p. 213) needed revision to meet the changing banking functions. The administrative and clerical staff in electricity supply (No. 5 see p. 212) needed to discuss a new salary structure with their employers, "with special regard for the need for remuneration in the higher posts being commensurate with responsibility". The merchant navy officers (see p. 217) were only to receive half a recommended increase in basic rates, the other half forming a pool from which each company could create a new salary structure. Increases in staff pay in insurance companies (No. 41 see p. 214) should be related to increased productivity estimated by work measurement and job evaluation in individual companies, which would result in a new structure. The chief and senior local officers (No. 45 see p. 224) and their employers were both supporting a system giving rise to "salary drift"; the remedy was to introduce a job-evaluated structure relating pay to responsibility and performance. A prime need for nurses (No. 60 see p. 227) was to improve the salary structure, hence the grading system recommended by the Salmon Committee should be introduced much sooner than the Ministry of Health intended.

Much of this was generalised by the PIB itself in its report on job evaluation (No. 83). The chaos of pay structures from which job evaluation produced order had often been the result of national collective agreements breaking down. Where these consisted of minimum rates for labourers and craftsmen, a wide range of rates was negotiated at the work place. Even without PBR difficulties as well, the national rates became increasingly irrelevant to pay determination. Fragmented bargaining with separate groups led to a continual struggle to remove anomalies. Increases in earnings as a result were far beyond nationally negotiated increases or productivity increases. Job evaluation was a contribution to solving this problem, as it generally aimed to rank jobs on common standards, though it could not itself determine a particular structure.

The experience of firms which had used job evaluation was mostly encouraging. Resulting structures were said to be more rational, which usually meant more equitable as well as more efficient. "Equal pay for work of equal content" was often demanded, especially of multi-plant firms, and job evaluation was a technique to determine the "equal content". Significantly, firms had also found that ordered systems gave them more control of costs.

Though job evaluation was essentially a management tool there had also been advantage for unions, since some found job-evaluated pay structures "helpful to the co-ordination of union wage policy". As the pressures on conventional pay systems were likely to continue, and as all the evidence suggested that job evaluation was a practical means of constructing rational and efficient pay structures, it was to be commended in general.

However, there were difficulties in the short-term context within which incomes policy had to be applied. Installing a reformed pay structure of a comprehensive kind could not be done without cost; it ought not to be done without benefit. But the cost and the benefit did not usually coincide, and unit labour costs would rise in a transitional period. The costs hump might be a long time disappearing while more systematic promotions arrangements, or extra reward for skill and responsibility had time to affect output. Yet the eventual benefits might be considerable.

The White Paper for 1968 and 1969 explicitly excepted reformed pay structures (together with productivity agreements) from the $3\frac{1}{2}$ per cent ceiling. However, more guidance than the White Paper rules alone was needed to sort justifiable schemes from ill-devised ones, and the PIB considered that job evaluation schemes would require "particularly rigorous examination" by the DEP to ensure that the eventual benefits outweighed the costs so that some gain might accrue to the customers. In particular, pay increases should not be made before the new structure was introduced. All firms should be required to provide information on job-evaluated structures costing more than $3\frac{1}{2}$ per cent on the pay bill about the method and construction of the particular scheme, job descriptions, numbers in each grade, personal or job allowances, and the proposed methods for control. It also warned that job evaluation could not of itself settle general pay problems. Job-evaluated structures were more likely to adapt themselves easily to changing jobs, but pressures would build up against any structure, especially in the form of claims for regrading at the border of one grade and another. There should therefore be "regular audits" of pay structures, at intervals of about three years, by senior management.

The pay and duty of light-keepers (No. 114) was referred early in 1969. A link had been established in 1962 between the pay of light-keepers and seamen in an award of the National Maritime Board in respect of seamen's pay, which had been mainly concerned with reductions in the seamen's basic working week. Subsequent agreements for light-keepers had not, however, translated these reductions into light-keepers pay, though negotiations on the subject had taken place each time. Narrow differentials and poor career prospects gave rise to problems of recruitment and wastage. Neither side could really defend the link, and the PIB concluded inevitably that it should cease.

A new pay structure must be devised, having regard to the long hours and interrupted social life of light-keepers compared with others. This time public-sector employees had suffered from an inappropriate link with private-sector workers. But the result was familiar: underpayment for the public employees.

In the case of the pay of ground staff at aerodromes (No. 128), the Government specifically referred the pay structure for investigation. Publicly-owned civil airports were operated by the British Airports Authority, local authorities and the Board of Trade, and each had their own pay negotiations, pay scales and conditions. The same work was carried out by workers in different grades at different airports and pay agreements were reached at different times for different airports. Pay structures inevitably diverged; and working practices in turn diverged. As usual, resentment over indefensible differentials accumulated.

Some employers had concluded productivity agreements with their respective groups of workers; but more could be done. In particular, the PIB considered that grading to enable each airport to make flexible use of its manpower was needed. Method study should be used to adapt working procedures to new equipment and the changing pattern of traffic. Work measurement should be used to establish realistic manning standards. A new joint negotiating body should introduce a common pay and grading scheme, associating improvements in efficiency with it. The new body would require the assistance of an expert advisory unit on efficiency to guide its work. The airport employers were in effect recommended to set up a Joint Industrial Board, as had been done in the electrical-contracting industry.

A special problem of pay structure was a main feature of the report on Smithfield Market (No. 126). This was a highly labour-intensive activity, and the labour involved was divided into a relatively large number of separate categories, separately organised, and paid on unrelated scales. Though many separate grades might be evidence of an efficient division of labour, in this case more interchangeability would clearly allow some improvement. Employers and union had agreed in principle on the interchangeability, but negotiations had repeatedly broken down on the rate to be fixed for combined jobs.

The overriding problem was the difference between the earnings of employed and self-employed men, which continually caused discontent among the employed workers. There was no shortage of self-employed workers to provide the service required (not surprisingly, in view of the fact that the PIB found them to be earning from £45 to £55 a week while the employed workers earned from £19 to £34). The collective bargaining machinery exacerbated the unsatisfactory situation. Though all classes of workers (including the self-employed) belonged to the TGWU, each section negotiated separately. Though there was a Central Co-ordinating Committee of unions it was in fact powerless to reconcile the interests of different groups of workers as it could not control the self-employed.

The only real remedy the PIB could suggest was to tackle all the problems in a connected way—including the general efficiency of the whole market's operations. Improvements in methods of operation and working conditions would have to be matched by changes in labour organisation, especially in industrial relations and pay systems. The PIB was not very optimistic about a practical solution being reached. It could only point out that the wide gaps in earnings of workers doing similar work side by side was "against the long-term interests of the market and should be either ended or at least extensively modified". A Joint Board of market tenants and workers, chaired by the Market Superintendent, might try to negotiate, or at least discuss, some improvement.

In the pottery industry the employers' association had already begun arranging a job evaluation for the whole industry when their pay structure was referred in the last phase of the PIB's life (No. 149). It was begun as a prelude to equal pay by 1975, as over half the labour-force was women. Equal pay was expected to raise many women's pay by nearly 50 per cent, and the potteries' wage bills would rise by 2 to 17 per cent (with a median of 10 per cent). Productivity and pay structure was clearly a more urgent problem in this industry than in many others.

Negotiations were apparently centralised and formalised. Time rates, fringe benefits, disputes procedure and the relationship of piece rates to time rates were all agreed in the NJC. There were few non-federated firms, or company agreements not related to the NJC. A small cost-of-living supplement and a large percentage "plusage" (a percentage addition to basic rates to increase earnings) made the structure both complex and confusing. Agreements were made annually, by a traditional ritual around Lady Day (25 March). Ostensibly it was an industry as strongly central-ised for pay negotiations as the plant bakers. But the PIB found that few male workers earned the NJC rates. More of the women were on the negotiated rates, but most men and some women were clearly as dependent on company pay agreements as on the central proceedings. A majority of women and a substantial minority of men were on piece rates negotiated at shop-floor level. Though the minimum ratio of piece rates to time rates was agreed, actual differentials were much greater. Negotiations over piece rates were often informal to the point of confusion, since setting proper work standards was not always distinguished from negotiating a price for the work. Employers had clearly built supplements on to rates in an attempt to stabilise their labour-force. Job classifications no longer matched the work in modern plants; and differentials for skill and responsibility did not match the functions actually carried out.

There was a clear case for a reformed pay structure, and the PIB recommended that a new classification could best be worked out by job evaluation. No one scheme was likely to meet the needs of all firms, and technological changes were still going on, requiring further changes in job grading. National framework agreements should be negotiated, covering a job evaluation framework, guidelines for PBR systems, guidelines for company agreements and a code of rights and duties for workshop representatives. Both the union and the employers' association would need strengthening for new activities, and the NJC would also have new functions in advising firms on pay matters, and perhaps investigating labour productivity.

In the water-supply industry (No. 152, see p. 153), it was the Training Board that had taken the lead in redesigning job contents in a wider range of more demanding work. But differentials were still too many and too narrow—as so often in the public sector. A few large undertakings had already reclassified jobs into broad bands with great advantage to managements and unions and the PIB recommended others to do so.

Another industry in the public sector, the National Freight Corporation (No. 162, see p. 123), needed a reform of pay structures, after a major reorganisation of control had been made but when more was clearly needed. The main constituent parts of NFC were NCL and Freightliners, inherited from the railways, and the two major British Road Services Companies, inherited from the Transport Holding Company. NCL and Freightliners were organised by the National Union of Railwaymen and their pay structures corresponded to the railway's pay systems. BRS (Parcels) and BRS Ltd were organised mainly by the TGWU and had developed pay structures of their own. But the purpose of creating NFC was to rationalise freight transport, a rationalisation that was urgently needed to restrain costs and improve returns. The labour-force in all the main operating companies would have to be run down, and their functions more specialised. This would entail workers transferring from one company to another, a process that could only be accomplished smoothly if job grades and pay structures corresponded. A plethora of negotiating bodies, some covering manual workers, some craft workers, some clerical and other salaried staff would have to be replaced by a few related joint committees covering all workers in all NFC's activities. Pay reform was necessary to improve efficiency and profits, and a major reform of negotiating procedure was necessary to make an appropriate pay structure possible.

All of these cases concerned pay structures where close links between pay and the jobs to be performed for the pay needed to be made. Many salary structures were of a different kind and offered more intractable problems. The link between pay and the job performed presents less difficulty than the link between pay and the performance of the person in the job. Any job, apart from the most repetitive machine-paced operations, is performed more or less effectively by one person and another in a way which is difficult to quantify. But there are significant differences between the problems arising from cases described in this chapter, and those arising from typical salary structures.

Reports

No.   8   Pay and conditions of British Railways staff (Cmnd 2873)

No. 18   Pay of industrial civil servants (Cmnd 3034)

No. 29   Pay and conditions of manual workers in local authorities, NHS, and gas and water supply (Cmnd 3230)

No. 24   Wages and conditions in the electrical-contracting industry (Cmnd 3172)

No. 120   Pay and conditions in the electrical-contracting industry (Cmnd 4097)

No. 91   Pay and conditions in the civil-engineering industry (Cmnd 3836)

No. 92   Pay and conditions in the building industry (Cmnd 3837)

No.   5   Remuneration of administrative and clerical staff in electricity supply (Cmnd 2801)

No. 45   Pay of chief and senior officers in local government (Cmnd 3473)

No. 83   Job evaluation (Cmnd 3772)

No. 114   Pay and duties of light-keepers (Cmnd 4067)

No. 128   Pay of ground staff at aerodromes (Cmnd 4182)

No. 126   Remuneration of workers in Smithfield (Cmnd 4171)

No. 149   Pay and conditions in the pottery industry (Cmnd 4411)

No. 152   Pay and productivity in the water-supply industry (Cmnd 4434)

No. 162   Costs, charges and productivity in the National Freight Corporation (Cmnd 4569)

15

Salaries

Salaries are distinguished from wages either by method of payment (usually monthly rather than weekly paid), or by function (staff rather than production workers). The distinction can be regarded as between manual and non-manual work, or between operators and jobs having supervisory, executive or advisory functions. For present purposes, the differences between definitions mainly involves different treatment of clerical salaries. The PIB itself chose to limit its definition of salaries to those above clerical level when it discussed salary structures in general. But as there were a number of salary cases which comprised clerical and higher functions together, clerical pay has been included in the present chapter.

The first White Paper said nothing specific about salaries: the words "and salaries" were simply tacked on to wages in relation to the norm and the four criteria for exceptional treatment. But this was not enough to constitute even a rudimentary policy. Very few salary-earners were low-paid (none were discovered by the PIB), and relatively few could make meaningful productivity agreements. This left only exceptional market pressures, or gross anomalies to justify anything more than the norm for some millions of salary-earners; and given the PIB's approach, these two exceptions would only apply to small groups of unusually specialised people. There was a case on social grounds for closing the gap between wages and salaries more rapidly; but it was never intended that this should be a consequence of the incomes policy. Nor was it intended that public-sector pay should lag behind private-sector pay, another inevitable consequence of particular restraint towards salaries as a whole. The PIB found very early in its activities that fair and equal treatment under the same policy required different rules for salaries; and eventually major changes in salary structures were included in the White Papers as an exception justifying pay increases above the norm or ceiling. This became a more important "escape route " for salary-earners than for wage-earners.

The first salary case (No. 5) was referred in June 1965 a few days before a strike was due to start. The dispute concerned negotiations between unions representing the clerical and administrative workers in the electricity-supply industry and the Electricity Council. The workers claimed that differentials between themselves and management staff, and manual or technical workers, had been unreasonably disturbed because both manual and managerial workers had recently concluded productivity deals. Managers and professional staff had had increments related to the volume of business as well as annual increases in salary scales. Manual workers had received substantial increases in return for major changes of working practice; and the engineers had agreed to work new patterns of hours to supervise the manual workers, again in return for a substantial increase.

However, only a small minority of clerical or administrative workers were required to change their working practices. There was no evidence that the industry's capacity to recruit or hold staff was any worse than similar employers, so their pay was not seriously out of line. The only question left, according to the White Paper, was whether there was a contribution to productivity that these workers could make, commensurate with the increase claimed. They could not, except by giving up a previous rule that shift-working could only be extended with the unions' agreement, and by taking into account the fact that more showrooms were remaining open on Saturday afternoons. But cost saving or extra income would be very small.

If the White Paper rules were strictly applied, clerical workers must be restricted to hardly more than the norm, while their colleagues in all other grades were getting annual increases several times the norm, and all in accordance with the policy rules. This conclusion was neither just nor calculated to promote efficiency in electricity supply. Nor would it endear the incomes policy to other salaried workers. Hence the PIB's pronouncement that the employers' offer of eight per cent could be justified. Where productivity agreements were concluded, greater changes were required from some groups than others, and general disturbance followed. The employers' offer could be regarded as reducing this "sense of disturbance".

The PIB, it was said, had invented a fifth criterion, a sense of disturbance. It had indeed. It had begun to fill the gap left by the previous failure to consider salaries, or salaried employees, as significantly different from wages and wage earners. But payment for disturbance could only be reconciled with the aims of incomes policy with difficulty. It would hardly help to restrain costs, nor encourage radical changes. It was not until late in its career that the PIB finally managed to grasp the nettle firmly. In a report on the salaries of ICI staff (discussed further below, p. 218), the PIB came to the conclusion that the staff, who claimed "disturbance", enjoyed their already high status and salary precisely because of their co-operative attitude to changes necessary for efficiency. Manual workers had recently adopted the same attitudes, and it was only right that the gap between themselves and salaried staff should be closed. In this respect at least, the PIB became more radical with the years.

The electricity clerks' case was typical of salary problems in large productive enterprises, where salaries have to fit into a hierarchy of pay, from nationally negotiated wages at one end to individual managerial salaries at the other. The PIB had reached a conclusion to meet these particular circumstances; but the solution turned entirely on internal relativities between groups. The question of relativities with clerical occupations elsewhere still remained.

The case of the salaries of Midland Bank staffs (No. 6) raised the question of the determination of clerical salaries, in relation to executive or managerial salaries. The large majority of the bank's staff was on a continuous scale with annual increments, mostly continued up to retirement age. Ability or creditable performance were both rewarded by merit increments, as well as promotion. General increases in salaries were negotiated annually.

The "production" of banks could be reckoned in the form of the volume, range and more complex nature of the services provided. There had been increases of product in all senses. There was no unequivocal evidence of an increase in the volume of transactions per staff member; but the work was more exacting, especially for the senior staff, as a result of rapid expansion in non-routine business. However, the referred settlement had little relevance to this, apart from raising minimum pay for manager. "But," concluded the PIB, "the acceptance of more exacting work by some employees cannot be regarded as a valid reason for exceptional treatment for all."

This judgment had significance for many other salary earners. There were thousands more employed in institutions increasing the range or complexity of their services. "More exacting work" was being performed, and it could have been said that exceptional increases in salary were justified in such institutions, to give equivalent increases in pay for many salary-earners (including some public-sector salaries). But the PIB considered that general salary increases would hinder performance of higher quality or more complex work, where those actually doing it received no relative advantage over the rest. New demands for a different mix of skills needed a new structure of pay to induce a matching supply.

Like its competitors, the Midland Bank was employing more women for the routine work and had no difficulty in recruiting them. But all the banks needed entrants with higher educational standards able to take decisions involving heavy commitments for their employers. A general salary increase might leave salaries still too low to attract and retain

H

high-quality staff, and too high for the routine jobs. While most wage structures needed simplifying out of a confused multiplicity of purposes, the banks' structure was too simple, and needed elaborating to recognise the changing needs of the job. The PIB recommended a dual salary structure, one part offering "more realistic conditions" to potential managers, the other appropriate rates for clerical and other routine work, not necessarily leading to posts of responsibility.

There were then no powers to rescind the Midland Bank's agreement, contrary to the incomes policy though it was. The PIB recommended therefore that the increase should be absorbed by paying no further general increases for 18 months.

Nearly four years later the salaries of all bank staffs were referred to the PIB (No. 106). A Joint National Council, negotiating for the clearing banks as a whole had been set up and national negotiations had begun. Effort had been concentrated on this, and hitherto little change had been made in the form of agreements. The referred agreement provided for pay increases averaging seven per cent, designed partly to level up pay between banks (the first consequence of national negotiation) and partly as a step towards levelling up women's pay to men's pay. An interim payment of $3\frac{1}{2}$ per cent across-the-board (the general ceiling on pay increases) had been agreed between the DEP and the JNC, on the explicit understanding that it would not be withdrawn later, no matter what the PIB recommended.

This decision presented the PIB with something of a dilemma. An increase in the salary bill of $3\frac{1}{2}$ per cent spread in such a way that anomalies (between banks) were corrected could be justified as a rationalisation of salary structures. But another general increase of $3\frac{1}{2}$ per cent could only be justified by increases in productivity, as none of the other criteria applied.

The PIB found that the staffs' contribution, including their co-operation, had amounted to rather over the necessary $3\frac{1}{2}$ per cent. The increase already paid was thus justified; though no further general increase ought to be made, until more savings (or improved services) had accrued generally. A new salary structure to attract better qualified recruits was being introduced, as had been recommended.

Several salary cases involving insurance companies came before the PIB, the first being the General Accident Assurance Company, referred in July 1967 (No. 41). The company had a special problem in losing experienced staff faster than similar companies, and to an extent that the management considered would prevent them from operating effectively. This was found by the PIB to be an exceptional situation, with clear evidence of salaries being out of line with strictly comparable ones. It was held therefore to justify a general pay increase, as well as changes in structure.

The report also advanced the interpretation of salaries by considering incremental scales. The main justification for incremental scales was to relate pay to experience. A new entrant's experience could be equated with age, and there was "no great harm" in age-related scales at recruitment. As time went on though, age was less connected with experience of value to the employer. It was the demonstrated ability of individuals that should then be rewarded, and not so exclusively the jobs individuals filled. The PIB suggested abolishing some grade scales, in favour of fixing salaries individually on merit. This would improve career prospects, and hence improve recruitment and efficiency, a change in the national interest as well as the company's. Merit increases should be paid in accordance with the criteria relating to salaries, namely that exceptional increases could be allowed for "progressions based on added experience, increased responsibility or special effort", and to provide incentives for better performance. The product would be improved by providing the insured with better or speedier service, and performance improved by incurring a smaller salary bill to do it.

The following year the PIB continued its study of labour use in insurance companies (No. 74). Two larger companies, the Pearl and the Prudential, had made agreements with their staffs for general salary increases. Both companies had already made substantial improvements in office procedures and work control; but in neither could it be said that any resulting disturbance had anything to do with the claim for extra pay. There was no evidence of failure to retain experienced staff. Both companies considered that their staffs had contributed generally to improved performance, and that the proposed increases were necessary to keep pay in line with comparable jobs. The case therefore raised the general question of the determination of salaries for clerical staffs. The PIB had to return once more to comparability, as it had done three years before for the railway clerks. Its view now was that the traditional justification for increases in clerical pay, comparability with others, was only acceptable if output could not be measured. Many repetitive clerical jobs had been measured successfully, and this practice should be extended.

Increases in clerical salaries for lower grades in the referred companies could and should be linked in future to improvements in performance. The proper increases in salary for their supervisors, and those with more complex or less measurable functions, would follow by offering proper rewards for responsibility and skill. In the last resort, salaries might need adjustment at certain points of market pressure, especially to avoid a loss of middle management, as General Accident had needed to do.

Measured increases in work would indicate appropriate salary increases at the bottom, after savings had been attributed to improved management or increased capital. The appropriate salary structure above the basic measured work load could be determined by job evaluation. But comparisons between one firm and another, even among insurance companies, could not be made with proper accuracy, since staff grading and the related jobs varied too much from one company to another.

The PIB had by now collected much more evidence of the lack of similarity in job content and methods of work even in apparently similar occupations at similar levels in one industry. At this stage, the weakest point of the PIB's principles was that they justified increases in salary in relation to internal needs firmly, but to external analogues only tenuously or prospectively. The best hope most clerks would have of general increases in pay (apart from good management of their own activities) would be that their fellows in sectors with internal relativities to fast-advancing wage-earners would move up enough to create "gross anomalies" in pay of clerks elsewhere.

The case of clerical staff employed in Bristol docks (No. 81) referred in May 1968, was just such a case. Bristol docks were then owned by the local authority, and the dock clerks' pay increases mostly followed automatically from settlements made for local authorities' clerical (and other) employees, where there were no clear relativities with wage-earners. Not unnaturally these arrangements resulted in pay levels that bore no reasonable relationship to the pay of the dockers, determined by different negotiating machinery, covering a different industry. The settlement referred to the PIB was for an increase of £1 a week for all the dock staff, intended to restore part of the traditional differential with the dockers' pay after considerable increases in dockers' wages, (as part of the arrangements for decasualisation of labour). The dock clerks had already received a rise of 3.4 per cent in common with other local-authority staff; but this still left them behind the dockers.

The extra £1 a week was not associated with any specific productivity agreement, so it clearly could not be justified easily. Increased work was being done by a smaller number of staff as a result of "co-operation and flexibility". Like the Midland Bank staff, the dock staff were considered to deserve some reward in recognition of their co-operation but this could not justify as much as the proposal. Nevertheless, the PIB eventually recommended it should be paid in full, but merely as "the tail end of a large number of increases consequential on the decasualisation settlement"—the end of a closed chapter. No further increases should be made, either following on changes in dockers' pay or on further settlements with local authority staffs, until the Government was satisfied that "an approach to efficiency" was also being made. Appropriate work standards should be set, and improvements in measured work duly rewarded.

The clerks would not be confined entirely to increases directly related to productivity. Proper differentials between dockers and their supervisors should be maintained. These supervisors were members of the staff, so the whole hierarchy would benefit from a consideration of internal relativities throughout. But until the staff were in a position to get direct productivity increases, they were not to get any others either.

The sum of the PIB's findings on all clerical-type salaries was thus: first, that many clerical activities were capable of measurement and should be measured. Current levels of performance would then be clear, and improvements in the level could also be quantified. Appropriate increases in pay could be related to these improvements without increasing unit costs.

Secondly, where activities could not be measured, levels of skill or responsibility could be described or delimited by job analysis. Such analysis would allow the levels to be related to a minimum, and perhaps would encourage the exercise of more responsibility at lower levels. Again, extra pay could be related to such changes, without increasing unit costs.

Thirdly, the performance of individual holders of a particular job might add materially to the quality of the service provided. Individual merit should be rewarded by individual payments, related as closely to the performance as the nature of the activity allowed.

Finally, the whole structure of clerical pay might in certain circumstances be related to wages or other salary structures. Clerical and adminstrative pay would need relating to wages within an enterprise, where salaried staff supervised wage-earning workers. There should be a proper differential at this point to safeguard the supply of competent supervisors. This would apply also to the points of supervision of clerical or other volume work. There should be a proper comparability of earnings between the staff of one enterprise and another, providing educational qualifications were similar, the jobs they were required to perform were exactly similar, and that career prospects were duly taken into account.

Many of these same principles had been derived from investigating salaries of other workers besides clerks. The question of the relation between the pay of supervisors and supervised had been posed in an acute form in a quite different environment during the period of severe restraint.

The report on the pay of merchant navy officers (No. 35) was the first report to make use of the first specific provision for the "proper development" of salary structures included in the fourth White Paper (after June 1967) to resolve this question. The settlement referred to the PIB had been reached following a new agreement with the seamen's union (after the costly and nationally disastrous seamen's strike of May–June 1966). The PIB had not been asked for its views on the seamen's agreement itself, because it had followed the report from a Court of Inquiry. The result for the seamen was increases in pay and shorter hours, the net effect of which would raise earnings by something over 10 per cent. The officers had settled with the employers for a consequential increase of 10 per cent. It was clear common sense that something of the sort was necessary, since differentials between manual workers and their supervisors were a crucial point in any pay structure. The consequences for the whole enterprise or industry should be considered when a pay increase was given to one group within it. The merchant navy officers' increase must therefore be allowed. But as an inducement to a radical overhaul of the pay structure the PIB recommended that half the increase be paid immediately, the other half being held by the companies as a fund to be distributed on different lines, after the whole pay structure had been reviewed. Both recommendations were implemented.

Differentials between wages and salaries in the same enterprise might be upset where there was no point of supervision, and no measurable volume of work to resolve the issue, giving rise to an inhibiting sense of disturbance. A later case where earnings had been increased substantially below a salaried group was that of journalists (No. 115). Productivity agreements in a number of newspaper houses had resulted in substantial increases to the (already high) earnings of production workers. Journalists' pay could not be regarded in isolation from production workers, especially as they were at similar levels. The productivity agreements with the production workers had not taken into account the consequential increases for journalists, justified though these might be in themselves.

However, the question of internal relativities did not in the end contribute directly to the PIB's conclusions. Method study to ensure "a more efficient flow of copy" between different groups of workers was recommended to improve performance. Salary drift had occurred, as merit awards, higher starting pay and rapid promotion had resulted in average increases in earnings well above agreed increases in minimum rates. This could be mitigated by introducing a new structure, based on job analysis, whereby all existing differentials could be reviewed.

By the spring of 1969 the PIB was reviewing staff salaries in a number of other cases. The report on the salaries of staff employed by ICI Ltd, was the second relating to the firm (No. 109). The PIB had already reported on the agreement ICI had proposed with their manual workers (see p. 166), which gave them staff status in return for abandoning practices inhibiting increases in output (or sales) per worker. Staff workers had also negotiated a new-style agreement, covering most of the staff other than executives. The company reported that its staff were already co-operating fully in changes of practice that had been, or would be required. They could not therefore, collectively speaking, "sell" any restrictive practices in a similar way to the manual workers. It would be unfair therefore, in the company's view, to leave staff workers without a pay increase broadly equivalent to the increases agreed (and approved by the PIB) for manual workers. In plants where the new structure for manual workers applied, anomalies affecting staff workers had already arisen, most acute difficulties, as usual, at the points of supervision.

The PIB verdict was this time that the virtue of co-operation must be presumed to have been rewarded already, and that present rewards for abandoning unco-operative ways were rectifying past unfairness, rather than creating a new injustice. The general implication of this conclusion was a radical one indeed, and would have involved a considerable squeezing of pay for most white-collar work, relatively to manual work.

The basis of the salary system in ICI was an assessment of job content. Consequently, when more exacting work had been required, this was taken into account by a reassessment of the jobs concerned. A regrading of the job would give its occupant a direct reward for more exacting work (whether his initiative—or virtue—were involved or not). Where an individual occupant contributed more, by experience, energy or ability, in a given job his personal contribution would be rewarded by a good performance increment. Long-service increments were also awarded. Outstanding individuals could even have the normal maximum salary attaching to their jobs raised. All this was in addition to normal promotion prospects.

The question then remaining for the PIB was whether the system gave increases consistent with the incomes policy rules. Salaries had gone up on average somewhat more than the permitted $3\frac{1}{2}$ per cent for productivity, and more than accounted for by changes in the structure of jobs, or in the age, seniority or ability of the occupants of the jobs. There were no grounds therefore in the PIB's view for approving a general increase in salaries of more than $3\frac{1}{2}$ per cent, other than would result anyway from the performance related increments for individuals. Moreover, it was the comprehensiveness, and even generosity of those increments (for the able and energetic) that led the PIB to take the general view it did.

The Government duly accepted the recommendations, and the DEP discussed it with the company. As a result, ICI announced that the balance of the increase would be withheld until November 1969, the end of the maximum standstill that could be imposed statutorily under the Prices and Incomes Act of 1968. But it also announced that on that date it would pay the full increase due since 1 January 1969, as originally agreed. As in the case of the banks, all that the Government had achieved in terms of immediate income flows was to postpone payment.

Another case involving clerical and administrative salaries in a large company was that of staff employed by BICC (No. 125). This company had not got so far as ICI in rationalising salaries, and was changing from salary scales to salary ranges with minima and maxima. Pay within the ranges would depend on merit awards, in place of pay-for-age or annual increments. A new agreement gave $6\frac{1}{2}$ per cent all round, and a further move towards the new structure. Accepting job evaluation, work measurement, flexibility of working between grades, common grades for male and female clerks (with a move towards equal pay) were also part of the deal.

The PIB found that the job evaluation represented a "significant strengthening of the Company's personnel and salary administration". But though the company had acquired assurance of co-operation from the staff, it was not proposing to use the new techniques immediately. Staff efficiency would increase with the merit system; the costs of introducing the new structure would be contained. But without estimating the possible gains, and setting appropriate objectives for management the Company could not hope to make full use of the "potentially valuable" assurance of co-operation they had negotiated.

The settlement was not subjected to a Standstill Order, so though the PIB found it was not according to the rules, it could not be stopped. The only solution was to urge the company to improve performance to justify the increases retrospectively.

However, the PIB had meanwhile been asked to provide guidance to industry generally on the factors affecting "the proper development of salary structures, and the methods by which this can be achieved" (No. 132). The PIB chose to discuss salary systems, rather than structures, so that all aspects should be included. A structure is a relationship existing at a point in time. But relativities over time, especially over career lengths, are as important a feature of salaries as relativities at a particular stage. It was not so much salary levels as the method of reaching decisions that was to be related to incomes policy. It was found that only about 60 per cent of staff (outside the public services) enjoyed salaries structured to the minimal extent of having ranges with known limits. Increments were mostly based on personal performance.

The PIB could not recommend any particular system as more desirable than any other. It was desirable that there should be a coherent system; but structures would differ according to whether firms employed few or many highly skilled and mobile staff, for whom there was a well-defined market. Also, some firms filled senior posts largely by internal promotion, others by outside recruitment. The general requirements were fairness, effectiveness and control of staff costs. The right system which might be revealed by job evaluation would achieve all three together.

Individual careers could not be arranged fairly and consistently unless pay increases arising from increments in one job were distinguished from those arising from general increases of salary level.

Then came the question of increments. Though the incomes policy was to be interpreted in the light of cost restraint and the requirement of economic management, "the simple statement that all incremental payments are additions to income and therefore must be directly related to existing incomes policy rules is based on a misapprehension", the PIB thought. The salary bill for a whole group was the proper subject of the policy. As one individual moved to the top of the scale, another would be coming in at the bottom, so that "the normal movement of salaries for the individual members of such a group set up what might be described as a circular process". Personal increments did not therefore need justifying by the policy rules.

General increases in salary bills beyond the norm could only be justified by a "contribution towards increasing efficiency, considered in the light of systematic information and planning". But preserving relativities with the wage structure in the same firm might also be a valid reason for exceptional increases.

The vexed question of matching market rates, the reason often given for salary increases, had then to be dealt with. The PIB distinguished between incompetent or ineffective attempts to meet general market pressures and accurate assessment of the market rate at particular points. Most firms used surveys of some sort to discover market rates. Technical difficulties concerning job descriptions and comparable levels of responsibility made much of this information of dubious value. The better surveys all showed a considerable spread of salaries for similar jobs. Surveys could not in themselves settle the market rate for a particular firm, unless it happened to be seriously out of line with the rest, i.e. below the bottom of the spread. Otherwise, uncritical matching of market rates was not only expensive but "unsatisfactory in any but the short term for salary earners, who are victims of the inflation to which these methods of salary-fixing contribute".

Accurate comparisons were necessary for small numbers of highly mobile people with scarce professional skills. At these particular points, salaries must be market-determined. But this need not entail raising scales, still less raising all salary levels. Firms should first try to meet their needs for scarce staff by the promotion and training of existing employees.

At all other points, salaries should be increased only in relation to the firm's scope for raising efficiency and containing staff costs. Managements would need information to monitor staff contributions to efficiency. General increases designed only to secure "staff co-operation" would not do. "Salary costs are not mere overheads, expensive but inescapable; the cost of salaries needs no less careful consideration in terms of return on outlay than other forms of investment." Directors ought to answer a check-list to assure that the salary administration of their companies was being efficiently conducted.

Salaries of directors were reviewed in the report on top salaries in the private sector (No. 107). This time the PIB's conclusions had to be applied to give a quantified result as it was asked to recommend salaries for Chairmen, Board members and senior management in the nationalised industries. The Government considered the problem to be concerned with "marked divergence of salaries between nationalised industries and private industry", which was supposed to inhibit the recruitment or retention of "suitable people". Distinctions and comparisons, invidious and odious, loomed again. But the PIB had taken a sufficiently secure position to avoid some of the pitfalls.

Companies, it found, over emphasised the importance of external comparisons to determine top salaries "with self-defeating results". Instead, salary structures to "induce internally the assumption of greater responsibility" and reward performance, should be established. Given a hierarchy of jobs, involving successively greater areas of responsibility, a hierarchy of salaries ought to follow. There ought to be personal differentials to reward exceptional devotion to those duties, or exceptional abilities in carrying them out. The implication of this was that the range of salaries should be extended and that the relatively well-paid would get greater increases than their unfortunate junior colleagues who qualified neither by job nor by personal contribution.

Nationalised industries should follow the same recommendation. Each should develop a sound salary structure to give adequate rewards for individual performance and greater responsibilities. The PIB's own recommendations for Chairman and Board members applied these principles, in that salary ranges were "designed to provide sufficient headroom below Board level" so that managements were able to establish appropriate levels of pay.

Comparability could not be disposed of altogether, since some senior posts had to be filled by outside recruitment and the evidence pointed to difficulties in attracting people of "suitable calibre". To overcome difficulties of promoting, relating reward to performance, and recruiting from outside, differentials on and below the Boards had to be widened. The PIB then stood away from comparisons as far as it could by adding that it was "not self-evident that pay in the public sector should entirely match whatever is paid in the private sector". There was no standard for an objective comparison of jobs; it must be largely a subjective judgment. Comparability refused to disappear, but it ought to correspond more exactly with market pressures actually experienced.

Large increases for nationalised industry Chairmen and Board members were recommended, beyond the $3\frac{1}{2}$ per cent ceiling, as a major reorganisation of structure justified on efficiency grounds. The increases would be staged, and would raise the salaries of Chairmen and Deputy

Chairmen to new levels, determined for three separate groups, varying with the size of the enterprise. Board members would have personal pay ranges depending on the "content and responsibility of each individual job". The range should be used by the Minister (who appointed them) to reward performance, according to the advice of Chairmen or Deputy Chairmen. The purpose of the increase was "to make good the undue compression of differentials which now occurs at the top and which makes salary policy an ineffective instrument of management". How the "instrument of management" would be used below Board level was a matter for the Boards themselves, except that progression should nowhere depend on age or length of service.

Some perplexing problems were still largely unsolved in relation to professional salaries, mostly in the public sector. Differences between jobs in the public and private sector were difficult to evaluate, as the PIB found in relation to the nationalised industries' Chairmen, and performance is often a matter of opinion, informed though it may be. Even where there was a market price for professional services, as in the case of solicitors and architects, how much the principals ought to be paid for their individual performance was not entirely settled by the market. Low incomes would tend to repel recruits, and high ones to attract them. But in both cases, the PIB also found it necessary to compare increases in their income with others of their class, and with changes in work content.

But where private practice or employment covered few or none of the professionals concerned, like teachers or civil servants, how a fair or "efficient" system could be devised had to be approached in a different way. There was little point in job evaluation where there was not much variation in jobs as in teaching, and some parts of the civil service. The important variations are in the performance of individuals in relatively uniform jobs. Equally difficult was the question how a profession's level of pay could be determined on any principle other than comparison with some other group. Comparisons might be done more carefully or objectively than before, but this was not to apply a different principle, and it did not conform happily to the policy. The PIB never found it easy to apply incomes policy to public-sector salaries, nor did their conclusions offer much clarification of the principles.

The Government had already divorced its operations as employers from national policy, as many groups, like the armed forces and the higher civil servants had independent review bodies to make recommendations on pay, using comparability as the governing principle. For higher civil servants, there was a Standing Advisory Committee that reviewed pay every three years, basing their recommendations on information about other salary changes collected by themselves. The increases proposed for the higher civil service (No. 11) were mostly within the current "norm" anyway (when spread over the period since the previous increase), and did not in the end need any special justification. Long-term problems of pay depended on the outcome of the report of the Fulton Committee (Cmnd 3638), which proposed a new management structure and recommended job evaluation to establish common grading. Having studied job evaluation as such (No. 83 see p. 204), the PIB was sufficiently moved to include a chapter on its application to the civil service. In particular, the main effect of successful job-evaluated structures was to replace confused structures by systematic ones. But the civil service already had a highly systematised pay structure. The effect of job evaluation in these circumstances might just be to limit the freedom of the unions to bargain. But so long as they fully participated in, and approved, the scheme, no harm need follow.

The PIB had another case involving administrators at the top of a complicated hierarchy in the public sector, local government chief officers (No. 45). A settlement giving increased pay lower down the scale had recently been reached, giving administrative, professional, technical and clerical grades a rise of seven per cent (spread over two years), and now the chief officers claimed at least as much, a claim the employers were disposed to meet. However, this settlement had been reached when the norm was still $3\frac{1}{2}$ per cent. But by the time that the chief officers' claim was being considered, the rules included no norm at all. But an answer to the case had, in effect, already been given in the case of the merchant navy officers, Preserving differentials for skill and responsibility, and observing the consequences for the whole when an increase had been given to a lower group, both led to the conclusion that the increase must be allowed. At the transfer points between A.P.T. and C. grades and chief officers grades differentials had been squeezed, sometimes to the point of extinction. A seven per cent salary increase was therefore needed to restore relativities at the lower levels.

The problems of deciding what public-sector salaries ought to be was nowhere more acute than in relation to the armed forces. The job required of the armed forces is in the nature of a service, determined by authority. Pay for the job is not subject to negotiation, and standards of performance are a matter of discipline rather than incentives.

The PIB's first report (No. 10) had to recommend whether an increase should be paid, according to the formula recommended by the Grigg Committee (Cmnd 545). The only material point discussed by the PIB was the difficulty of recruitment. Though pay was probably not the sole factor in recruitment, the PIB concluded that it could hardly be improved without an improvement in pay. The biennial review in the Grigg formula could be regarded as a commitment. Failure to honour it might reduce recruitment even more. The commitment must therefore continue, unless and until due notice were given.

The next report (No. 70) was the first under a standing reference of the armed forces, and contained only the proposals for immediate increases in pay. The PIB found difficulties in recruitment and retention (as before); but a new pay system could not be introduced for two years. Pay should therefore be increased by the seven per cent proposed by the Ministry of Defence.

Meantime, the PIB's feasibility studies showed that job evaluation of the armed forces was a practicable basis for a proper pay structure The results were published in two parts, one a year and the other 21 months later. The first (No. 116) announced the principles for the future. A pay structure for the armed forces ought to compare sufficiently well with equivalent civilian earnings to attract and retain the necessary manpower, and reward recruits suitably for the jobs done. The existing system was so complicated that it was difficult to convey to recruits what their earnings were likely to be, and servicemen themselves had some difficulty in calculating their earnings. Whether the actual level of pay was right, in relation to its two purposes, was another matter. The lowest pay went to single men, though the Services were particularly anxious to attract them. It was doubtful whether the various trades and ranks were fairly rewarded. Then there were the peculiar disadvantages of military life (which the PIB chose to call "the X factor"), which must be rewarded to attract and keep recruits. When the job evaluation was complete, the PIB recommended that all Servicemen should receive a military salary, a gross taxable money sum (for single or married men), from which food and accommodation would be paid for. The salary would comprise three elements: pay according to the content and demands of the job, a supplement for "the X factor", and a few special allowances, like flying pay, which clearly deserved special reward. Working out the details of the new salary would take many more months. Meantime, a further interim increase of $3\frac{1}{2}$ per cent in pay on the old system was recommended, from 1 April 1969.

The recommendations for pay on the new system, to date from 1st April 1970, were set out in a further report (No. 142). The job evaluation showed that the Services had not arranged their pay structure at all badly compared with civilian counterparts, and that internal relativities through the ranks were not badly awry either, for all the eighteenth-century nomenclature. However, major amendments were needed, mainly because some Service trades, apparently comparable with civilian jobs, turned out to be more demanding.

The effects of the whole of the recommendations were difficult to summarise, even for PIB itself. The combined effects of levelling up pay for single men, paying according to evaluated jobs, and adding in the remaining special allowances varied extremely widely from one individual to another. The PIB's own estimate was that the average increase was 15 per cent.

It may well be asked at this point what all this had to do with incomes policy. It must be said, in terms of the explicit rules of the White Papers, not much. The increases in pay in No. 116 were questionably in accordance with the current norm, since a seven per cent increase only a year before was specifically intended to last two years. The further 3½ per cent for 1969 was justified on the grounds of acute difficulties of recruitment, as there undoubtedly were; though PIB itself observed: "More important than immediate pay is the prospect to a potential recruit of life in the Services"—the radical pay review to come. When the final restructuring report did come (plus report No. 158, on separation allowances), its recommendations were not related to White Paper principles at all. They were intended to be generally more sensible and more effective than the preceding system. A fresh look at an old problem from first principles produced desirable changes. This was undoubtedly in the spirit of incomes policy, even if it would be difficult to accommodate it precisely within specific rules.

The final instalment of the PIB's review of Service pay was only added after the change of Government: indeed the pay of senior officers was the only reference made by the Conservative Government before it finally decided to destroy the PIB (No. 157). By that time, senior civil servants had had an accelerated pay increase (recommended by the Plowden Committee, and not of course referred to the PIB). Doctors and dentists had also had a substantial pay increase (also not referred to the PIB). The PIB was thus in a similar difficulty to the one it faced over university teachers, that it had to make recommendations on one pay structure, having obvious close links with others it had not investigated. The only solution was some form of comparisons.

As senior officers worked alongside senior civil servants, and sometimes filled the same jobs, a close comparability in pay must continue. However, career prospects and pension rights were different in the two services; so exact correspondence of pay was not justified. Exact levels clearly had to be decided by some common sense principle. The chosen solution was to equate pay at the most senior level (Field Marshal, Admiral of the Fleet, or Marshal of the Royal Air Force) with the highest-paid Permanent Secretaries.

Another early case which appeared to be similar to the armed forces was that of fire service pay (No. 32). The performance required was also a service, and a service where standards of performance do not depend on pay. But there were equally clear differences. Pay was the subject of negotiations by collective bargaining, and the employers consisted of local authorities, instead of a central department.

Neither low pay nor comparisons seriously out of line with analogues were found to apply. But once more (like the banks and civil servants) there was found to be a real problem of recruiting up to the higher standards required to meet changing needs. However, it did not follow that a general, across-the-board increase was therefore to be recommended. The cost of providing the required service varied with service per man, something which could be influenced by pay structure. An increase in pay ought to be made in such a way that a more effective use of existing manpower was encouraged. The employers had already offered a higher rate of pay for extra shifts worked, in an extended duty system. The PIB recommended a higher rate still. This, it was thought, would allow or encourage extended duty arrangements (per man per week) to be developed where they did not already exist.

In respect of using pay to induce workers to make more of their time available to their employers, the case of the pay of BOAC pilots (No. 88) was most closely related to fire service pay. In both cases, by agreeing to work more hours they could directly reduce the cost of the service, and so make possible the accompanying increase in pay.

An even larger public service, where the service required was expanding in face of chronic labour shortage, was the National Health Service. Nurses and midwives pay was dealt with in report No. 60. The cost of hospital care was largely labour cost; so the use of nursing labour was the most important determinant of total hospital costs, and the quality of the service. But neither extended duty—already overextended for many nurses—nor incentive schemes were relevant. It was a matter of investigating any other possibilities there might be of getting better service, increasing pay and restraining cost at the same time.

The jobs actually done by nurses varied widely. A job analysis had already been done for senior nurses (ward sisters and above) in the report of the Salmon Committee, which gave job descriptions for all nurses having management functions; and the pay scales to be related to the Salmon grades had specifically been referred to the PIB. But job description did not throw much light on pay or performance in the wards.

The general assumption about nurses was that they were in vastly short supply and were vastly underpaid. But taking all grades actually doing nursing jobs, nurses were found (surprisingly) not to be in seriously short supply. Recruitment was suprisingly good; there was thus no direct evidence of pay being in general seriously out-of-line. But retention was bad, and distribution between well and poorly staffed hospitals and services abysmally uneven. Fully trained nurses were in short supply in most hospitals. Failure to retain trained staff and gross maldistribution suggested two associated problems to the PIB: imperfect management of nursing staff and a distorted pay structure.

The relevant criterion for an exceptional increase was again the proper development of salary structures to provide incentives to improve performance. Performance of nursing duties in most hospitals could be improved by different methods of supervision and control; in poorly staffed hospitals, nurses were at once overworked and spending too little time actually nursing. But nothing was to be gained by attaching even a small part of pay to standards of performance resting on standards of management somewhere further up the hierarchy than the wards. Improved management there ought to be, to justify the cost of a better salary structure. But pay changes themselves could not induce it in the PIB's view—even by "career prospects" attracting recruits of better managerial ability. Hence it was an essential part of the PIB's recommendations on salaries that the new management structure for senior nurses be implemented forthwith (instead of in the very easy stages proposed by the Ministry of Health), to simplify and unify grading throughout the NHS and provide better promotion prospects for the ablest and best qualified senior nurses. The pay structure could be improved by giving the highest rate of increase (14%) at the points of most serious wastage and shortage: senior students and staff (qualified) nurses.

Serious shortage of nurses was found in long-stay hospitals, both psychiatric and geriatric. Exceptional increases in pay were therefore justified at both these points in the PIB's view. There should be a "lead" of £100 a year for all nurses in psychiatric or geriatric hospitals (in place of the existing £50 for psychiatric hospitals alone).

A similar case in some respect was the pay of university teachers (No. 98). Here too, pay levels could encourage or inhibit recruitment, within the limits of numbers qualified in the right age group, and of competing demands. Here too, recruits tended to stay within the sector, though mobility between one institution and another was high. But the case was far more difficult for the PIB to resolve satisfactorily, even with a standing reference (given to it in 1967). The profession had no hierarchy of jobs with management functions, and it had no variety of function (like the armed forces or the civil service) which would lend itself to job evaluation. The question of comparisons was the main theme of the report, though a negative one, since the PIB decided to jettison the whole principle. It held that salary increases generally had "exceeded the national increase in productivity and (had) therefore been inflationary". And any claim based on "a movement in salaries which had been inflationary would, if conceded, add further to that inflation". Therefore, though recognising the harshness of the conclusion, the conclusion must stand. "Any attempt to break the endless chain of increases because others in general have had increases may seem hard to those waiting at the point where the chain is broken. Not to attempt to break it, however, would be to help to perpetuate a national situation of recurring financial crises." Comparisons were therefore no reason for an exceptional increase.

The PIB interpreted improved performance as a need to contain costs per student, and encourage a shift from research to teaching. (However, most unusually in PIB reports, the extent of the need was not demonstrated factually.) Because of the special difficulties of recruitment, there should be a "restructuring", by increases of 10 to 17 per cent at the bottom of the scales, sharply tapering up to two per cent at the top. Because of the desirability of improving "performance" in teaching, each university "should have freedom within four per cent" of its annual salary bill to make discretionary payments, depending on teaching quality.

The PIB's attempt to relate pay to performance was in this case abortive. After widespread protest, the discretionary supplement was whittled down to $1\frac{1}{2}$ per cent of the salary bill, the rest being added to the general increases.

The reference still stood, however, and the PIB had to begin a further review after the lapse of about a year, leading to a second report (No. 145). Evidence on which to base any different judgment was only then collected, and it threw little light on the problem. The PIB had somewhat changed its attitude in the meantime, as it had found that comparisons could not be ignored. For some public-sector professional employees, like doctors and dentists, there was an independent review body. For some, like higher civil servants, pay was explicitly negotiated on the basis of "fair comparisons". "In practice," observed PIB, "the Government is in very much the same position as a large industrial concern which makes settlements affecting one group of employees today and another group tomorrow; the settlement with the first group may predetermine the negotiations with the second." By way of comment, PIB could only repeat its observation in the first report: that the system resulted in unfairness. Last time PIB had decided not in mitigate what "unfairness" there was in the interests of general restraint of inflation. This time it accepted that an increase for university teachers was necessary. Taking into account "the recent movements in salaries in the public sector and of earnings in both the private and public sectors" the increase should be nine per cent.

In general, salaries should, on the PIB's principles, always be related to performance. The level of pay at certain stages might have to be determined by market rates; so that the whole structure would be hung on these points, or based on recruitment pay. Wherever it was possible to measure performance, it should be measured. This applied generally to clerical occupations, where work study and work measurement was underdeveloped compared with occupations more directly concerned with production.

Where measurement of work was not possible, the primary requirement was an analysis of the job to be done, job description or job evaluation as appropriate. A structure having been constructed, hung on its points of market pressure, the pay scale for individuals would depend on the content of the job they were required to do. The point on the scale at which they were paid would depend on their own performance in the job. Both job and worker would be suitably rewarded, taking into account career prospects, as well as current pay.

The PIB always looked to internal relativities to set the structure in the public services. Relating the structures one with another, or with structures in other sectors of the economy proved a more intractable problem on which the incomes policy rules were not much help. Yet every public-service case, even the less successful ones, showed the need for a periodic objective view of pay problems in these occupations above all on general grounds of either equity or efficiency.

Reports

No.   5   Remuneration of administrative and clerical staff in electricity supply (Cmnd 2801)

No.   8   Pay and conditions of British Railways staff (Cmnd 2873)

No.   6   Salaries of Midland Bank staff (Cmnd 2839)

No. 106   Pay in the London Clearing Banks (Cmnd 3943)

No. 41   Salaries of staff of General Accident Assurance Co. Ltd (Cmnd 3398)

No. 74   Terms and conditions of staff of Prudential and Pearl Assurance Cos (Cmnd 3674)

No. 81   Pay awards by City of Bristol to staff in its docks (Cmnd 3752)

No. 89   Office staff employment agencies charges and salaries (Cmnd 3828)

No. 25   Pay and conditions of merchant navy officers (Cmnd 3302)

No. 115   Journalists' pay (Cmnd 4077)

No. 109   Pay of salaried staff of ICI Ltd (Cmnd 3981)

No. 125   Salaries of staff of BICC Ltd (Cmnd 4168)

No. 132   Salary structures (Cmnd 4187)

No. 10   Armed forces pay (Cmnd 2881)

No. 11   Pay of the higher civil service (Cmnd 2882)

No. 83   Job evaluation (Cmnd 3772)

No. 45   Pay of chief and senior officers in local government (Cmnd 3473)

No. 70   Pay of the armed forces (Cmnd 3651)

No. 116   Pay of the armed forces (2nd report) (Cmnd 4079)

No. 142   Pay of the armed forces (3rd report) (Cmnd 4291)

No. 158   Pay of the armed forces (5th report). Separation allowance (Cmnd 4529)

No. 157   Pay of the armed forces (4th report). Pay of senior officers (Cmnd 4513)

No. 32   Fire service pay (Cmnd 3287)

No. 88   Pay of pilots employed by BOAC (Cmnd 3789)

No. 60   Pay of nurses and midwives in the NHS (Cmnd 3585)

No. 98   Pay of university teachers (1st report) (Cmnd 3866)

No. 145   Pay of university teachers (2nd report) (Cmnd 4334)

Part 4

Conclusions

16

A National Policy for Prices

The national policy was intended to keep the general level of prices stable, and to this end each White Paper gave detailed rules governing the conditions in which prices should or should not be raised. Individual managements were given rules of behaviour designed to bring about the national objective, rather than a specific instruction about prices. It was only during the standstill and severe restraint, 12 months in all, that managements were required by statute to keep prices and charges unchanged (at the level ruling on 20 July 1966), unless certain exceptional circumstances could be demonstrated to exist. This applied generally to public-sector pricing, as to the private sector, though the rules of required price behaviour for public enterprises differed in detail.

The PIB dealt with seven price cases during the standstill and severe restraint, and only two of these raised any question of how the statutory requirements of stability were to be applied. Thus, the great majority of the price cases concerned the general rules intended to promote a stable price level in aggregate.

The price level is an abstract concept, the stability of which can only be represented by an index. Had the policy aimed at stability for all prices throughout, deciding whether any one price change conformed to the policy would have been more straightforward than it was. Aiming at an aggregate result meant that whether any one price change was consistent with general stability was much more controversial; indeed predicting the possible effect of generalising particular conclusions was the only way to reach a decision, where cases concerned a product or service with a small market. Where they concerned widely-used products, especially industrial inputs like fuel, transport or steel, the general consequences elsewhere of raising prices had to be analysed; and the conclusions following from the policy's rules for a stable price level were mostly in conflict with the conclusions following from the rules given to individual enterprises. The result was that the PIB had more difficulties over price cases than pay cases.

The credibility of the policy and the PIB depended on public under-standing and support. The distinction between stability of the price level and stability for all prices was not likely to impress the general public favourably, even where it was understood (and it is not necessarily public understanding that is to be deprecated). The distinction was not explicitly drawn in the White Papers, let alone subsequent speeches and reports "explaining" the policy. Consequently the PIB was almost continually torn between demonstrating that it intended to achieve stability in as many instances as possible, and applying the rules as sketched in the White Papers.

The price rules were, that prices should be raised to the extent that the cost of bought in materials increased; or that taxes (or similar charges) were increased; or that profits were insufficient to allow desirable investment to take place; or when increases in pay consistent with the incomes policy could not be paid without them. Prices should rise (and fall) with costs, these being reckoned after all possibilities of improving productivity were exhausted. If markets were fully competitive in the private sector, this is broadly how firms would be induced to behave eventually. The very fact that such rules had to be administratively applied was an admission that many markets were imperfectly com-petitive, or time lags too long for cost or price restraint to follow. The PIB's experience provided a lot more evidence for this view.

Public-sector price cases had to be treated differently by the PIB because special pricing rules were imposed on them by the Government, and because of the special function it was given to review efficiency when major price increases were proposed. Competition had long been absent or limited for most of their products, and for this reason alone public-sector cases would have raised some special problems.

Private-sector price cases fell into three groups: where markets were highly competitive, where there were monopolies and all the others lying between. Competitive activities usually had a large number of firms, many of them relatively small, though there might also be a few large firms with a national market.

Among large manufacturers in this group, effective price competition was found where technical progress was pushing down costs exception-ally fast (as in compound fertilisers), where there was competition from imports (as in some of Hoovers' products) and where small specialist firms had enough advantage to make inroads into the market against national producers (as in secondary batteries). Effective market pressure of a different sort could also be found, where the customers themselves were large manufacturers (as in electric motors). In cases like these, effective price competition was not usually obvious from outside, especially to the customers. There was point therefore in having proposals to increase prices in line with costs, or to restore profits, reviewed independently. In every such case, the PIB's report had positive recommendations to make about the extent of uniform increases that ought to be made, even though market pressure would dictate the size and timing of particular increases.

Also in this group were most of the cases involving distribution and services (other than food distribution). Typically, capacity consisted of premises, or premises staffed with a skilled salesman or engineer, rather than equipment; and operating units were relatively small, whatever the overall size of the parent firm. Competition exerted pressure on all prices or margins, in spite of differences in product, quality of service, selling expenses, and management methods.

The prices policy had relatively little relevance to this group, since market pressures already usually kept prices in line with costs more effectively than administrative intervention, and returns on capital were usually no more than adequate. The PIB found no reason to recomment a particular price in any of these cases. It could only confirm that markets were competitive enough to stabilise prices or protect consumers.

But even in these cases, there were ways in which competitive pressure on prices was attenuated. The industry's trade association could adopt pricing policies inhibiting competition, as in road haulage and wholesale fruit and vegetable distribution. Alternatively, a remarkable spread of charges might persist, not corresponding very closely with standards of service, the whole drifting upwards because the customers were not sufficiently informed about charges, or not active enough in seeking out the best bargain. A typical reaction of both business and individual customers in such cases was to complain to authority (MPs, Government departments, the PIB, Chambers of Commerce). Laundries and dry-cleaning, garages, office staff agencies and cotton yarn were all instances of this. The prices policy provided customers with grounds for objecting to anti-competitive practices, and a procedure for lodging complaints. The PIB suggested ways of removing obstacles to competition, whether the fault lay with the suppliers or the customers. Market pressures might well have achieved the removal eventually. The policy could possibly increase the speed of the response, by providing a (free) management consultancy service not otherwise available to firms too small or too inert to seek it as their sales and profits fell.

The dividing line is notoriously difficult to draw between monopoly and partially competitive markets dominated by a big firm. The PIB dealt with nine cases where the firm or pricing organisation was clearly a monopoly (cement, Mallory Batteries, butyl rubber, Orkney and Shetland Shipping, IBM rentals, TV relay services, viscose yarn, plasterboard, and Ever Ready batteries). Prices in all these industries were administered prices virtually unrestricted by price competition. Approval of prices had to turn on what profits ought to be, as there were neither gross operating inefficiencies nor exceptionally bad industrial relations in any of the nine instances. Some of the firms were less profitable at the time of the reference than they could endure for long, some much more so: in all cases the PIB related profits to the prospective demand for their products. But only in the first report on cement and on Mallory batteries did the PIB find serious fault with price increases proposed.

It has long been recognised that there is a case for a public body to have powers to scrutinise monopolies or monopolistic practices, where prices can be too high because profits are unjustifiably high, or because no market pressure restrains rising costs due to slack or complacent management. The Monopolies Commission existed long before the PIB, and in two cases (cement and viscose yarn) the PIB dealt with industries already reported on by the Monopolies Commission. The PIB's function was different from the Commission in that it was applying a prices policy meant to affect all firms alike, whether monopolies or not. But since the prices policy rules amounted to requiring firms to fix prices as though market restraints were effective, both bodies ought to reach broadly the same conclusion about the right prices. But the PIB was obliged to make a specific recommendation about prices, and might incidentally comment on efficiency and general policy, while the Monopolies Commission had to comment on general policy and efficiency, and might only incidentally propose specific prices. Part but not all of the investigations might overlap, if neither institution took the other's reports into account, nor had access to the other's records.

Even if the PIB had never succeeded in trimming any proposal, it might nevertheless have exercised a useful function in satisfying the customers that dominant sellers were not unfairly (or illegally) taking advantage of their dominance to raise their prices and incomes. The PIB's results showed that most of the monopolies investigated were not particularly inefficient, mostly no doubt because they were large enough to employ highly skilled professional managements. Nor did the PIB find that monopolies exploited their customers particularly savagely. But it was possible and sometimes happened, that a monopoly charged its customers in a way that would not be possible in competitive conditions, and that was not justified in relation to the costs involved (as happened in IBM rents for old customers, some TV relay charges, and Mallory Batteries). But equally, some monopolies did price according to cost and desired returns on capital without trying to reach the maximum return the market would allow (plasterboard, cement and Ever Ready batteries). Furthermore, some undoubted monopolies may be in no position to do other than minimise their losses (Orkney and Shetland Shipping and butyl rubber), though an independent investigation of pricing may be no less desirable than in the profitable cases.

In the third of the private-sector groups, we have all the various degrees of partial competition, ranging from detergents, dominated by two international giants (another industry investigated by the Monopolies Commission), to bricks with one firm (just short of the Monopolies Commission definition of a monopoly) dominating hundreds of smaller ones, or chocolate and confectionery, with four big firms dominating a longer tail of small ones, or breweries, in the throes of amalgamation into a group of competing giants. In this group also came building societies and clearing banks, with competing enterprises, in competition restricted by legal and administrative rules and inherited conventions.

The PIB's conclusions on pricing were reached in a roundabout way. The case for price changes had to be discussed in the light of the long-term interests of the customers and the national economy as well as the immediate issues. Whether more or less competition would give a better result on the whole could also differ according to the circumstances. Markets mostly had every characteristic of competition to the managements; but market pressures might work in such a way that inefficient firms could realise planned profits, sales and output, in spite of competition and in the absence of inflation. The market might allow the efficient to increase their margins or costs, rather than forcing the inefficient to reduce them. In an expanding market, if the efficient firms found themselves with profits rising beyond the levels required to provide the investment to maintain their market share, they might increase capacity faster than the expansion of demand (because too many expected to increase their share of the market). The extended capacity would then be underused, unit costs would be unnecessarily high and profits lower than expected. But the inefficient as well as the efficient might remain in production, with market shares changing very little.

The situation might then be changed, either by the existing firms competing in marketing, rather than production; or by the merging of firms. Market share and profits could be increased by greater selling efforts, in a competitive and efficient way. But competition of this kind does not reduce or constrain total unit costs and prices. The greater the emphasis on selling, the more likely that prices will be pushed up. This was against the national interest in a stable price level, in order to reduce the inflationary pressure from which all consumers suffer, whether or not the customers of the particular industries were harmed by it.

Where there was chronic under-use of capacity, competition in selling might also lead to a struggle to keep up output or turnover rather than profitability, in a (probably vain) attempt to reduce unit costs by using capacity more fully The attempt would be thwarted by the extra costs involved in keeping customers, if orders for small lots and non-standard sizes or specifications were accepted or sought, although unit costs increased even more because of the frequent interruptions in production. Once having adopted such a policy, it might be difficult for an industry to get out of such an impasse without some sort of collusion. Although clearly in the interests of all to bring prices more in line with costs (and drive the small or fussy customers to specialist or stock-holding firms), no one firm would risk being the first to act, for fear of not being followed. Rounds of cost and price increases, with intervals of stagnation and low profits might then appear, until demand climbed steeply enough to overtake the industry's expectations and investment plans.

When demand is restrained or pushed down for national economic management purposes, as it was in 1966–68, the upward pressure on costs, and in particular on selling costs may be increased even more. It is therefore a situation that a policy for stabilising prices must seek to influence. But whether demand is restricted or encouraged nationally, and whether inflation is advancing or retreating, price stability cannot be taken for granted as a consequence of market forces. The value and consequences of a prices policy must stand or fall mainly in respect of such industries.

That all these things happen was amply borne out by the PIB's cases in this group. That the upward pressure on prices was made worse by Government restraint of demand, was shown in cement, bricks (in spite of relatively high labour use), aluminium, Hoover appliances. But the forms and degrees of competition were almost as various as the cases. The PIB's attitude to them was entirely pragmatic. Each was investigated as thoroughly as time allowed, and attempts made to discover the special problems of the trade, as well as more general characteristics. There was no general presumption that costs, prices or profits were unjustifiably high, nor that marketing activities were less desirable than production. In fact in many cases, in spite of its responsibility for prices policy, the PIB finished by advising the Government that pricing, in some or all its aspects, was a matter of commercial judgment to be left to the managements. But this did not mean an abandonment of policy. That PIB tried to light on a strategy appropriate to each case for restraining or at least monitoring costs and prices as effectively and economically as possible. Its general endeavour was to set prices as nearly as possible to a level a more competitive market would induce, and then frame recommendations likely to bring them about.

Prices in the public sector naturally figured largely in PIB's investigations when the special functions of investigation were given to it. In Report No. 56, the first published after their new functions, the PIB set out its own general policy towards them more explicitly than it ever did in respect of the private sector. In making the efficiency audits, the PIB intended to avoid duplicating the work of management, the sponsoring department, or consultants. It would "choose areas which have significant implications for prices" meriting investigation because market constraints were lacking.

The Prime Minister's statement (announcing the new function) gave recognition to the peculiar importance of prices in the public sector, both because the nationalised industries were creatures of the Government, and because they were large basic industries. Price increases therefore affected the prices of many other goods, "but in addition industry generally regards Government's pricing activities as evidence of Government's own good faith as regards price restraint". For both these reasons, either the industries themselves or the Government had already postponed price increases which might well have been made in the private sector. This alone presented the PIB with difficult decisions. Cost increases had been accumulating for the public as for the private sector, but exceptional restraint on prices had left an exceptionally urgent need for future increases.

Though the nationalised industries were subject to competition in varying degrees and forms, the PIB set itself to consider whether there was enough to encourage operating efficiency and the adoption of progressive management technique. If not, measures such as introducing more competition or "other forms of constraint" might be required. But this would not be sufficient to determine prices, which ought to be in line with long-run marginal costs, to induce the most economic employment of resources. Identifying these costs was usually more difficult in public enterprises than in the private, because of the complexities of the industries, and because some costs impinged elsewhere in the economy; and these social costs had to be taken into account in determining both prices and the financial returns.

Furthermore, the PIB's preoccupation with inflation also presented it with difficulties in applying its principles to the public sector. Rising prices in the public sector might be more inflationary than in the private sector because the inevitable publicity encouraged a belief that the general price level was increasing, and wage increases might be advanced. Alternatively, if public enterprises did not raise prices when their costs unavoidably increased, incomes available for spending on private-sector products would be larger, and their prices consequently higher. Moreover, the Government would have to borrow more heavily to finance the public sector, and this in itself might be inflationary. The PIB therefore considered there were no general rules to be laid down on the inflationary consequences of raising or not raising public-sector prices. Particular problems in each industry, and the national or monetary consequences of price increases had to be considered separately.

Concerning financial obligations, the PIB repeated its view in the first of the nationalised industry cases, that the percentage rates of return were "indications of a trend to be met rather than figures regularly to be met year in year out". The underlying purpose of the targets had to be kept in mind in weighing up their relative importance compared with prices policy. The financial objectives were supposed to be an incentive to management and a standard of success or failure. But most public enterprises could meet them simply by putting up prices as costs increased: they did not control costs. The Government presumably intended to further "their ultimate ideal", as set out in the latest White Paper on nationalised industries (Cmnd 3437), in referring cost and prices to the PIB. But investment according to the proper criteria, and prices according to long-run marginal cost would give a more rationally defensible result than any financial target. Ideally, the right prices and the right investment standards should be consistent with the financial targets; but the calculations necessarily rested on a whole series of estimates and forecasts, all of them liable to doubt or error.

Nevertheless it was also the PIB's view that there should be some financial standards. The quality of top management was to be judged "in the main only by the overall performances expressed in monetary terms". Such a standard was essential to a minister, and to the public's judgment of a minister, in exercising his or her right to retain or to dismiss top management. There was also the relation between public and private sectors, as the standard of success in the private sector was profits. The best managers might not be attracted to the public sector if it did not use a comparable standard. Also, profitability was a common standard by which a desirable distribution of resources between sectors could be assessed.

This was a set of standards for pricing difficult to apply in any situation. Public-sector price increases were peculiarly likely to be inflationary in the nature of things; therefore increases ought to be avoided wherever possible. Public-sector capital should be suitably rewarded to maintain management standards and to guide resources to the right uses; therefore returns to capital ought to be maintained at the right relationship between public sector and private, and restoring it might require price increases. Prices must be judged in relation to long-run marginal cost; but public enterprises with a heavy burden of fixed costs, might not cover their outgoings, let alone build up any reserve if they did so, and though economic logic might not justify reserves, management or political logic did, as a safeguard against uncertainties and a protection against undue dependence on Government departments.

In practice, public-sector price cases were treated in much the same way as private-sector monopoly cases. Public enterprises were required to meet their target returns, a requirement the PIB was specifically instructed each time not to question, and which was never relaxed, except during 1966 and 1967. On the contrary, the targets tended to rise, as interest rates and returns required by the private sector both rose. The important public-sector industries were either labour-intensive, and struggling with increasing wage costs and a difficult market (coal, transport and the postal services); or they were capital-intensive and expanding (gas, electricity and telecommunications), and unable to contain their prices effectively in face of high and inflexible returns on unusually heavy capital formation.

The Government's overriding insistence on the financial obligations also prevented the PIB from considering the national consequences of increasing public-sector prices. Only in the case of steel, where targets had not then been set, were the total consequences of the industry's proposals reviewed. In the cases of electricity, gas, coal, transport and post office charges, no such review was possible consistent with the ubiquitous targets. Even where the industries were struggling to cover their costs, it would surely have been desirable, in the context of the prices and incomes policy as a whole, to consider the indirect consequences of the size and timing of the increases, as the PIB pointed out in each of the reports on London fares. Prices had their part in determining demand, and hence investment. It was undesirable to stimulate demand by unduly low prices, and prices that fail to cover costs must be unduly low. But if a steep or ill-timed price increase pushed demand so far below capacity that unit costs rose further, or if the consumers' dismay at the price increase added to their determination to seek (successfully) for higher incomes, inflation would actually have been stimulated by insisting on financial rectitude.

The PIB report on steel prices also illustrated another unresolved conflict of principle concerning public-sector price increases. All the industries reviewed wanted price increases, to raise their revenue by a stated amount. But the possibility of increasing revenue by this or that amount, and the consequences of doing so, could only be analysed by reference to the specific price increases proposed. Detailed consideration of markets and marketing policy tended to be the most resented of the PIB's "interference", not unnaturally, as it was precisely where the Boards of nationalised industries were supposed increasingly to exercise their commercial acumen. Yet leaving nationalised Boards to exercise commercial judgment would effectively have removed any possibility of reviewing their efficiency. Product prices determine total revenue, and total revenue determines returns on capital, given whatever costs the corporations feel obliged to meet. Outside pressure to restrain costs can only be effected through outside pressure on product prices. The PIB itself repeatedly pointed out that financial "discipline" (avoidance of borrowing) did not impose any particular restraint on costs, except where there was competition, or where managements chose to use the financial targets as a means to cost control.

The effectiveness of the prices policy in general was greatly tempered by other economic policies and circumstances. High rates of return on capital, in the private and public sectors tended to accumulate through the economy, since much of the product of capital-intensive producers as brought by other firms. The capital-intensive producers put up their prices, and these became unavoidable cost increases for many more. The cumulative process would only stop when the passed on increases hit firms in process of major improvements in working practices or technology, which brings us back to productivity once more, as the means of counteracting inflation.

The policy required that prices should be increased only in relation to unavoidable rises in operating costs. Raw materials costs did not give rise to any great difficulty until devaluation (late in 1967). Even then, the PIB did not find much reason to object to proposed price increases. Where the substitution of cheaper materials was possible, it had mostly been done before the case reached the PIB (soap, electric motors, Hoover domestic appliances and margarine and cooking fats).

Cases involving increases in taxes were not quite so straightforward. The biggest and most frequently encountered increases affected service and distribution trades (SET, taxes on oil, vehicle licences, rates), or labour-intensive activities generally (employers' National Insurance contributions). Many of these were relatively competitive industries where the state of the market would normally restrain prices. But common notorious tax increases gave firms a ready-made opportunity to increase prices on a well-founded assumption that others would follow suit. The PIB's function was to calculate the actual incidence of the tax, assess the capacity for offsetting it, and hence hasten the settlement in market prices that competition would no doubt have eventually secured, given time.

In all industries prices were also pushed upwards by industry-wide agreements on pay. Complacency about labour costs pays off even in competitive industries, where complacency over selling costs would not. All firms know that their rivals have to pay broadly the same increases at the same time; and there is no compelling reason to avoid putting prices up to the same extent as pay. Even where labour costs are a small part of total costs, profitability will eventually be threatened unless prices are raised. Cases where prices increased following wage increases were at the heart of prices policy, since it was this link that was supposed to be the main cause of inflation, and a main target for the policy. In its first report on road haulage charges, the PIB chose to make labour practices and wage determination the main theme. In the second, on printing, such an attitude was required of it, since pay was referred with charges. In the third, on bread prices, most emphasis was put on improvements in labour use, even though returns on capital were low. Improvements in labour use by the *Daily Mirror* were made a prior condition for a price increase, and hence for improved returns on capital, and (much later on) by the steel industry. From 1967 onwards, most of the labour-intensive industries referred were in the public sector (coal, postal services, transport). Requiring changes of practice as a prior condition of allowing price increases was not possible to any great extent, because the possible improvements in productivity (beyond what was already proposed) were generally speaking not to be had in a short space of time. So long as the target rates of return on capital had to be taken as a sacrosanct, year in and year out, it was not practicable to suggest any such condition, and these cases became basically a question of returns to capital.

But this treatment of price cases was not continuous. Industries such as breweries, laundries, bricks passed by with only light passing reference to labour productivity or pay agreements. Investigating labour use is commonly itself a laborious activity, and significant results therefore slow (especially in relation to the PIB's timetable) in coming. The PIB did not enjoy the resources necessary for systematic investigations of labour use in relation to cost or price references until it had built up its own enquiry team, from 1967 onwards, and its own management team, which was not fully staffed until 1970.

Of the 32 private-sector price cases referred after September 1967, only 13 (at most) could be described as labour-intensive. Four of these had appeared before (bread, bricks, newspapers, and garages), and of the remaining nine, only three involved a report on a particular price increase, rather than a general comment on costs, prices, or efficiency. It could hardly be said that the PIB had an adequate opportunity to review private-sector labour use in connection with costs and prices, throughout the period when it was equipped to do so.

If neither raw material costs nor tax increases were important, and if labour cost was not investigated deeply or not quickly to be reduced, the sole criterion for price determination was the return on capital employed, the overwhelming theme of so many price reports. The PIB defined capital employed and proper returns; but for all its efforts, the PIB itself was not satisfied. In its final report it confessed that "the assessment of an appropriate level of returns was a problem we do not claim to have entirely solved".

The problem was partly technical and partly political. Some progress was made with the technical aspects, if only by systematically applying best practices as the PIB saw them.

Where expanding demand justified the expansion of capacity, the rate of return should cover the average cost of the new capital needed, using the cheapest source open to the enterprise. Rates of return were calculated by comparing the discounted cash flow with cost of capital, since expected rates of return over the lifetime of the investment compared with the expected expenditure flow would determine profits and the maintenance of investment. The discounted cash-flow method was advised because it gave proper weight to the phasing of expenditure and the life of capital; and the timing of cost and price changes was particularly important to prices policy. But the PIB's experience showed that the method itself was only a first step. Feeding the right information into the calculation was a more difficult problem in practice.

A DCF calculation is very sensitive to the rate of discount used, and the imputed life of the investment. High interest rates involve high discount rates, which inhibit investment. An imputed life which turns out to be shorter than actual life also inhibits investment (and there is still much investment not subject to rapid technological obsolescence).

The PIB managed to mitigate some price increases by recalculating demand forecasts, a field in which its expertise built up. Sometimes improved accounting actually made price stability more difficult to achieve. Where depreciation charges had been calculated on the historic cost of capital (or something between historic and replacement cost), calculating prices in relation to returns on new capital instead, was almost certain to justify price increase. Even when new capital was not needed, valuing capital on the basis of current costs by itself established a case for a price increase, because returns were "too low", when measured against a higher base. In the interests of price stability, the PIB recommended that revaluation should not be done precipitately if this involved a significant increase in price. In gas and steel, accelerating technical advance produced a similar effect, in that the potential life of equipment, some of it only recently installed, was significantly shortened by new techniques.

National economic management could also influence the calculations, through changing prospective demand. Calculated returns depend on calculated extra revenue; the lower prospective sales or prices, the less worthwhile the investment. Hence, where prospective demand is reduced, the required return on new investment might only be possible with a price increase to compensate lower sales. There was a relatively large number of PIB cases where profits had fallen because demand and output had fallen well below capacity. In almost all of them Government policy was at least partly to blame for the recession. The PIB's view was that if prices rose to maintain profits when excess capacity appeared, they should go down again when the excess disappeared. Prospective unit costs should always be calculated assuming average capacity use as much in industries suffering the consequences of Government policy as in those where surplus capacity was the result of overestimated demand in the past.

Firms where capacity utilisation had been low because of unexpected technical difficulties were in a different situation. Both Fisons (fertilisers) and Esso Chemicals (butyl rubber) had made low profits because of such problems. So far as past losses were concerned, firms should not expect the customers to pay for them (though electricity consumers in effect had to pay for past mistakes in the industry). New investment in each process was justified by prospective demand; and for each the PIB calculated prospective returns with less optimistic costing. Price increases were therefore justified in both.

The political problem involved in assessing proper returns to capital is a formidable one which the PIB was never intended to touch, and could not do so. The tacit assumption of the prices policy rules was that all enterprises were to stay in business, unless market conditions dictated otherwise. It is true the PIB did consider the capacity of the whole industry, and the justification for its existence in relation to newsprint (but only relating to overseas suppliers), and considered the effect of its recommendations on whole industries sometimes. But its view of a proper price was mostly one which would allow existing enterprises to reach returns high enough to stay in business in their existing form, with existing managments. Some prices might have been higher on this standard than they need have been, given structural or managerial changes, where market pressures would not (or did not) secure them.

What the best strategy should be in the interests of the policy as a whole still remained the most important problem, even when demand and supply prices had been reconciled for any one firm or sector. The result of the technical analyses, according to the White Paper criteria, did not necessarily promote price stability in general. In the overwhelming majority of price cases PIB had to recommend a price increase though it was often less than that proposed to it. Nevertheless its recommendations clearly showed no undue severity as far as prices are concerned. This followed from the way rules worked. An economy generally needing growth and modernisation, needed new investment at a higher rate than in the past. Many enterprises could make a good case for a price increase on those grounds alone. When direct costs are also rising—some of them, like taxes and licences, as a result of Government activity—the price increase justified according to the policy became still higher. The exceptions were cases where turnover was increasing rapidly, or where there was rapid technological improvement; these were cases which neither needed nor received official investigation.

The PIB had to apply its rules to a very biased selection of cases on any standard. Most of the nationalised industries came before it because of its special responsibilities. In the private sector, the food industries were fairly well represented, by bread prices (three times), flour prices (twice), beer prices (twice), fruit and vegetables, meat (through Smithfield), milk distribution, chocolate and confectionery, ice cream, margarine and cooking fats, and food distribution as a whole. Among industrial materials there was cement (twice), bricks (twice), bright steel bars, newsprint, plasterboard, fertilisers, cotton yarns, synthetic fibres, dyestuffs and aluminium semis. The engineering industry was represented by electric motors (small). Private-sector transport was represented by London taxis, Orkney and Shetland Shipping and road haulage. Batteries appeared three times, and domestic electrical appliances once (but only the Hoover variety). Printing, TV rentals, ITV companies and national newspapers represented the communications-entertainment industries. Laundries, dry-cleaning and garages represented domestic services, and solicitors and architects professional services. Banks and building societies represented the monetary sector. Only four of these covered pay and prices in the same reference.

On any classification of the private sector, it was a baffling bunch. Most sectors were represented somewhere. But it was certainly not a selection that could by itself indicate whether or not the price level was being stabilised.

The outstanding features of the PIB's pricing activities were, first that they were concentrated on the public sector. Secondly, it was narrowly confined, especially in the public sector, by the Government's insistence that returns to capital were maintained at a time of high and rising interest rates. Thirdly, it was confined to a curious selection of cases, less and less related to labour use and pay as time went on. Within these limits, the PIB did its best to propagate two principles of pricing: price according to the extra costs incurred in providing a particular product or service, and price to cover the market return on extra capital needed to meet potential demand. Beyond that, the efficiency of all monopolies, public or private, needed supervision if costs were to be restrained, and the nature and degree of competition in all other industries ought to be carefully examined before it could be assumed that the market will in fact press upon unjustified increases.

17

A National Policy for Incomes

There were two influences propelling incomes upwards in an inflationary manner, one a general attempt to keep up with the rise in prices, and the other the attempts of groups of workers to keep up with their fellows. Prices policy had to remove the inflationary force from the one, and incomes policy the other.

Whole industries or occupations might try to keep up with other industries or occupations, or with the general level of earnings elsewhere; or, smaller groups within an industry might try to keep up with those below and above them. The policy therefore had to achieve four things. It had to keep aggregated pay increases more in line with productivity increases and less with prices. It had to unhitch the links between one industry and another by outlawing external relativities (comparability). It had to scrutinise the steps in a hierarchy of pay, so that internal relativities (differentials) should match job content. Finally, it had to promote a general improvement in productivity, the overriding purpose of the whole policy.

The PIB's own role was in practice more complex. A strict interpretation of the White Papers could have led to the conclusion that only modest pay increases were justified, if any at all. This would have been a tolerable result if the prices policy really had induced a stable price level. But even the ingrained optimists expected nothing more than a slackening in the rate of increase (apart from the short interval of standstill). Incomes had to rise to some extent, to make the policy acceptable or fair.

Above all, the PIB had to make its recommendations acceptable. It had to find ways of recommending increases in pay consistent with the White Papers and the general aims of incomes policy. Furthermore, if recommendations could be made in such a form that further increases consistent with the policy were in prospect, so much the better.

The first general aim was to establish a "norm", equivalent to the overall national increase in productivity. It was a fair presumption in 1965 that any pay settlement lower than previous ones would bring the

I*

national flow of incomes nearer to the norm. But just as most enterprises were exceptional in their own eyes in respect of the price policy, most groups of workers were exceptional (and their employers mostly agreed) in respect of incomes policy. This was not merely due to "greed" or "irresponsibility" so much as the impossibility of the bargaining parties being able to predict the national consequences of any particular settlement. It was the purpose of the policy to bring such predictions into the reckoning; and it was the PIB's function to make the prediction.

It first concentrated on relating the policy rules to pay and not to wage rates. Many national pay negotiations had become a complicated ritual related to "basic rates" and "standard working week", which bore an increasingly tenuous relationship to take-home pay and hours worked. In report after report the PIB commented on negotiations taking place in total ignorance of the facts about actual earnings, and hence in ignorance of the probable results of the negotiations. National statistics also were prolific on formal wage rates; meagre, late and ill-classified on earnings.

The PIB decided how the norm was to apply to weekly or annual earnings; and it followed the interpretation put on it by most negotiators, that the norm was the rightful expectation for all groups. Two of the first three pay cases were referred after a settlement had been reached (printers' pay and Midland Bank staffs, see p. 131). Both of these were relatively highly-paid, in relation to the rest of the working population, if not to their own aspirations. To have suggested that settlements be upset (or should not have been made) would have been of no effect whatever, with no powers of enforcement. The only practical way of influencing pay was to suggest what was required in future to justify similar settlements in accord with the policy, including the norm.

The first unsettled claim related to the public sector, and to some of the most highly-paid of all public servants, the higher civil service. Because the Government was the employer, there was always the danger that public-service workers would have the full rigour of the incomes policy applied to them, while private-sector workers lingered longer in the habitual routines, paying lip-service to the policy. It would have been very awkward indeed to make a show of rigorousness in respect of civil servants, highly-paid though they were. They too got the norm. After this it would have been difficult to think of a group which might have qualified for something less.

The more exceptions were allowed, the more the national flow of income would rise above the forecast increase in national productivity. If the norm was the minimum to which exceptional increases had to be added, the policy had to be concentrated on discovering any and every opportunity to increase labour productivity, with the leverage of pay. The PIB diverted most exceptional cases into this channel the first of the four criteria, major changes in working practice. Few cases were ever recommended for exceptional increases because of low pay, anomalies or market shortages without productivity-linked pay arrangements.

The PIB could not ignore general trends and consequences. In 1965 and early 1966, the accumulating statistics showed that pay was still rising much faster than could be tolerated, in the interests of the balance of payments, or of greater price stability. Diverting as many groups as possible to seek rises through productivity bargains could keep incomes nearer in line with national productivity. But it did nothing to change the relation between one level of pay and another. Pay might still be cranked up step by step, on a base of exceptional increases (perhaps for productivity), followed by exceptional increases to preserve differentials. The PIB did not find it necessary to explore this issue until early 1966, when pay in the whole of the industrial civil service was referred. It then got increasingly involved in the question of pay structures within enterprises or sectors.

In this respect, as in no other, the PIB itself created incomes policy. There was no criterion in the first White Paper, to cover consequential increases when part of a labour-force had increased pay through productivity (or other) increments. If clerks were separated from manual workers (as in electricity supply, see p. 212), the rules as originally drafted would have to apply to the separate groups, with manifest injustice and resentment to the clerks. Heterogeneous collections of workers who happened to be parties to one set of negotiations (industrial civil servants, local authority manual workers, or NHS ancillary workers, see p. 201) were also in need of the reform of differentials, though this could always be done, on the PIB's interpretation, by applying the policy rules to the total wage bill, and rearranging the structure within the recommended total increase. But where enterprises or industries required a mixture of radically different kinds of work, attaching pay to productivity endowed production workers with privileges, against workers whose effect on output was indirect. Many large enterprises, especially in the public sector had difficulty in measuring output at all. But altering differentials might nevertheless be necessary to perform the work at less total cost. Reforming pay structures therefore also deserved exceptional treatment to promote cost restraint or increase labour productivity.

The extra criterion was added to the White Paper relating to the period after June 1967. "A proper development of salary structures" designed to "provide incentives to improved performance" could take place, even while there was still no norm. It applied on this first appearance specifically to salaries, since it was here that most of the PIB's difficulties had arisen. In the next two White Papers, it appeared in relation to pay generally. In the one relating to 1968–69, "reorganisation of wage and salary structures" could be allowed if they were "justified on the grounds of economic efficiency" under the productivity criterion. By 1969 it was required only that they "opened the way to substantial improvements in the efficiency with which labour is used", and such increases might well be "above the normal range". A restructuring scheme might well contribute to efficiency in a general way, eventually, while the immediate effect was to increase the flow of income quite considerably.

Having early attached itself so strongly to productivity as a condition above all else for pay increases, the PIB was early in a position to generalise its principles and advice. The reports on productivity agreements, payment by results, job evaulation, salary structures, and efficiency agreements were essentially a series of handbooks on a fair and reasonable interpretation of the policy, or on a reasonable determination of pay on any policy.

The general rule was pay according to performance. Pay was everywhere graded, usually distinguishing many separate functions, as well as seniority, responsibility or levels of skill and the grades (structures) must relate to the performance required as closely as possible. There was no uniquely best relation of pay to performance; rather a one-way progression from relatively primitive pay schemes to more refined ones. The best scheme in any particular case depended on history and conventions and the current needs of the enterprise or industry.

The first requirement of a coherent scheme was work analysis, the sort of analysis used—method study, work study, work measurement —depending on the nature of the work. Job description or job analysis, to make explicit the work expected and reasonable standards of performance, would complement it. Some large volume, repetitive or machine-paced work still lacked general standard times or standards of performance established by work measurement. The PIB recommended work study and work measurement in many activities, from clerical work to repair and maintenance work in garages, to laundries and hospital kitchens.

Where there was no measurable output, or where the work varied, method study could establish the scope for improving the use of skilled or experienced workers' time, or the relevance of existing job definitions, to the functions required. Even in as unpromising an environment as hospital nursing, some management committees found ways of making better use of nursing skills, as a contribution to controlling mounting costs. Work analysis and job analysis helped to improve management, since systematic work description and explicit objectives provided vital information for matching performance to requirements.

Incentive schemes, such as payments by results, were the most direct relationship between pay and performance and ostensibly in the spirit of incomes policy. But many of the most difficult problems in the determination of incomes occurred where such systems had been abused. Nevertheless there were many activities, especially in service sectors where simple incentive or piece-rate systems represented an advance over ineffectively supervised work on time rates.

However, payments-by-results schemes seemed to degenerate fast. Though all might begin with a close link between pay and performance, there were various ways in which the link was stretched. With an unchanging job or piece, the rate might still be increased unduly, where local (plant or workshop) piece-rate increases were added to increases in nationally negotiated minima. With frequently changing jobs or pieces the prices for new jobs could be settled more and more generously.

It was often difficult to renew PBR schemes in such a way that the problem of drift would not recur. So the remedy was to move to productivity agreements. Instead of relating individual pay to individual performance, a productivity agreement ought to relate pay increases for a whole group or labour-force to methods of work, standards of output, or other aspects of performance. In return for improvements in output per head, or a reduced total wage bill, extra pay could be offered out of the savings to the enterprise. Extended overtime, worked to make up pay rather than to meet the needs of the enterprise; over-generous manning standards, especially in relation to new technically improved machinery; too narrow a range of functions for distinct groups of workers, especially between maintenance and process workers, were all circumstances in which workers and management could find a common interest in altering working practices so that labour productivity, and possibly capital productivity, could be improved, providing extra pay was matched to it.

Productivity agreements could only be negotiated if pay and working practices were discussed together, at the same time, by the same negotiators. When the PIB started work, many collective bargaining bodies could not or did not do any such thing. Productivity and pay were discussed in separate committees, sometimes with different membership and procedures. Wages Councils were actually prevented by the nature of their powers from recommending anything but minimum pay rates and conditions of work. Voluntary negotiating procedures varied from over-rigid national bargaining, imposed with much adaption in suitable and unsuitable circumstances alike (as in the public sector), to the over-fragmented bargaining at plant or workshop level (as in private-sector manufacturing like engineering). Getting more reasonable pay agreements depended on more reasonable negotiating procedures; and the PIB examined procedure and institutions in almost all the productivity agreement cases. The confusion of national and local bargaining was inflationary, and was generally to be overcome by differentiating their functions, rather than attempting to brush one or the other aside. National negotiations were needed to set a framework for proper local agreements. National agreements might set minimum and maximum pay and establish working practices to be the subject of local productivity agreements. Work standards and grading of work or jobs might also be agreed nationally. Local agreements, at enterprise or plant level, could then fill the framework with the details of jobs and pay.

Where the nature of the work did not allow productivity agreements, an efficiency agreement was the recommended substitute. The work of an enterprise or institution could be arranged more or less effectively, or at greater or less cost, even where it could not be measured. There might be major changes of working practice, such as less convenient working patterns, wider ranges of function or responsibility, that would allow such increases in efficiency, and extra pay should be associated with the performance. Also, enterprises already having installed productivity agreements might find themselves with less and less to bargain about in future negotiations. These too might need to consider an efficiency agreement, specifying general arrangements to allow management greater control over labour costs.

Salaried staffs might earn pay more closely related to performance through the use of job evaluation. Job contents could be analysed more objectively and in more detail than was commonly done, and jobs in different departments of a complex enterprise classified on a reasonable common standard. Some producing services, or enterprises in the public sector, already used job evaluation with good results: more could do so. But it could equally be used with profit by industries where technological development was changing job content or the skills required (as in civil engineering and building).

The more employees approached salary-type pay structures the more relevant efficiency agreements, reform of pay structures and job evaluation would become. Relating pay to the personal performance of the holder of an evaluated job, as well as the job itself, would also become more important. If direct measurement of results was not feasible, there could still be agreed procedures to assess merit. Rewarding individual quality would increase efficiency by keeping specially skilled or experienced people in the job for which they were best suited, as well as encouraging extra effort from above average workers. It might encourage more responsibility to be exercised at lower levels, so that eventually the levels in the hierarchy could be reduced. It would also help to meet market pressures where there was a shortage of a particular skill, without having to raise the pay of a whole class of workers.

Job evaluation and individual assessment would bring greater control of staff costs, and hence, eventually, a reduction in unit costs. But new pay structures had rarely actually been installed without an immediate increase in the salary or wage bill. Often carefully devised schemes of a type approved by the PIB, had meant an immediate increase of a multiple of the norm or ceiling. Eventually, improved performance would balance the extra cost. Meanwhile the extra cost added to the excess of the flow of national income over national output. Universal progress in the improvement of pay structures would not necessarily contribute to universal stability of costs. Indeed the more concentrated the effort to devise and install new schemes, especially where nothing like them existed before, the greater the aggregate effect of the accumulation of jumps in pay bills. Moreover, not all reformed pay structures would be well founded. It was only too easy to under estimate the time necessary for negotiating a scheme, getting effective (as opposed to formal) agreement to it, installing it, getting rid of the unpredicted difficulties, and actually getting results. The greater the haste, the more likely somewhat fragile schemes would be tried, and the more incomes and costs would rise ahead of prices.

Labour-markets were, in the PIB's view, much less important than the institutions and conventions of pay determination. Labour-markets, and market pressures on pay existed alright: indeed it would have been somewhat surprising if the PIB had failed to find any such thing. But the limits and the nature and extent of market pressures were so varied, and so much influenced by the institutions and conventions, that beginning from a presumption that there were labour-markets analogous to product markets was virtually useless. Nevertheless, the nature of market forces was constantly an important question for the PIB, since where they did exist, they might well be more powerful than Government policy, legal powers notwithstanding.

All the PIB's enquiries led to the conclusion that labour-markets were much more complex than was often supposed. At any one time, there were only relatively few people deliberately choosing between occupations or employers, even in industries of areas with notoriously "high" mobility. At any one time, there were relatively few employers deliberating matching extra units of labour, at the "going rate" of pay, against the value of their product. Moreover, even in active markets, workers and employers were both commonly badly-informed about the facts, a result of pay structures so complicated that the recipients sometimes had only a vague understanding of the system. The market process went on, in a jerky, hit-or-miss fashion, with the decisions of both workers and employers often being made on false assumptions about actual pay and conditions. Time after time the PIB's endeavours to find "market rates" revealed a range of rates, beyond what could be explained by differences in conditions, experience or productivity. This was no trivial matter since the ranges were commonly wider than the alleged gaps to be made good by pay claims or offers. It was not surprising therefore that employers who raised their rates of pay to correct a labour shortage seldom succeeded in doing so. Where demand for specialised skills was expanding strongly or rapidly, pay increases could be effective in attracting workers and encouraging new recruits to seek training in scarce skills. But even here, employers had found that re-training or reorganising their existing labour-force was a better and cheaper way of overcoming the shortage.

The PIB's attitude to labour-markets was that markets needed careful definition, the nature and causes of pay differences being examined case by case. Often the relevant facts had not previously been collected; and when they were, they showed that jobs with similar titles and descriptions, especially in non-manual occupations, in fact had markedly different content or responsibilities. Different employers required different qualifications and experience. Career prospects could also vary widely between employers. All this needed taking into account to assess the reasons for the big differences in pay between one individual and another, or between the pay offered by one employer and another. With universal knowledge of the facts, the differences might be market-determined: with universal ignorance they could hardly be so.

But even if labour-markets were adequately informed, and if pay was negotiated by institutions corresponding rationally to the boundaries of the market, it still would not follow that pay differentials, let alone pay levels or the national flow of incomes were determined in any particularly rational way. The great majority of workers are committed to their occupation, industry or employer, and paid on some system, scale or rate, which would have been market-determined some years before. The pay level is increased from time to time, according to bargaining strength, and (possibly) to the market strength of new recruits. But pay structures often persist unchanged, especially in the public sector. It is not in the least true that most workers are paid "as though" they were in an active labour-market. This was indeed the reason why comparability became so strong an influence, propelling all pay levels up together.

Given the circumstances it found, the PIB's general verdict was that employers should think less about market pressures, and relate their existing labour-force more closely to their existing needs. Pay structure was an integral part of this, since changing needs meant that jobs and pay would have to change as well. Due regard for fairness and consequences for others required taking account of pay and conditions elsewhere. But, within reason, pay differentials should be set in relation to the needs and aims of each enterprise, each structure having only a few points of coincidence with market rates, in cases where there were active markets.

The labour-market was indeed elusive, and belief in its solidarity might actually do harm. Employers short of labour might each believe that the shortage was due to his pay being below the "market rate", and increase it to correct the shortage. If other employers acted in the same belief, there might be a higher level of pay all round with no change at all in the distribution of labour between enterprises. In many occupations, the size of the labour-force depended more on demographic or social trends, on educational opportunities, and influences, than on the relatively few entering and leaving competing jobs. Even the few actually choosing between jobs might well be moving for reasons other than pay.

There were limits beyond which "market pressure" in the form of pay differences began to inhibit recruitment and retention in a major way. There were two special cases where the PIB found that salaries were slipping towards the lower limit of a market range with undesirable effects, both relating to high salaries in the public sector. In the early case relating to higher civil servants, it was held to be desirable to pay proposed increases so that career prospects should be sufficient to recruit and retain the quality of entrant required. In the much later case relating to the Chairmen and Board members of nationalised industries, a defect of the existing structure of salaries was that recruiting from outside to senior management or Board level was not always possible because of the pay offered (among other things). However, in the same section of the same report, the PIB went out of its way to emphasise that there was no reason for public-sector salaries to match those in the private sector, as the jobs were clearly different. It was a case of removing a disparity of pay so marked that some market response built up beyond considerations of the special nature of the jobs.

Another reason for recommending a revision of salaries in the nationalised industries was that increased responsibility at senior management level was not being suitably rewarded. The PIB frequently observed that the differentials for responsibility were unduly compressed. The supply of "supervision" or willingness to undertake more responsibility might respond to market rewards more than supply of basic skills, since it usually required no further technical qualification than the jobs supervised, and the PIB took the view that the quality of supervision and extent of responsibilities responded to pay increments at relevant points. This was another view not necessarily leading to cost restraint. Its immediate effect would be to draw out a pyramid of pay. The pay of the supervisors and managers nearer the top would increase faster relatively to the rest. The aggregate effect would be to swell the national flow of income in relation to output, until the better performance of better supervisors and managers attracted by the higher rewards should have their effect on costs. The only way to counteract the swelling of the income flow would be to reduce the levels of responsibility and increase areas of supervision. Initiating such changes and getting better performance would require high standards of management at the top.

The relation between pay and performance is the main preoccupation of trades unions and professional associations. To some degree therefore, pointing out the need for a radical reform in this relationship

was pointing a need for radical change of attitude or policy on the part
of unions and associations. But the stream of PIB reports on pay form
an extended lecture on better management standards, fully as much as a
homily on better trade-union policies or practice. Describing desirable
reforms and costing them must be a management function—however
"co-operative" or "unco-operative" a union might be. The total size of
the wage and salary bill in relation to output must in the end be a
management function. At the stage of a particular set of negotiations,
performance to which pay should more clearly relate must have been
suitably described and measured for the result to have much influence
on productivity or cost restraint. Assessing standards of performance
and methods of work to create the framework for pay arrangements
more in the national interest than before had to be initiated by management.

Though some of the strictest and most rigid conventions for the
determination of pay occurred in the public sector, the PIB's strictures
on management were by no means all addressed to the public sector
(in spite of their salary disadvantages). Most nationalised industries compared favourably with private industries of a comparable size in standards of labour and pay management. Nor did particular unions appear
more creditworthy than others. Whatever their general political attitude
towards prices and incomes policy, the big unions were actually
occupied, in some sectors some of the time, in altering the institutions
and practices of pay negotiations in tune with the aims of the policy.
Circumstances, conventions and institutions—and the attitude and state
of organisation of the employers—were more important in determining the unions' style of negotiations than attachment to general philo-
sophical principles.

The general development of the incomes policy was greatly hampered
by the crisis of 1966 and the devaluation of 1967. The emphasis had
to be not so much on discovering and encouraging better methods
of pay determination as on enforcing the letter of the law designed
primarily to cut down the flow of income.

It was not until 1969 that advance could be renewed in two major
problems still outstanding. One was improving the relative rewards to
the low-paid. The other was the right principle for determining pay in
the public sector. Putting so much emphasis on improving productivity
to make the low-paid less low paid, put these workers in the hands of
management. But low pay associated with low productivity was as likely
as not the result of poor management. Inducing unions to put pressure
on managements to improve productivity might be effective, providing
the barriers were mild lethargy, or remediable bureaucratic procedure.
Where they were poor standards of management (possibly accompanied
by poor work standards or bad industrial relations) any improvement
could at best be slow. Meanwhile, the more productive and highly-paid

workers in better managed enterprises would forge ahead, even if they all conformed strictly to the policy rules. Something more than productivity bargaining was needed to make the low-paid relatively better-off in most low-paying, ill-organised industries.

The White Paper to apply after 1969 itself described this problem at greater length than before. It recognised that the problem was different from what had been assumed when the first White Paper was prepared, the relevant rules of which had been repeated ever since. "The first step must be to identify who are the low-paid, and why they are low-paid." The PIB itself had pointed out that there were low-paid pockets in many highly-paid industries as well as low-paid occupations. The low-paid could only be made better off if differentials above them were squeezed. There would have to be "a conscious decision of their fellow workers that they will accept a re-assessment of differentials both between different industries and within an industry". The only practicable way of tackling the problem was to investigate case by case, the scope for making the low-paid relatively better-off to the rest. The PIB would be asked to do this, rather than being asked to comment on pay in a whole activity, all of it presumed to be low-paid. But when the three special references on low pay were sent to the PIB in 1970, all referred to low-paying industries.

The special problem of women's pay was also (at last) specifically discussed in the 1969 White Paper. "Women comprise the great majority of low-paid workers. Any policy designed to lift the levels of low pay will therefore be concerned to a very great extent with women." Legislation to enforce equal pay would change the principles. But if its practical effect was to make women less low paid in relation to men, again traditional differentials would have to be squeezed. The three low pay references all concerned women's occupations. But the PIB's reports were not notably helpful in improving women's prospects.

The general problem in the public sector was that the PIB had been unable to suggest a general substitute for comparability between public and private sectors for determining the level of pay. Only some parts of the public sector would be able to keep up by means of productivity or efficiency agreements. Even job evaluation or reforming pay structures was not very relevant to sectors like education where there was not so much a variety of different jobs, as a variety of ways of doing very much the same job. Performance was often too remote from pay and differences in pay to give any precise or practical guide about what pay ought to be.

The White Paper began by pointing out (as usual) that the rules were generally to apply to the public sector as to the private. Nevertheless "some special problems" arose: output could not be measured and it did not have a market price. Employment opportunities for certain professions (doctors, nurses, teachers, police) existed to only a minor extent outside the public sector, and "unduly low" pay would not create market pressures. Moreoever, the Government was under particular pressure to make fair settlements. This meant that "where close comparisons with similar jobs in the private sector are not possible . . . regard will have to be paid to more generalised comparisons with pay elsewhere". The reinstatement of comparability should not mean that efforts to link pay to performance should cease, but no general rule could be prescribed. The PIB would investigate the cases, and advise accordingly.

The rules and terms of reference were set for a new stage in the PIB's efforts to reform pay structures. But no such development ensued in the public sector. The DEP, having promulgated its new more elaborate rules, gave the PIB virtually nothing to work on, while it was getting more and more involved with battles over changing institutions (and in turning the PIB into the CIM), and over the general legal framework of industrial relations (through the Industrial Relations Bill). The references on low pay were made a year after the White Paper; and one of the outstanding omissions in the public sector and professional pay references, doctors' pay, was only referred in June 1970 after the Kindersley Committee (an independent review body) had recommended a 30 per cent increased, and then only in respect of half the increase. But it was already too late. The change of Government at once removed the PIB's powers and influence. One of the first actions of the new Government was to withdraw the doctors' case even though the PIB's investigation had been completed—the only time any withdrawal was ever made. The low-pay reports were among those allowed to go on, but their academic flavour and lack of positive recommendation must have been due, directly or indirectly, to the Conservative Government's withdrawal of support.

The PIB's own view of its attitude to incomes cases was given in the final report: "We tried to contribute to the improvement of industrial relations by helping to develop situations in which management had a more effective control of the work-situation based on the co-operation and consent of the workers concerned."

18

Success or Failure?

When the PIB was created, prices and incomes policy was a term to conjure up a benevolent glow, a hope of better ways of settling pay and prices. By the time its destruction had been arranged, prices and incomes policy had become, it seemed, a vain hope, if not a term to conjure up a sneer. The PIB itself enjoyed something of the transferred benevolence in the early days; and even towards the end of its life, it did not attract the antipathy generated by the policy, either among its three sponsoring parties, or among a wider public.

We clearly have no unquestionable success to celebrate so far as the policy is concerned. One purpose was to develop general public acceptance of its aims, and this at least had failed. Many industrialists were refusing to continue early warning of price increases by early 1970 and trade-union leaders were refusing to contemplate even a norm or clearly defined rules for pay determination, much less any powers to enforce them. At the same time, the obvious and well-publicised acceleration of price and wage increases late in 1969 and throughout 1970 discouraged any great faith in it. But even though the new Government lost no time in repudiating the already unpopular policy and killing off the PIB, the idea of a prices and incomes policy reappeared in general public comment in a matter of a few months.

Equally clearly we have no unequivocal failure of either the policy or the PIB to bury. Our conclusions must sum up the short but productive history of both the policy and the PIB in terms less stark or presumptive than these. There are degrees of success and failure to examine.

We have seen that the policy was designed to achieve national economic management aims, namely to restrict the increase in the total flow of incomes to the increase in productivity, and induce a more stable price level. But in spite of the emphasis with which these aims were announced, no one imagined that they would be entirely achieved, as they very obviously were not. However, that a particular norm was not reached does not in itself argue failure. We must rather examine whether the policy failed to bring the rate of increase of incomes— nearer to the increase in productivity, or to restrain price increases, or to raise productivity, any more than would have happened without it.

During the first period of the policy, from April 1965 to the summer of 1966, the record was not impressive. There are a range of indices relating to the price level, incomes and productivity, and they give various figures for rates of increase. But all agree in recording rates of increase in 1965 and 1966 closely matching 1964 to 1965. Moreover in both periods, the increase in pay was considerably in excess of the increase in productivity, which (though less than two per cent a year) was not far from the average of the previous decade in both years. Wage and salary costs per unit of output actually increased faster than before, as hours worked (at high employment levels) were coming down more rapidly than before (or since). The prices and incomes policy, in its first voluntary period, was not accompanied by any notable worsening in the situation; but neither was there any noticeable improvement.

Then the economic environment of the policy was abruptly changed by the freeze and squeeze crisis policies imposed in July 1966, followed by severe restraint during the first half of 1967. During the standstill (freeze), earnings did not increase but retail prices rose by something less than $1\frac{1}{2}$ per cent. Then, during severe restraint, earnings rose by two per cent while prices rose again by $1\frac{1}{2}$ per cent. The most important change was the increase of some $2\frac{1}{2}$ per cent in productivity, and in manufacturing about twice as much. A most welcome corollary of this was that export prices increased by only one per cent, instead of two to three per cent as in previous years.

From late 1967, through 1968 into 1969, the situation was again drastically changed by devaluation in November 1967. Retail prices went up by $4\frac{1}{2}$ per cent between 1967 and 1968; but earnings went up even faster, by some eight per cent. This was partly due to increased hours worked (compared with the days of standstill and severe restraint), and partly to increased output per hour. Productivity continued to increase at a higher rate than the average for the previous decade. It looked as though trends had changed for the better, judging by productivity indicators.

The year from 1968 to 1969 was shaped by the severe budget of April 1968, designed to counter the inflationary effects of devaluation. Prices rose still faster, by $5\frac{1}{2}$ per cent over the year. Earnings were still climbing higher at an increasing rate, at an annual increase of nearly nine per cent. But productivity was still climbing higher also, and had now reached some four per cent a year. It was partly this that carried earnings with it. Prices and earnings were both increasing faster than in the previous decade, but so was productivity.

Meantime, the era of deflationary demand management had begun.

As a result of the squeeze (in the form of credit restriction, and cuts in projected Government expenditure) imposed at the same time as the standstill, unemployment rose to nearly $2\frac{1}{2}$ per cent in 1967, and stayed there in 1968. In 1969, it crept slowly upwards, while the total national product increased only slowly. From late 1969 onwards, the rise in output ceased and productivity started to fall. Prices and earnings still continued to rise, with an acceleration of the rate of increase during 1970. More significantly, earnings were still rising faster than prices, in spite of the fact that neither extra output, extra hours of work, or extra productivity accompanied them. Increases in unit costs were going on at the same time in both capital-intensive and labour-intensive industries, the one because of the squeeze on demand and credit, the other because of fast rising incomes. It was difficult to conceive an alternative to further deflation to prevent the inevitable further round of price increases, pushed by costs and allowed by incomes—except a renewal of prices and incomes policy.

The policy was clearly a failure in restraining incomes or stabilizing prices, except for the six months of standstill. Even then prices went up by over one per cent (some $2\frac{1}{2}$ per cent annually, not far from the average for the previous decade). Then, as the standstill relaxed into severe restraint, and severe restraint into the nameless "period after June 1967", the pace increased. Earnings overtook prices from 1967 onwards; though there was still some cause for hope, in that productivity was increasing faster also. The annual increase in "income-cost" per unit of output still climbed, but more slowly than before. If a further acceleration of pay increases could have been avoided, while the productivity increase continued, the upward propulsion of prices might have died away to more tolerable rates. But the devaluation of 1967 introduced its own propulsion. There was no time for an effective post restraint policy to have any results.

Could it be said that the policy was responsible at any stage for mitigating the upward pressure of pay and prices, or for securing increases in productivity? This is a question that cannot be resolved beyond doubt. There were too many other influences on the price level, and on the total flow of incomes to isolate any one with precision. The most that can be claimed for the policy is a weight of evidence suggesting some influence.

The PIB itself made some of the most sustained efforts at the time to test the evidence of the impact of the policy on national aggregates. Any such analysis has to be based on a selection of assumptions about the relations between variables. The PIB analysis assumed that increases in wages and salaries were determined partly by concurrent increases in the price level, partly by the level of unemployment (measuring the state of demand for labour), and partly by independent factors such as rising expectations (real terms in intention). Increases in the price level were in turn partly determined by wage increases, partly by import prices, and partly by independent factors, such as expected demand and the nature of the market. When formalised in equations, the results fitted the statistics then available well enough to lend some confidence to the results, (for further details see Appendix A. 3rd General Report Cmnd 4130).

During the voluntary phase of the policy, up to the summer of 1966, there was no convincing evidence that the policy had begun to have any effect on incomes, prices or productivity. The most that could be said was that there might have been some effect: price increases might have been somewhat postponed because of the early-warning arrangements. The standstill of July 1966 was accompanied by credit restriction and some demand deflation, so the statistics reflect all three policies. The standstill directly prevented wage rates from rising at all from July to December 1966. Earnings also ceased to rise. Though they might well have risen further through the freeze by a certain amount of drift, the squeeze prevented it. There is no doubt that the policy of combined freeze and squeeze worked during the standstill.

Severe restraint allowed considerable relaxation of the prices and incomes policy, if not of monetary restraint. All existing commitments on 20 July 1966 were allowed in full after six months postponement, even if they were not consistent with the policy. Naturally the effect of this began to swell the total flow of incomes again, early in 1967. The PIB's view was that the increase in wage rates, which also began early in the year, was that it was due mainly to increases for low-paid workers, who were still entitled to exceptional treatment. However prices never ceased to rise mainly, perhaps entirely, due to Government action. At a time when pay was effectively frozen, this was bound to lead to resentment and to the conclusion that the policy was a failure.

The Government's policy, especially the imposition of SET, probably gave even competitive industries an opportunity to increase prices that they otherwise might not have had. The rules of the price policy made exceptions for unavoidable cost increases, specifically mentioning taxation; so passing on SET was entirely excuseable within the bounds of the policy. With falling profits, as turnover failed to rise as fast as costs, SET allowed traders to increase margins by putting on SET "surcharges", as was widely done in retailing, restaurants, hotels, and many other service trades. In competitive trades, the policy was doomed to failure eventually. But adjustment to changing conditions, even in highly competitive markets, takes time. A new tax that had the effect of widespread increases in retail prices, including food prices, appeared to be the very opposite of prices policy. The timing also could not have been worse, as it turned out. Though announced in April, SET did not become effective until September, after the pay standstill had started.

Prices and margins cannot have increased much in the end as a result of the 1966 SET (see the first report of the Reddaway Committee, which found that the tax did induce greater efficiency rather than raise prices). But by the time prices of services were settling down again, other prices were rising for other reasons.

The squeeze policy, coming on top of a deflationary Budget in the spring of 1966, pushed demand down, as it was intended to do. But output was pushed down with it, partly to help reduce the upward pressure on incomes. As output fell appreciably below capacity working, unit costs automatically rose. But the price policy rules specifically allowed profits to be restored by means of exceptional price rises, where it could be shown that this was necessary to finance investment. A number of industries could claim to come within these exceptions. Raising productivity in capital-intensive industries is likely to need new investment anyway, and not all companies had been so profitable in 1965 and 1966 that they needed no more reserves by 1967. It was the special cases which came to the attention of Government Departments, some of which were referred to the PIB (newsprint, fertilisers, cement, bricks). The PIB was in the circumstances, given its terms of reference, unable to refuse the increases.

However prices might well have risen faster during this period than they did, had not the Government also adopted a policy towards the public sector that undoubtedly promoted price stability. The financial targets of the nationalised industries were temporarily withdrawn in favour of price stability. Perhaps the fact that the 1961 targets had only related to the quinquennium up to 1966, and that discussions on those for 1967 onwards were still going on (and not finally concluded until late in 1967) made it easier to ignore the targets for a short breathing space. The exception—inexplicably—was for the bulk electricity supply tariff in 1967, a decision which dealt another major blow to public toleration of the policy after severe restraint.

Earnings overtook prices again after the end of severe restraint. But the PIB itself pointed out repeatedly that aggregate changes shown in the statistics were not good indicators of events as they affected individuals, whether consumers or industries. The retail price increases were not very steep, but all consumers must have been affected to some extent by them. By no means every family had an increase in income. Even among those in work, in any period as short as half a year, aggregate pay increases are made up of a number having above average increases and a number having no increase at all. During severe restraint, the difference was more marked than usual, since there had been an unusual interval of standstill in the normal round of pay increases. Many families suffered a reduction in real income, considerably bigger than the deceptively shallow reduction suggested by national aggregates. They were balanced by some who had kept up, either through salary increments or promotion, or through a recent pay increase. Public opinion on such matters is inevitably dominated by those who endure falling standards, rather than those whose standards are rising.

By the end of severe restraint the prospects for an orderly emergence into a less restrictive but effective post restraint policy were not encouraging. The figures for 1967 to 1968, aggregated though they are, offer incontrovertible evidence of the "catching-up" process in pay. Earnings rose rather faster than before the prices and incomes policy began. It looked as though the prophets of gloom would be right, and restraint would be followed by a readjustment back to the level which would have been reached with no policy. The fall in real income of 1966–67 had been offset—in aggregate anyway.

But devaluation altered expectations and, it seems, the underlying relationships between prices and incomes. After increasing for a time (at three to four per cent a year), real consumption had to be compressed once more. As in the summer of 1966, so in the post devaluation situation, the prices and incomes policy was only one of a group of policies all having effect on prices and incomes. Devaluation itself was expected to raise the retail price level by three per cent. But this would not be deflationary if it induced a parallel (or faster) increase in earnings. In any case home demand had to be restrained so that extra exports could be supplied in the absence of much surplus capacity. Little was done at the time of devaluation to inflate demand, surprisingly little in the opinion of most commentators. Devaluation would not have its full effect on prices, or on export supplies for some months. The time lag between payments for imported materials and final sales of the goods containing them was to be reckoned in months rather than weeks; and it was difficult in November to forecast either the price level or incomes for the following April. But postponing a decision itself had an effect on the matter. The inevitable conclusion was drawn by the public, aided by the legions of press, radio and TV experts: devaluation required deflation to accompany it, as the Government had admitted. Not much deflation of demand had yet been announced; therefore a fiercely deflationary budget was to come in April. Two further influences were thereby introduced into the determinants of prices and incomes in 1968, confident expectations of tax increases or further credit restriction to come and the actual deflationary measures of the Budget of April 1968. Anticipation of deflation was an opportunity for both pay and prices to be pushed up as far as bargaining strength or competition allowed, to protect real consumption or profits. Bargaining strength allowed a degree of effective pushing in both, in spite of rising unemployment, climbing interest rates and credit restriction. The PIB's own view was that expectation of steeper price increases was the main cause of higher wage claims pressed more urgently. But some of the increase in earnings was matched by increased output and increasing productivity. Output, hours worked and output per head all increased at the same time, and all of this was reasonable, within the policy rules. No doubt the aggregate flow of incomes was increasing faster than the policy rules ought to have allowed, but the excess was not equal to the difference between the rise in earnings and the rise in prices. More significantly, wage-cost per unit of output was hardly rising.

When the Budget eventually came, it included a number of tax increases adding to prices and a steep increase in SET, again not to be effective for six months. Once more enterprises had been given an excuse entirely within the rules of the policy to increase prices. For 1968 to 1969, the prices policy was not stability, but an increasing price level of at least $4\frac{1}{2}$ per cent. The ceiling for pay had become $3\frac{1}{2}$ per cent, with exceptions only for productivity or reformed pay structures. The prices and incomes policy was being used again (among other things) to reduce real consumption in aggregate. But the deflation of demand cut down output again, and the opportunities for maintaining or increasing pay by working overtime, or getting production bonuses. Unless bargaining strength was reduced with proportionate effect, the pressure for more pay would be on general increases in rates or scales.

In face of its inconclusive evidence, the PIB tried to estimate the order of magnitude of the impact of the policy. Its tentative conclusion was as follows. The national flow of income had increased more slowly than would otherwise have happened to the extent of about one per cent a year, over the whole period from the beginning of the PIB's existence to the end of 1968. This was a result of considerable importance to economic management. The one per cent smaller growth in incomes was equivalent to an improvement in the balance of payments of £100 million a year (due to the slower growth in wage-costs per unit of output, allowing lower export prices, higher export earnings, lower imports and lower expenditure on imports). Regarded as an alternative to deflating aggregate demand and output, a one per cent reduction in the rate of increase of incomes by prices and incomes policy was equivalent to 100,000 extra jobs.

We therefore conclude our examination of the policy in a similarly tentative way. There is evidence, not yet directly refuted, that the rate of increase of incomes and also therefore of prices was checked by the operation of the prices and incomes policy, imperfect though it was. There is evidence moreover that the extent of the improvement was enough to make a worthwhile impact on a national scale. Indeed accepting the PIB's figure of £100 million improvement in national earnings of foreign currency, this was a rate of return on the extra resources employed to satisfy even the greediest capitalist.

Our main concern is with the activities of the PIB. By itself the PIB could not achieve any economic management purpose directly, as it could only proceed case by case, applying the prescribed rules. We next enquire whether the PIB applied the rules in such a way that the pay norms and price stability were more likely to be achieved.

The containment of costs, in the longer term as well as immediately, was its overriding purpose, and to promote productivity and tighter management generally. The PIB also tried to mitigate price increases, even when the Government's policy was pushing them up, to make the incomes policy more tolerable and effective. Relating pay to productivity or performance was an overriding need, even when particular policy rules did not explicitly require it. On the face of it, a list of price cases and incomes cases, showing where price increases were approved, modified or disapproved, and where pay increases up to the norm (or ceiling) had been recommended would demonstrate its effectiveness. But such a list would be at best misleading. Most price cases included a specific price proposal on which the PIB commented. But these were not always made independently of the PIB's investigation, or of an expected examination by a Government Department or the PIB itself. (Such a strategy was not unknown in relation to pay claims also where the PIB recommended less than the proposed increase, it might have done nothing more than market pressure or bargaining would have achieved anyway.) Where this was clearly not the case, as for instance in public-sector cases, the PIB was often in the position of being compelled by its terms of reference to allow proposed increases immediately. But it always took the opportunity of pointing out alternative policies and recommending longer-term changes which might eventually be more important in promoting productivity, or restraining inflation, than the immediate refusal of a price increase would have been. Equally, immediate refusal or scaling-down of a pay claim could be less important than recommendations opening opportunities for further increases in the next round.

Taking all these considerations into account, the impressionistic evidence is nevertheless reasonably clear. The PIB allowed price increases more than it refused them, and on the whole, it failed to find cases for price reduction. It does not follow though that this was PIB's failure. It could only operate on the cases referred to it; and applications for price increases came in the main from firms having a reasonably good case. If the early-warning arrangements did nothing else, they made increasing prices more trouble, and hence probably delayed them, strengthening the case where costs were rising steadily. Only a few of the applications made to Government Departments were referred to the PIB, and on the whole only those where the case was urgent enough for enterprises to resist administrative pressure to withdraw or modify their proposals. Moreover after 1967 most price cases related to the public sector, most with the financial obligations. This almost always meant that there was little alternative to an increase of the size proposed.

Incomes cases were even more varied as particular increases were neither asked for nor recommended in some of them. In others, claim and offer might mean very little before negotiations were completed. Moreover, recommendations other than a particular pay increase were the most important part of the many reports. Nevertheless the impressionistic evidence is again clear, that the PIB adopted a generous view of the incomes policy rules. In the great majority of cases where it scaled down claims, it set out conditions in which the increases could be paid in future in accordance with the policy. There was a constant danger, borne in mind by the PIB, that its clients would be discriminated against because it had no power to alter its rules, widely though it might interpret them. Other highly paid and well-organised workers were clearly getting increases outside the rules and were not referred throughout the PIB's existence, except during the standstill. It could not always avoid being in a weak and acutely uncomfortable position, as a result of the limited selection of cases, especially concerning public-sector pay.

As the PIB had no power to refuse references, nor to choose its own, it tried constant prodding of Government Departments through its annual reports. It suggested a selection of price cases, fairly representing goods and services heavily weighted in the retail price index, and a representative selection of cases where taxes had been newly imposed. It suggested selecting private-sector industries where competitive pressure on prices was low, to balance public-sector price cases. It suggested investigating export industries, those competing with imports or protected by tariffs, after devaluation. It pointed out the unjust consequences of referring some professions' pay, but not others. It asked for second references on pay cases where the consequences of important agreements were not clear. Occasionally, usually in income cases, the requests were granted. More often especially on price cases, the selection of cases remained as bizarre or sparse as before. There was, it seems, too little organisation or thought for a general strategy to appear.

The PIB's capacity for dealing with a flow of cases was always limited. It could not have handled a fully representative sample of price cases, and perhaps not of incomes cases. It certainly did not do so. But in spite of this, it had to draw its conclusions so that they could be generalised to similar cases, as well as making practical sense in the particular circumstances of the case in hand. The evidence on this has appeared in Parts II and III of this volume. In general, it can be said that the PIB recommended little that was not already practised by some enterprise, often in the sector being examined, as much in the public sector as in the private. It urged unions to negotiate minimum earnings rather than basic wage rates, as some were already doing. Other unions were already looking more to production bonuses on productivity bargains rather than to basic rates of increases. The PIB recommended the

K

details of applying such broad principles, and applied them more widely than the parties were doing themselves. It was spreading best practices in labour management and cost control as in pricing and operational efficiency. Though it was a reforming body the PIB never tried to impose any general rules, either derived from the White Paper or from its own interpretations, on a particular industry or firm, without first investigating the circumstances from the beginning. It usually had before it studies of the history and institutions of the particular activity, as well as analyses of costs, earnings and so on. Having its own information, often more complete than anything before available to Government Departments or to the industry itself, it could consider ideas and techniques in the light of the facts. It was at pains to discover what markets were like: whether prices were competitively determined, or whether a labour-market could be found with the characteristics usually assumed. It could always claim that it paid more attention to the facts than its critics. We may conclude by suggesting a degree of success for the PIB, in that the soundness of its judgment was accepted and its independence approved by relatively expert and uncommitted observers. Where there were disputes, or the possibilities of dispute between the Government and its employees, or between the Government and industry over incomes or prices, it became an accepted, recognised, beneficial way out to refer the matter to the PIB.

Abundance of sense would have been of no avail if no one was led to behave any differently after PIB reports from what would have happened without. The impact of the PIB reports on particular industries or firms was also relevant to success or failure. The effect was likely to be different in respect of public- and private-sector cases anyway, since Government decisions can to some degree be enforced throughout the public sector, while in the private sector legislation is necessary. In practice, the distinction was not so clear. Public-sector managements could be more or less recalcitrant in face of Government pressure, especially since Government Departments were reluctant to direct them. Private-sector management could be more or less amenable to Government pressure, since there was often a degree of indeterminateness about prices and investment, especially about the timing of changes. Nevertheless the PIB's reports inevitably had their maximum impact on the public sector. Pay recommendations were mostly implemented, though longer-term or general recommendations to improve productivity or performance were not always followed in the spirit of the PIB's intentions. However it could never be said that action did not follow. In the private sector action did not always follow. Immediate, specific recommendations for pay or prices were usually implemented. But how much impact more general recommendation for alterations of the conventions had needs the sort of detailed investigation the PIB did when the cases were referred to them. This has not yet been done, except where the PIB itself did so by means of second references.

In general terms we must therefore leave the question of success or failure at the level of particular cases still open. Some degree of success relates to public-sector cases, and some, possibly smaller, degree to private-sector cases. But at least, even in relation to the most hostile private-sector parties, the PIB reports often changed the basis of discussion about the industry's future policy.

In the end, the policy and the PIB had to depend on public toleration of its aims and the applications. Concerning the policy only one conclusion is possible, that it did not become acceptable. The standstill and severe restraint undoubtedly affected incomes severely, but it appeared that prices were not so strictly confined. Though incomes were increasing faster than prices by the end of 1967, the news about the policy and the PIB always tended to be in terms of limits and restraints. There was a widespread belief among workers in restraint of incomes. By the summer of 1968 (after devaluation and the deflationary Budget), the policy was no longer tolerable to trade-union leaders, except in a purely voluntary form as in 1965. Whether so powerless a version could have achieved any economic management purpose is doubtful: there is little evidence that it did in 1965.

On the other hand, managements observed in 1968 that prices were rising less than Government expectations, and drew the conclusion that prices policy was unfairly restrictive. There was no evidence at all to support such a view. Prices rose less than costs, and profits lagged; but the deflationary budgets and credit restriction were more likely causes than prices policy. The PIB was by now getting only a trickle of price cases, and the private sector ones were mostly relatively trivial. Significantly, early warning of price increases was only half the level of the previous year. Once the immediately post devaluation increases were out of the way (in 1968), it was either not necessary, or not possible (in 1969) to increase prices much further. The PIB's own interpretation was that the relative stability of prices later in 1968 was to be explained by the stability of wage rates during the standstill and severe restraint. This, together with increasing productivity through 1967 and 1968, meant that unit costs were not yet rising much. At the same time, the deflation of demand made it more difficult to increase prices in anticipation of the effect of current pay increases. But by 1969 the upward pressure on costs was resumed, due to the faster increase in pay in 1968; and more widespread enjoyment of higher incomes made it possible to raise prices again.

By early 1970, unit costs were pressing on prices, and industries and firms were sufficiently persuaded of the effect of the policy to take the trouble to withdraw their agreement to early-warning arrangements. To some extent, this was probably an essentially political gesture to put an end to prices policy, although it had already ceased to have any effect. It could equally have been an indication that the early-warning arrangements, plus threat of PIB investigation, at least had the effect of delaying price increases.

By late 1969 or early 1970, there was no doubt that public acceptance of the policy was much reduced. This was partly a consequence of the trades unions' refusal to tolerate it. It was also probably due to the renewed rise in prices. When the Government itself finally announced that the policy would no longer be backed by statutory powers, and that the functions of the PIB itself would be absorbed by a new body, it was widely assumed that prices and incomes policy could be allowed to die as a failure—regrettable perhaps, but complete.

With the change of Government in June 1970 the policy and the PIB were wound up. But we cannot finish our assessment of the success or failure of the policy, or of its public acceptability without recording a remarkable (as it seemed at the time) restoration of the idea. In six months from the change of Government both prices and incomes rose at an unprecedented rate. This alone made it more plausible to believe that rates of increase of over eight per cent in earnings in 1968 and 1969 and an increasing price level were compatible with the policy and the PIB having had some impact after all. Widespread apprehension of the consequences of returning to fiscal and monetary policy alone for economic management, also kept the idea of a prices and incomes policy alive, somehow to be made more effective than before.

So short a history has led to no very clear conclusions. Neither the policy nor the PIB can be written off as complete failures, in accordance with the evidence. Nor can it be said that the policy proved to be misconceived, in that it was based on false assumptions about the determinants of prices and incomes.

Neither prices nor incomes are fully determined by market forces, nor are they fully determined by one another. Old habits and inherited institutions influence pay negotiations, the gaps between one rate and another, and the intervals of time between related settlements. The total flow must in consequence depend also on these. Market pressures cannot fully determine prices, still less price structures where many different products or services are offered where monopolistic tendencies exist. Price competition exists in some sectors, though it is not nearly so widespread as appearances suggest. The price level is clearly not fully determined by the market. The timing as well as the size of changes depend on many other circumstances in both public and private sectors.

Neither the PIB nor the policy can be hailed as completely successful, if misunderstood. But through all the vicissitudes of the policy, the PIB was not a target for criticism, except occasionally by disgruntled subjects of reports. If it was less effective than it ought to have been, it was because the Government gave it too little effective to do. It was the policy rather than the PIB that failed in public esteem (in spite of the Government making use of the PIB to raise public-sector prices, especially fuel and fares).

Looking back on the whole development of the policy, the conclusion is not so much that the policy failed, as that it was never really tried. The main reasons for believing that prices and incomes policy (in association with demand management and monetary policy) could provide a means of running a more stable economy, with less waste of resources, was that there was an important direct link between prices and incomes, working both ways and that this could most readily be altered by direct intervention in pay and price decisions. The policy was adopted by agreement between the Government, industry and the trades unions, because any one of the three parties could frustrate the good (non-inflationary) intentions of the others, and each acting alone was relatively powerless to achieve more stable price or incomes, even though more stability was in the interests of all three.

Using fiscal policy alone to reduce prospective demand by increasing indirect taxes, might have been a good policy. But it made nonsense of prices policy. If money incomes did rise in reponse to price increases, tax-created prices increases were just as inflationary as excessive profits. The Treasury might distinguish between good and bad parts of a price rise, but the customers did not. Similarly, monetary policy in the form of high interest rates might have been justified in itself. But as they resulted in prices of all capital-intensive goods and services going up, especially transport, fuel and house rents, for which the customers have long-term commitments, it was just as inflationary as greedy shareholders, or irresponsible workers, or rising international prices, or slack cost-control. To rely on raising prices to deflate demand was tantamount to an admission that the prices policy was not taken seriously. Insisting that nationalised industries met financial obligations might have been a well-justified policy, as the PIB itself pointed out. But a price rise to reach the target might be just as inflationary as a price rise to compensate for lax management, especially as increased prices of basic services were passed on to the final consumer (and the retail price index).

The PIB produced 170 reports, five of them general. Of the 165 cases, 79 concerned incomes, 67 prices, and 10 both. The remaining nine were studies of productivity, prices and incomes in whole industries or sectors, and most of these were referred late in the PIB's history. Report No. 170 was its valedictory general report, and the PIB attempted its own summing up. It wished to be remembered by six virtues:

It had gathered its own information, keeping oral enquiries informal to encourage frankness and overcome hostility. "In many cases—though not all—we . . . established a real understanding with those whose affairs were referred to us."

It had adopted a constructive approach. "Our main intention was not to stop people from doing things, but to suggest how things could be done more efficiently and economically. From the early days we put the emphasis on containing unit costs so that a pay increase could be justified or a price rise avoided. We tried to widen people's understanding of their problems, both in particular areas of industry or commerce and in the country as a whole."

It acted with whatever mixture of speed and depth was possible in the time available to it.

It built up a board and a staff of various experts, and "their effectiveness (was) the greater because they acted as a single instrument of investigation".

It found indeed, as the policy had supposed, that prices and incomes were "inextricably bound together". It could only regret the separation of the problems once more in its successor organisation, the Monopolies Commission and the Office of Manpower Economics.

Finally, its staff became "blended into a highly efficient and effective team. . . . To the end Board and staff functioned as a team and effectively completed the tasks that had been given to them."

The tasks given to them were the critical limit on its general function.

"The usefulness of a body such as ourselves depends primarily on the readiness of the Government to give it significant tasks and to follow up its recommendations."

APPENDIX A

The Statement of Intent

1   The Government's economic objective is to achieve and maintain a rapid increase in output and real income combined with full employment. Their social objective is to ensure that the benefits of faster growth are distributed in a way that satisfies the claims of social need and justice. In this way general confidence will be created in the purpose of the national plan and individuals will be willing to make the utmost contribution towards its implementation.

2   Essential conditions for the achievement of these objectives are a strong currency and a healthy balance of payments.

3   The economic situation, while potentially strong, is at present extremely unsatisfactory. Drastic temporary measures have been taken to meet a situation in which the balance of payments was in serious deficit, with exports falling behind imports. But these measures can provide only a breathing-space.

4   To achieve a more permanent solution we must improve the balance of payments, encourage exports and sharpen our competitive ability. Our longer-term interests lie in reducing the barriers to international trade. We must take urgent and vigorous action to raise productivity throughout industry and commerce to keep increases in total money incomes in line with increases in real national output and to maintain a stable general price level. Unless we do this we shall have a slower rate of growth and a lower level of employment.

5   We, Government, management and unions, are resolved to take the following action in our respective spheres of responsibility.

6   The Government will prepare and implement a general plan for economic development, in consultation with both sides of industry through the National Economic Development Council. This will provide for

higher investment; for improving our industrial skills; for modernisation
of industry; for balanced regional development; for higher exports; and
for the largest possible sustained expansion of production and real
incomes.

7   Much greater emphasis will be given to increasing productivity.
Government will encourage and develop policies designed to promote
technical advance in industry, and to get rid of restrictive practices and
prevent the abuse of monopoly power and so improve efficiency, cut out
waste, and reduce excessive prices. More vigorous policies will be pursued
designed to facilitate mobility of labour and generally to make more
effective use of scarce manpower resources, and to give workers a greater
sense of security in the face of economic change. The Government also
intend to introduce essential social improvements such as a system of
earnings-related benefits in addition to the improvements in national
insurance benefits already announced.

8   The Government will set up machinery to keep a constant watch on
the general movement of prices and of money incomes of all kinds and
to carry out the other functions described in paragraph ten below. They
will also use their fiscal powers or other appropriate measures to correct
any excessive growth in aggregate profits as compared with the growth
of total wages and salaries, after allowing for short-term fluctuations.

9   We, the representatives of the TUC, the Federation of British Industries, the British Employers' Confederation, the National Association of
British Manufacturers, and the Association of British Chambers of Commerce accept that major objectives of national policy must be:

> to ensure that British industry is dynamic and that its prices are
> competitive;
> to raise productivity and efficiency so that real national output can
> increase, and to keep increases in wages, salaries and other forms of
> income in line with this increase; to keep the general level of prices
> stable.

10   We therefore undertake, on behalf of our members, to encourage
and lead a sustained attack on the obstacles to efficiency, whether on
the part of management or of workers and to strive for the achievement
of more rigorous standards of performance at all levels; and to co-operate
with the Government in endeavouring in the face of practical problems,
to give effective shape to the machinery that the Government intends to
establish for the following purposes:

> (i)   to keep under review the general movement of prices and of money
>   incomes of all kinds;

(ii) to examine particular cases in order to advise whether or not the behaviour of prices or wages, salaries or other money incomes is in the national interest as defined by the Government after consultation with management and unions.

11 We stress that close attention must be paid to easing the difficulties of those affected by changing circumstances in their employment. We therefore support, in principle, the Government's proposals for earnings-related benefits and will examine sympathetically proposals for severance payments.

12 We, Government, management and unions, are confident that by co-operating in a spirit of mutual confidence to give effect to the principles and policies described above, we and those whom we represent will be able to achieve a faster growth of real incomes and generally to promote the economic and social well-being of the country.

APPENDIX B

List of goods subject to early warning, 1965

PART A

Bread
Flour
Biscuits
Cakes
Breakfast cereals
Sausages
Meat pies
Canned meats
Canned fish
Frozen fish
Margarine
Lard and compound fats
Jams and marmalade
Chocolate and sugar
  confectionery
Condensed milk
Canned fruit
Frozen vegetables
Processed vegetables
Pickles and sauces
Soft drinks
Ice-Cream
Tea
Processed coffee
Spirits
Beer

Electric motors
Primary and secondary
  batteries

Chains
Ball and roller bearings
Contractors' plant
Agricultural machinery
Tractors
Commercial vehicles
Cars
Bicycles and motorcycles
Tyres
Prams
Domestic refrigerators
Gas and electric cookers
Washing machines
Vacuum cleaners
Gas and electric fires
Electric storage heaters
Domestic boilers
Domestic water-heaters
Electric lamps
Cash registers
Typewriters
Domestic sewing-machines

Sole leather and soles
Rubber footwear
Textile yarn, thread
  and fibre
Paper and board
Wallpaper

National daily and Sunday
  newspapers
Oxygen and acetylene
PVC and polyethylene
Nitrogenous fertilisers
Household soap and
  detergent
Glass jars and bottles

Radio and TV sets
Bricks
Cement
Glass
Sand and gravel
Plasterboard

Petrol
Derv
Fuel oils
Coal
Coke
Manufactured fuel
Gas
Electricity

Rail fares
Rail freight charges
British Road Services
  charges

PART B

Food prices subject to constant watch by Ministry of Agriculture

Meat
Bacon
Poultry
Eggs

Fresh fruit
Fresh vegetables
Fish

Sugar
Cheese
Butter

APPENDIX C

Early warning and constant watch arrangements for 1968 and 1969

PART A

Goods and services subject to early warning

Bread
Flour
Biscuits
Cakes
Breakfast cereals
Meat pies
Sausages
Canned fruit and vegetables
Jams and marmalades
Margarine and cooking fat
Milk products (including condensed milk)
Pickles and sauces
Processed vegetables
Frozen food
Ice-Cream
Soft drinks
Chocolate and sugar confectionery
Soup
Table jellies
Tea
Processed coffee
Pet foods
Animal feeding stuffs
Beer
Cider and perry
Wines and spirits

Domestic refrigerators (electric)
Gas and electric cookers
Washing machines
Vacuum cleaners
Gas fires
Electric storage heaters
Domestic boilers

Domestic water heaters
Electric lamps
Household electrical wiring components
Cash registers
Photocopying machines
Typewriters
Sewing machines (domestic and industrial)
Chain-link fencing
Domestic power tools
Electric motors
Primary and secondary batteries
Contractors' plant
Agricultural machinery
Tractors
Commercial vehicles
Cars
Bicycles and motorcycles
Radio and TV (including components)
Copper cylinders and boilers
Galvanised cisterns and tanks
Plastic cold water tanks

Fertilisers
Glass jars and bottles
Insurance premiums
Man-made fibre and yarn
Sewing thread
Paint
Paper and board
Wallpaper
National daily and Sunday newspapers

Polyethylene
Polyvinyl chloride
Rubber footwear
Tyres
Household soap and detergent
Acetylene and oxygen
Coastal shipping rates

Asbestos cement
Cement
Bricks
Glass
Glazed floor tiles
Ceramic sanitaryware
Plaster and plasterboard
Pitch fibre pipes
Roofing felt
Clay pipes

Petrol
Derv
Fuel oil
Bottled gas
Coal
Coke
Manufactured fuel
Iron and steel
Gas
Electricity

Rail fares
Rail freight charges
BRS parcels rates

PART B

Goods where the trend of prices is kept under review

Carpets, mats and matting
Cotton and spun yarn
Footwear
Electric power cables
Wool yarns for weaving
   and hosiery

Knitting wool
Clothing
General chemicals
Hosiery and knitwear
Leather

Building blocks
Sand and gravel
Ready-mixed concrete

PART C

Food subject to constant watch

Meat
Bacon and ham
Poultry
Eggs
Fresh fruit

Fresh vegetables
Lard cooking and edible
   oils
Fish

Sugar
Cheese
Butter
Cream

APPENDIX DI

Statutory Instruments made under Part IV of the Prices and Incomes Act, 1966

Statutory Instrument Number	Date	Firm or Industry	Notes
1321/66	24/10/66	Laundry Industry	Standstill imposed on proposed increases in certain laundry and dry-cleaning charges.
1365/66	2/11/66	Thorn Electrical Industries Ltd	Standstill imposed on proposed salary increase for supervisory staff.
1380/66	5/11/66	National Newspapers	Standstill imposed on proposed increase in the cost-of-living bonus for workers engaged on the printing and distribution of national newspapers.
1444/66	21/11/66	Rockware Glass Ltd	Standstill imposed on proposed increase in payment for "hot work" by maintenance workers.
1468/66	24/11/66	Metropolitan Police Receiver	Standstill imposed on proposed salary increase for draughtsmen employed under the Receiver for the Metropolitan Police District.
1630/66	31/12/66	Printing Ink Industry	Standstill imposed on proposed pay increases for certain workers in the industry.
98/67	31/ 1/67	J. E. Hanger & Co. Ltd	Standstill imposed on proposed salary increase for limbfitters.
106/67	2/ 2/67	J. Bourne & Son Ltd	Standstill imposed on proposed pay increase for stoneware workers employed at the Denby Pottery.
216/67	23/ 2/67	Crown Bedding Co. Birmingham Ltd	Standstill imposed on proposed pay increase and reduction in the working week for road-transport drivers.
217/67	23/ 2/67	Press Association Ltd and the Exchange Telegraph Co. Ltd	Standstill imposed on proposed pay increase for certain workers.
424/67	21/ 3/67	Birmingham Corporation	Standstill imposed on proposed pay increases for certain Engineering Staff and Stores Personnel employed in the Transport Department.

Statutory Instrument Number	Date	Firm or Industry	Notes
515/67	31/ 3/67	Car Delivery Agents	Standstill imposed on proposed pay increase and reduction in the working week for employees of certain firms of car delivery agents.
608/67	18/ 4/67	Royal Burgh of Rothesay	Standstill imposed on proposed salary increase for administrative, professional, technical and clerical staff.
617/67	19/ 4/67	Electrical Contracting Industry, Scotland	Standstill imposed on proposed pay increase for electricians.
830·67	1/ 6/67	Harland & Wolf Ltd (Belfast)	Standstill imposed on proposed salary increase for certain supervisory staff and related grades.
1035/67	18/ 7/67	Metropolitan Police Receiver	Standstill imposed by SI No. 1468 of 1966 revoked.
1105/67	28/ 7/67	Thorn Electrical Industries Ltd and Birmingham Corporation	Standstills imposed by SIs No. 1365 of 1966 and No. 424 of 1967 revoked.
1106/67	28/ 7/67	Harland & Wolff Ltd (Belfast)	Standstill imposed by SI No. 830 of 1967 revoked.

Part IV of the Prices and Incomes Act 1966 expired on 12 August 1967. All the Statutory Instruments imposing standstills on pay or price increases above automatically lapsed on that day.

APPENDIX D2

Statutory Standstills under Part II of the Prices and Incomes Act, 1966, and the Prices and Incomes Acts, 1967 and 1968

Title of reference	Date	PIB Report	No. of Statutory Instrument	Notes
1 Agreement and award relating to terms and conditions of employment in road passenger transport industry.	27/ 1/68	63	816/68 1188/68	The first order extended standstill to the maximum six months, in the Act of 1967. The second extended it to eleven months allowed in the Act of 1968.
2 Agreement on terms and conditions of employment of draughtsmen in certain companies in engineering.	20/ 2/68	68	905/68	The direction and notice to extend the standstill applied to the Steel Group and Beckman Industries. The order applied only to the Steel Group.
3 Award on terms and conditions in road pasenger transport in Rochdale.	30/ 5/68		No order	
4 Two awards relating to pay in Bristol docks.	30/ 5/68	81		PIB reported in favour.
5 Agreement on sawyers' and wood-cutting machinists' pay.	21/ 6/68	82		PIB reported in favour.
6 Agreement on pay of platform staff in Dundee.	13/ 8/68	85		Agreement rescinded after PIB report.
7 Settlement on pay in thermal-insulation contracting industry.	16/ 8/68	84		PIB reported in favour.
8 Agreement on pay in road passenger transport in Wigan.	10/ 9/68	95		Agreement rescinded after PIB report.
9 Agreement on pay in road passenger transport in Great Yarmouth.	10/ 9/68	96		Order applied and extended.

Title of reference	Date	PIB Report	No. of Statutory Instrument	Notes
10 Agreement on pay in civil engineering and building.	13/12/68			Agreement suspended before directions came into force.
11 Agreement on pay in workers employed by the Electrical Contractors' Association in Scotland.	24/12/68	108	544/69	
12 Settlement of pay in the exhibition-contracting industry.	18/ 3/69	117	953/69	
13 Agreement on pay of workers in the film-processing industry.	8/ 8/69	131		No order made.

Appendix E

Members of the Board

The Rt Hon. AUBREY JONES, BSc (Econ). 1965 to 1970 Chairman. Formerly Chairman of Stavely Industries Ltd; previously Minister of Fuel and Power and Minister of Supply. Subsequently Chairman, Laporte Industries.

The Lord PEDDIE, MBE, JP. 1965 to 1971. 1965 to 1968 Full time Member; 1968 to 1970 Joint Deputy Chairman; 1970 to 1971 Chairman. Formerly Director of the Co-operative Wholesale Society Ltd and the Co-operative Insurance Society Ltd.

The Rt Hon. H. A. MARQUAND, MA, DSc. 1965 to 1968 Joint Deputy Chairman. Formerly Minister of Pensions (1948–51) and Minister of Health (1951).

D. A. C. DEWDNEY, BSc, CBE. 1965 to 1969. 1965 to 1966 Joint Deputy Chairman; 1966 to 1969 Part time Member. Managing Director of Esso Petroleum Ltd and subsequently Chairman, Anglesey Aluminium Co Ltd.

R. TURVEY, BSc (Econ). 1967 to 1971. 1967 to 1968 Full time Member; 1968 to 1970 Joint Deputy Chairman; 1970 to 1971 Deputy Chairman. Formerly Chief Economist with the Electricity Council.

Dr JOAN MITCHELL, MA, PhD. 1965 to 1968. Part time. Reader in Economics, University of Nottingham. Housewife.

R. G. MIDDLETON, DSC, LLB. 1965 to 1968. Part time. Senior Partner in Coward Chance & Co., Solicitors.

J. F. KNIGHT, BA, FCA. 1965 to 1967. Part time. Financial Director of Unilever Ltd.

P. E. TRENCH, CBE, TD, JP, BSc. 1965 to 1968. Part time. Director of the National Federation of Building Trade Employers.

R. WILLIS. 1965 to 1967. Full time. Formerly Joint General Secretary of the National Graphical Association.

Prof. H. A. CLEGG, MA. 1966 to 1967. Full time. Formerly Fellow of Nuffield College, Oxford.

Prof. B. R. WILLIAMS, MA. 1966 to 1967. Part time. Stanley Jevons Professor of Political Economy, University of Manchester.

Prof. W. B. REDDAWAY, MA, FBA. 1967 to 1971. Part time. Director of the Department of Applied Economics and subsequently Professor of Political Economy, University of Cambridge.

R. C. MATHIAS, OBE. 1967 to 1968. Full time. Formerly South Wales Regional Secretary of Transport and General Workers Union.

E. BROUGH, MA. 1967 to 1970. Part time. Head of Marketing Division, Unilever Ltd.

Prof. H. A. TURNER, BSc, MA, PhD. 1967 to 1971. Part time. Montague Burton Professor of Industrial Relations, University of Cambridge.

Prof. JOAN WOODWARD, MA, DPSA. 1968 to 1970. Part time. Reader and subsequently Professor of Industrial Sociology at the Imperial College of Science and Technology, London.

W. L. HEYWOOD, CBE. 1968 to 1970. Full time. Formerly Member of the Restrictive Practices Court; previously General Secretary of the National Union of Dyers, Bleachers and Textile Workers and member of the General Council of the Trades Union Congress.

M. B. FORMAN, TD. 1968 to 1970. Part time. Personnel Director, Steel Tube Division, Tube Investments Ltd; Director of Steel Tube Division Services Ltd.

The Lord WRIGHT OF ASHTON UNDER LYNE, CBE. 1968 to 1971. Part time. Formerly General Secretary of the Amalgamated Weavers' Association and Chairman of the Trades Union Congress.

J. E. MORTIMER. 1968 to 1971 full time and 1971 part time. Formerly a National Official of the Draughtsmen's and Allied Technicians Association and subsequently Board Member for Industrial Relations, London Transport Executive.

G. F. YOUNG, CBE, JP, MIMechE. 1968 to 1971. Part time. Chairman of Tempered Group Ltd, and formerly Pro-Chancellor and Chairman of the Council of the University of Sheffield.

Admiral Sir DESMOND DREYER, GCB, CBE, DSC, JP. 1968 to 1971. Part time. Formerly Chief Adviser (Personnel & Logistics) Ministry of Defence; formerly Chief of Naval Personnel & Second Sea Lord.

Dr H. G. REID, BSc, PhD. 1969 to 1970. Part time. Formerly General Manager (Commercial Services), Imperial Chemical Industries Ltd.

SECRETARIES TO THE BOARD

A. A. JARRATT, CB 1965 to 1968.

K. H. CLUCAS, CB 1968 to 1971.

Index